Praise for PREPARING FOR SABBATH

—Nominated for the Books in Canada Award for First Novels—

—Selected as one of the Ten Best Jewish Books of 5741 by Steven Arts Features—

"What Mary Gordon [in FINAL PAYMENTS] does for the Catholic girl growing up, Nessa Rapoport does in a brilliant novel about . . . growing up in a Jewish family."
—Bestsellers

"A beautifully wrought first novel . . . Judith's sexual awakening is one of the most beautifully written love scenes I've ever read."
—Judaica Book News

"Intense, emotional, often poetic, the book catches and holds the reader."
—Milwaukee Journal

"A religious book in a way that is uncommon among contemporary novels . . . It speaks to anyone who has ever struggled with the pursuit of her spiritual identity in an often unsympathetic world."
—Manhattan East

"An elegant love story . . . For those wishing to deepen their understanding of the agony as well as the joy of spiritual search, this is a highly recommended and important work."
—American Jewish Congress Monthly

"Places Rapoport among original Jewish women writers of the 80s . . . The early years are described in an extremely sensual style somewhat reminiscent of Marcel Proust."
—Jewish Frontier

"The story of a young Jew's search for spiritual meaning has been written before, but not from a woman's point of view. An incisive, lyrical novel."
—Flare Magazine

PREPARING
FOR
SABBATH

PREPARING FOR SABBATH

by

Nessa Rapoport

Introduction By Rosellen Brown

BP
BIBLIO PRESS
Sunnyside, New York

Printing History:
Wm. Morrow & Co., NY, edition published March 1981
Seal Book (Bantam) edition published May 1982
Biblio Press edition 1988

Library of Congress Cataloging-in-Publication Data:

Rapoport, Nessa.
        Preparing for Sabbath/Nessa Rapoport: new introduction by
        Rosellen Brown.
            p.   cm.
        ISBN 0-930395-05-0 (pbk.) $9.50
        I. Title
PS3568.A627P7 1988
813'.54 – dc19   87-36491 CIP

Printed in the United States of America

For the children of Rav Tuvyah
Srulke, Shabse, Perele, Tsipele, and Bella

Introduction
By Rosellen Brown

Our shelves are full of books about growing up. We have read about English childhoods — off to boarding school at seven or eight, to cold suppers and all those beatings grimly administered by masters and by classmates. We have surely read about American childhoods — on the plains or on the Mississippi, in the ghetto, this kind or that, Black, Irish, Jewish. And we have spent many vicarious hours at WASP dinner tables, watching the children watching their manners. Not all these books have been by or about boys becoming men, as some feminists will claim: there is *Jane Eyre,* there is *My Antonia,* there are Alice Munro's new classics, the bleak Canadian girlhoods in *Lives of Girls and Women* and *The Beggar Maid.* Kate Simon has recently given us a Jewish girl's growing up; in her two superb memoirs, *Bronx Primitive* and *A Wider World,* the immigrant child takes her new country at its democratic word and becomes a bold and outspoken American.

But Nessa Rapoport has done something quite different from all these chroniclers. She has written from within (and finally, because this is what generates passionate fiction, from without) a community not often represented in full and rich detail. Her Judith Rafael is a perfect representative of the "ordinary" reality of middle-class observant Judaism, the world of the day school, the religious summer camp, the idealistic sojourn to Israel. Many thousands have grown up like Judith in the United States and in Canada — she lives in Toronto — but their lives tend to pass too unremarkably for the heightened purposes of fiction as they take their places stolidly in the professions, as parents, as pillars of the synagogue.

Chaim Potok writes chiefly about young men caught between the Orthodox and the secular worlds. His heroes represent a generation seduced by the forbidden wonders of the "outside," and each provokes a desperate and heretical encounter between father and son, old devotions and new. Philip Roth, on the other hand, never deals with the spiritual side of Portnoy (if, indeed, he has one), or of Zuckerman. Both grapple with their fathers and their fathers' worlds but not precisely with their Judaism; only, one might say, with the behavioral expectations, the social demands and restrictions of their backgrounds. Nor has Roth written with anything close to affection or even acceptance of the Jewish community. He and many of the others who have set their work in the Jewish world have tended to concentrate, always critically, on the less endearing and unserious aspects of middle-class *nouveau arrivé* Jewish life; the results, however acute and amusing, always depict a world narrowly but blessedly escaped.

Preparing for Sabbath, in contrast, is not a search for the means of rejection. The girl whom we follow to womanhood, typical of women throughout history, is, rather, trying to find a way to accommodate all the conflicting calls upon her affections, to live comfortably but intensely in a world in which "there would be work, there would be love." Judith may want to expand ecstatically on the bourgeois life of her childhood, but she has no desire to turn her back on the faith with which she grew up. She does not want to reject her parents (who, granted, are half a generation more "civilized" than Portnoy's and Zuckerman's, more relaxed, that is, and better educated—they are, in fact, of a different class).

The question for Judith turns on how she, a Jewish woman of high seriousness, descended from a long line of rabbis, can bind the various aspects of her life into a single living braid as many-stranded and graceful as a havdalah candle. She is looking for a balance between constraints, not for "freedom." And while she is, like many of her generation, hungry to open the barred gates of traditional Judaism to women like herself, hers is not an extreme or exclusive feminism that would remove her from the possibilities of love or marriage. Of course she considers her religious and her erotic life more intense and complex than her mother's—her mother is comfortable, cheerful, perhaps a bit complacent—but superiority in matters of passion and commitment are the tasks of every generation. She wants to feel everything profoundly, but she does not, in fact, really want to bolt and run.

From our wonderful introduction to Judith, aged seven, who wishes she could marry her best friend, Janie, Judith's childhood is memorable for its very un-memorability. Rapoport renders perfectly the necessary smugness of the status quo, the private sense that "mine—ours—is the only right way to be" of most children as they first encounter the world beyond their front doorstep. But what is especially interesting in Judith's case is that, added to the particulars of every family's habits and expectations—her father's custom in winter of flooding the back lawn so that the children can ice-skate on it, her mother's last-minute morning dash across the street holding her children's hands, in a coat that covers her pajamas, a whole litany of "this is how we do it"s and "my mother always says"s—there are the special demands and rituals of an observant Jewish family.

Since Judaism makes its way in the world by creating distinctions (between holy and unholy, *shabbes* and the rest of the week, kosher and *treyf*) her life is strewn with prohibitions and with sanctions, with "you may"s and "you must not"s. Judith, growing up among them, is an enlightening example of how the child takes anything for granted: these are not difficulties, they are simply *the way it is;* she lives surrounded by others who don't question any more than she does.

Outside her world, however, there are—leaving out goyim, anti-semites and proselytizers for other faiths—two kinds of familiar stranger: one is exemplified by her beloved Janie's mother, Jewish herself but not observant, who feeds her non-kosher meat, which Judith accepts with some confusion because "she thought that since they ate chicken every Friday night it was all right," and who suggests that if Judith rides with her on the Sabbath, "no one would know." This time Judith is prepared. "God," she thinks, "would know because he knew what a person thought even alone in a room, and he could see Judith getting undressed at night, if he wanted to." The other kind of stranger is her piano teacher, also nominally Jewish, who dismisses "those Orthodox superstitions" and insists that a great musician has to practice every day, even Saturday. If this were Potok, such a challenge could easily be the first drum-roll in a painful campaign in which the young pianist-to-be affronts his father and his faith by playing scales when he should be chanting Torah. But this is Rapoport, and Judith is (for now) serene. Later she will allow herself some doubts: "What was it like for (her friend) Rachel to be Jewish in a small midwestern town where there were only two Jewish boys in her class...What a different language people who weren't Jewish spoke...And yet how narrow Judith's world was, Judith who did not have a single non-Jewish friend, who spent her long days with Jews and came home to a practicing Jewish house. Was Judith blessed or deprived? Neither of them was sure."

But even these necessary questions of a sensitive girl in the assimilated world never draw her very far from her security. She may want to expand her tolerance for the secular or pluralistic realm but she has no desire to lose her "differentness." There is a fine line between security and insularity, between pleasure in the strength of one's community and complacency in its unchanging habits, and Nessa Rapoport lets Judith find and walk it with convincing care.

There is a moment when the full-bodied accuracy of her portrayal of this closed-but-not-sealed world is marvelously manifested. Judith, far from her first true love, Ori, is living in England for the year, and giving all her attention to a young Oxford student named James. He takes her home to Devon to meet his parents. "They know you're Jewish," he assures her, as if to say "No problem: *they* won't be upset." But Judith, of course, is the one upset, and the moment is beautifully documented without ever becoming didactic. What we see, because we have lived with her in her world, is the enormous force with which Judith registers the inexorable difference between the fathers and mothers with whom she has grown up and James's perfectly nice parents. "James's father wore flannels and his mother wore her knit dress with pearls. During their chat at tea Judith found that his father had served with the British in Palestine in 1948. He was perfectly genial telling her, it was long in the past...James led her through the rooms of his childhood...His family had always lived in these parts...and the cathedral in town held the ancestral crypt where someday he too would lie. It was one of the greatest cathedrals in England...."

Later that night, as she and James slip out through the garden to walk in the English mist, James goes first. "She would not tell him he was disappearing ahead of her, the dark mass of him shuffling through the undergrowth." Though she waits, later, for him "to capture her in his arms," we haven't much doubt that James, lord of an alien realm, will not, cannot be a part of Judith's real life for very long.

In fact the "real life" of a woman who takes her Jewishness seriously is fraught with so many dangerous distinctions that to make mischief one needn't even bother to go outside the faith. Earlier, as a teen-ager, wracked with all the expectable insecurities about her worth as an object of love, Judith watches, worshipfully, a beautiful Orthodox girl named Anna in the throes of courtship by a boy in the grade above them. But alas, the boy is not Orthodox and "Anna could never hurt her parents, who had survived the concentration camps." So there is no appeal to them. (An irresistible contrast: Alice Munro's young women grow up on places like fox farms or in the whitebread towns of Ontario, not far from Toronto but as distant as Martians from such heated parochial anxieties!)

With intimate divisions and animosities like these, and a shared history of pain, every Jewish life is a potential drama: one walks into difficulties headlong or averts them by cunning or compromise, but, Rapoport seems to be saying, every passage is complicated, every safety conceals a threat, every choice the opening of one door and the closing of another. Judith's woman friends and her brilliant, searching, confused Ori try many variations in their search for satisfaction. Judith, betrayed by some, helpless in the face of others' frustration, learns slowly and painfully how delicate is the balance of fidelity to friends and family and faith.

Flannery O'Connor, a writer most luminously and gratefully bound to the specifics of her South and her Catholicism—perfectly poised contrasts to Rapoport's North and her Judaism—talked about the way "the writer operates at a peculiar crossroads where time and place and eternity somehow meet." She says of the South that it is "a society that is rich in contradiction, rich in irony, rich in contrast..." If we substitute "Jewish"—explicitly, proudly "Jewish"—for "Southern" in these excerpts, we can see how universal specificity can turn out to be. Nessa Rapoport's

Judith, a child growing out of her easy certainties into the more provisional certainties of adulthood, transcends the narrowness of her situation. Though one question succeeds the next for her, like an endless Talmudic interrogation on a text as yet unwritten, the future finally seems limitless for this probing young woman who knows, understands and loves the limitless Jewish past.

ROSELLEN BROWN is the author of six books, including the novels Civil Wars, Tender Mercies *and* The Autobiography of My Mother. *She and her husband, Marvin Hoffman, are the authors of a documentary play about Russian Jewry,* Dear Irina, *produced in Houston in 1987. Her book of poetry,* Cora Fry, *will be reissued by Unicorn Press in the spring of 1988.*

ONE

She was seven years old. She was in love with Janie, who lived twelve houses away. They went to a wishing well and dropped in two pennies. Janie's mother said: Make a wish, but don't tell what it is. Afterwards, when they got home, they whispered their wishes. They were the same. They wished they could marry each other.

Judith didn't understand why they couldn't, if they really wanted to. Janie's mother and father laughed when they told them. Her father made them each a wire S to wear around their necks. It was for their secret clubhouse.

Janie's older sister hated Judith. She thought Judith was a bad influence. She went to high school and got her hair done every Friday. Sometimes when she was out Judith and Janie would sneak into her room and look at her things.

Janie's mother was wonderful. She let them sit at her dressing table and put on makeup. She had a box with tiny drawers, and each one had a lipstick or an eyeshadow. They put blue and green sparkles on their eyelids, and drew on red mouths. Then they laughed in front of the mirror. Judith liked to walk home with her makeup on. She said to Janie's mother: Maybe I'll meet a man on the way home who'll think I'm a little lady. She would stare into the eyes of every man she passed, wondering if he thought she was beautiful.

Janie and Judith had met at a barefoot party that Janie's mother made for her birthday. Judith was one year older than Janie. She didn't want to go to the party, because she didn't know Janie or anyone on the street, and Janie had a dog. When she got there, she had to take off her shoes to sit at the picnic table. It was the rule of the party. It felt good to put her bare feet on the grass under the table, until the dog came and licked her toes. Janie's mother said: Don't worry. He's just friendly. He never bites.

After that Judith and Janie were together all the time. They slept over. They walked each other home, back and forth. They couldn't stop talking. They had the clubhouse closet in the attic, and the bike game they made up, and a code to call outside the window if one of them wanted the other. They prayed that some-day they would live next door, and then they could have a telephone made of two cans and some string that would go be-tween their bedrooms, provided their windows were on the same side of the house. They prayed that they would be. They had teas in ballroom dresses of yellow and blue tulle that Janie's mother bought at an auction. They ate in the living room off little china plates.

Janie's family wasn't kosher. Janie's mother wanted to take Judith out to a Chinese restaurant, and Judith's mother had to explain about being kosher, and that Judith couldn't eat most of the food there. Janie's mother said she'd only give her the food that was permitted. She took them to *The Bartered Bride* opera, which they read about from the blue opera plot book that Judith's father had. Then she took them to a restaurant and said: Don't worry. You don't have to eat anything you're not allowed to have. Judith had some vegetable things with no meat in them. Janie's mother ordered chicken, and offered some to Judith. She didn't know if it was allowed, but then she thought that since they ate chicken every Friday night it was all right. She forgot the point of chicken and kosher. The point was, it's the way the chicken is killed that makes it kosher or not. She'd just learned it in school, that's what made her so mad at herself. Her mother didn't yell at her. She knew it wasn't her fault. She thought she prob-ably shouldn't have let her go.

Janie's mother didn't understand about being Jewish, even though she was. Judith didn't ride on the Sabbath. Janie's mother said: Couldn't you do it just once and come to the country with us? No one would know. She didn't realise it was a law, and God would know because he knew what a person thought even alone in a room, and he could see Judith getting undressed at night, if he wanted to.

Miss Zamora, her piano teacher, didn't understand either. She said: How can you be so limited? She cooked food that smelled funny, and grew her own herbs in little squares of earth in a box in the kitchen. Judith wouldn't want to eat that food. Miss Zamora was Jewish, from an old Sephardic family, but she didn't care. She said a person could never be a great musician if she didn't practise every single day, including Saturdays. Judith probably wouldn't be a great musician anyway, even though she was very intelligent, Miss Zamora said. She didn't understand how an intelligent girl like Judith could believe in those Orthodox superstitions.

Judith said: We're not Orthodox, we're observant. Her mother didn't believe in Orthodox, Conservative and Reform. Labels divide, her mother said. There will always be Jews more observant than we are, and Jews who are less. All Jews are responsible for one another.

Judith's mother said that Miss Zamora thought it was superstitious because she didn't understand the reasons for it. She thought it was something people from the old country did, instead of a way of life. Judith felt sorry for her. Miss Zamora thought music was more important than anything. In school Judith's teacher told her that idol worship was not only bowing down to statues made by people but also worshipping money, or even something good like art.

One side of Judith's street was good, and one side was scary. The good side was where she and Janie lived, with old houses, each one different, and old trees that shaded the sidewalk and dropped seeds every spring that they could stick on their faces like a nose. On the other side lived the five Tchaszetski boys, who weren't Jewish and said they'd beat Judith up if she stepped foot on their lawn. There were the new houses, all the same except for different coloured doors, and the house with the old lady who everyone thought put razor blades in the apples she gave out on Hallowe'en. Also, once Judith's little sister Naomi was walking on that side and a man made her lift up her dress.

Naomi was a bug. She wanted to play with Judith and Janie,

and Judith's parents said: Be nice to your sister. They didn't understand about the clubhouse and secrets and being younger, even though Naomi was almost taller than Judith already, and she was only five. Judith's mother said: Anyone who looks at your eyes can see that you're older.

Judith looked in the mirror a lot. She thought she looked exactly like her father. Everyone told her she did. Naomi and Riva looked like her mother. Riva was the baby. When Judith's mother brought her home from the hospital, her face was all crinkled up. She was screaming her head off. When Judith tickled her she didn't laugh. Her mother said she was too young to know how.

Her father said: The right way to wear a necklace is to tuck the chain under your collar and let just the stone show. Judith's father also knew how to roll up her sleeves so that they were the same on both sides. He did it for her in the morning before school, even though it made him late. He was very neat, and so was Judith. When he came home from work every night, he put his briefcase in the den and went upstairs and changed his clothes while he told her mother about his day.

Her mother was cheerful. She helped Judith with her home-work without yelling and sang Hebrew songs to put her to sleep. She said the Sh'ma prayer with Judith in bed, which said: And you should teach your children to say the Sh'ma. It was hard to say a prayer about saying a prayer.

They lived on 64 Valley View Drive, Toronto, Ontario, Canada. They had a backyard with a big tree in the middle that gave a lot of shade. In the winter Judith's father went out every night to flood the lawn, even though it would ruin the grass in the spring. That was to make a skating rink, but it came out very bumpy and it wasn't nearly as much fun as the Valley View rink that they had to drive to. Judith didn't tell her father that, because he worked so hard every night and came in with his hands freezing.

They also went tobogganing in the winter. On Sundays they bundled up, and Judith's mother made them wear leggings although Judith was too old. Then her father stood at the top of the hill and laughed the whole time. Tobogganing was scary, especially if she was in front. She wrapped her scarf around her face until only her eyes showed. She put on her gloves and tucked her sleeves into the elastic at the wrists. She put her feet under the curled part of the toboggan and divided the rope evenly between her hands. Every time Judith went first she screamed to Naomi: Why am I doing this? Naomi screamed it too. Every time she forgot how scary it was, and she wished she could make it stop but it was too late.

After tobogganing they came into the house covered with frozen snow that melted on the hall floor. When they took off their boots to take them down to the cellar, their socks got wet. Then her mother made hot cocoa for everyone, and French toast if it was lunchtime, and all the girls sat on the kitchen chairs shivering, holding their cups with both hands.

They were allowed to watch TV only on Sunday nights. They watched Walt Disney and Ed Sullivan every week. Her father watched it all the time. He read his medical journals in front of it, and slept with it on. Sometimes they'd sneak into the den on Friday nights and watch Lawrence Welk with him. Her mother read in the kitchen after supper. She didn't approve of TV, especially on Friday night, which was the Sabbath—Shabbat. She said it was against the atmosphere of Shabbat, so her father tried to turn it on only for the late show.

TV was the one thing that relaxed him. He worked very hard saving people's lives all week, and when he came home he had to unwind. He also ate supper himself in the dining room, away from the noise. Her mother carried it in on a tray for him, with a napkin and a toothpick.

They made a lot of noise at the table. Sometimes they got very silly, and then the dining room door swung open and her father came in with his yelling look on. Judith hated it when he yelled, and if he was really mad he chased her around the table and sometimes all the way upstairs. Her mother said he couldn't help it. She said he forgot about it five minutes later.

The most fun was when they got her mother to laugh. If she was trying to be mad, they pointed their fingers and said: Mu-mmy's laugh-ing, Mu-mmy's laugh-ing, until she couldn't keep a straight face. She went into the bedroom and closed the door to stop herself, but they followed her in.

Her mother's drawers were a mess. She kept trying to straighten them. She turned them upside down on her bed, and scarves, lipsticks, pins and little pieces of paper fell out in a big pile. Then she spent all afternoon sorting, and put it back in order. Then it got messy again.

Judith couldn't understand why her mother didn't just make it neat for once and for all. Judith couldn't be messy if she tried. She slept in her bed so neatly that she didn't have to make it in the morning. She did her homework over and over again until the page was perfect. When she did theory exercises for Miss Zamora, she filled in each quarter note until no white was showing.

She took piano lessons because when her father was young his father tried to get him to practise violin, but he wanted to play football so he quit. Now he was sorry. When you're old, you don't play in teams anymore, but you can always play an instrument, he said.

Judith really wanted to take ballet. She loved ballet. She had a history of ballet book that showed all the famous dancers, from the 1700s, when they could hardly move in their clothes, until they were allowed to show their ankles. She couldn't decide if she liked the princess dresses that came down to their knees or the tutus better. Her mother said: You know, you don't get a tutu right away, and Judith tossed her head and said: I know that, with scorn in her voice, but actually she was shocked. She thought she would, it was one of the main reasons she wanted to take it.

Her parents said: You can't take piano and ballet. They thought it would be too much for her, since she stayed up too late with her homework already, copying notes over. They didn't want to be like those parents that give their kids a million kinds of lessons. They said: When you're forty you won't be able to do ballet, but piano lasts forever.

A lot of girls in her class took piano, but they went to Conservatory. They all had the same books, one for piano and one for theory. When they were halfway through a piece they got a silver star at the top, and when they were done they got a gold star and moved on to the next one.

Miss Zamora was very against Conservatory. She thought Judith should play all the notes the composer wrote, not a made-for-Conservatory version. She thought each child was different, and she gave different pieces to every one. It meant Judith had a lot more piano books. Judith and Janie had their first lesson together. Miss Zamora said Judith was more musical. They were afraid she would split them up, and she did, and gave Judith harder pieces.

Judith's mother said that anything Judith played was musical. She said that right from the beginning Judith made the simplest pieces sound like music. She said she had never been able to play that way. Judith's father said she had golden fingers. Once in a while when he called home to talk to her mother, her mother would say afterwards, do you want to say hello to Judith, and hand her the phone. If Judith took it right away and listened, she sometimes heard him talking to someone in the room. My oldest girl, he was saying, she can do anything. So intelligent. Does so well in school. Then she'd hurry to say hello and pretend she just got on. It made her get a warm lump in her stomach. It also made her scared, because he didn't know how bad she was.

She got into a lot of trouble at school for talking. She whispered and passed notes the second the teacher turned around, and kept going even after a warning. When Mrs. Wilkinson made them cut off the erasers on top of their pencils and throw them away so she could see what mistakes they made in writing capitals and smalls, Judith sneaked one out of the garbage can and kept it hidden in her desk in case she made a really bad mistake.

She didn't practise piano enough either. Miss Zamora said a half hour a day at least and work up to an hour, but she never did. Some weeks she didn't practise until the night before her lesson. Sometimes after a week like that she'd play a piece and Miss Zamora would say: Very good. I can see you've really worked this week. When she walked out afterwards she'd take a deep breath and think: A whole week until the next time. I'll practise every night, and then she'll really see what I can do. But the next day was Thursday, one day before Shabbat. If she didn't practise Thursday night, and she couldn't practise Friday night because of Shabbat, and Saturday night was the weekend, and Sunday night was for the homework that she'd put off doing Sunday, then there was only Monday and Tuesday before her lesson, and Monday was the hardest night because all the teachers piled on homework at the start of the week.

Every morning at seven o'clock Judith's mother knocked on her door. Then Judith wriggled out of her covers right away. She ran to the bathroom to wash her face, and hurried back to put on her navy blue tunic and white blouse that were ready on the chair. In the pocket on the right-hand side of her tunic was a folded Kleenex and two student tickets for the bus. She also had navy blue knee socks and oxfords, which she hated but her mother made her buy so she wouldn't have problems with her feet later on.

Judith carried her school bag downstairs to breakfast. Her mother made porridge the night before, ready on the stove, and toast and cocoa. The toast was piled up in stacks, it was soft with margarine on both sides and tasted really good. Usually she had room for only one piece, though. Then she and Naomi took their lunch bags out of the fridge and checked for their own names, brushed their teeth, put on their coats and ran.

If they had enough time they went to the light, to cross Bathurst Street for the bus. But sometimes they were late, and then her mother put her coat on over her pajamas and jaywalked them across. She always said she knew she shouldn't do it, because it was dangerous, and they weren't allowed to do it on their own. The Rosenberg boys, who lived down the street, did it every morning. They didn't wear coats, even in winter, and their shirttails flew out behind them when they ran across, right in the middle of the cars.

Once when her mother was taking them, a man in a white car got really mad and yelled out: How can you risk your children's lives, you stupid woman? Her mother wasn't stupid. Her father said she was smarter than he was, but her mother said her father was smarter. Then she said: We're each smart at different things. After that morning her mother stopped for a while, but soon they had to start doing it again. Judith always wondered if one day a policeman would stop her mother and take her to court, where she'd have to talk to the judge in her pajamas.

Judith and Janie went to a Jewish day school. They went from eight-fifteen in the morning until four-fifteen in the afternoon every day, much longer than the public school kids. They had half a day Hebrew and half a day English, all the subjects the public schools had plus Bible and literature and history in Hebrew, and homework in every one. They had no time for other activities, and if they stayed after school for any reason, it got past four-thirty and they couldn't use their student tickets anymore, which wasn't fair to Jewish kids.

Mrs. Jacobs, the principal, told them to behave on the bus, because everyone knew they were Jewish and they had to set a good example. But they were pretty bad, especially the boys. They ran up and down the aisles and threw spitballs, and in the winter their hockey sticks got in the way. Judith looked at the old ladies in their pink and blue coats with fur collars and their tight grey hair in nets, and she could imagine that behind their little mouths and disapproving eyes they were saying: Those Jewish children are a disgrace. Mah yomru hagoyim meant: What will the gentiles say? It was a consideration.

When Judith got out of school, Janie was usually waiting for her at the door. If they had time, they walked two blocks to Variety and got snacks to eat on the way home. In the summer they got Nutty-Buddy ice cream cones. They peeled off the paper top and unwound the sides, and then there were crunchy nuts and chocolate on top of vanilla ice cream, and a sugar cone at the end. If they bit off the bottom, they could suck the ice cream through the hole. In the winter they bought five-cent bags of Hostess potato chips, which they sat on before they opened them on the bus, to make more. The tiny pieces always tasted better than the big ones, they didn't know why. They also bought Coffee Crisps, which were the best chocolate bar.

The way Judith ate a Coffee Crisp was to undo the yellow and brown waxed paper that said COFFEE CRISP IT'S A NICE LIGHT SNACK, and scrape off the top coating of chocolate with her teeth. Then, if she did it right and didn't bite too hard, came a layer of biscuit, and then a layer of coffee cream icing, then another layer of biscuit, and so it went, starting from one end, the other wrapped in the paper so the chocolate wouldn't melt all over her fingers. If she was good at it, she could eat one Coffee Crisp most of the way home.

Getting home in the summer. The days were long and full of afternoon light, thick and gold on everything. There was time to play before supper, and Judith raced up the street to Janie's house, or Janie came to hers. They played tag, when there were enough kids around, or they went biking. They walked in the ravine behind Janie's house, looking at lilies of the valley, ivory waxen bells that looked fake, they were so perfect. Janie and Judith breathed deep.

The first flowers were the forsythia bushes. There was one on each side of the house. Yellow bumps in green cases came out on the skinny stems, and then overnight the bush was a blaze of yellow she could see halfway up the block. Then in the beds under the living room windows were violets, dark and mossy near the ground. Behind them tall sticks of leaves turned into daffodils. Then came tulips, standing straight up, red and orange. In the backyard the big old tree got fuzzy and green, and hard knobs of peonies had ants crawling all over them, licking them open, Judith thought. Bleeding hearts, that was the name of the tiny hearts she could pluck from their stems and unpeel down to the thin pink core.

Later in spring the lilacs hung in fat purple and white gobs. They smelled so strong it made her feel faint. At twilight she lay on her back and watched the bushes grow black into the still light sky.

When the lilacs started to get brown, Judith's mother said: Take the high chair outside and cut some for the house, because soon they'll be gone. Her mother didn't believe in picking flowers, because in a vase they'd last only three days but outside she could appreciate them all summer. Judith felt a great pain in her heart, when she took the yellow high chair out to cut lilacs.

Fall was the worst time for pain in the heart. The trees were so bright they hurt her eyes, and when she looked up, the branches were cutting the sky into little blue shapes. Turning around and around, she couldn't tell what was ground and what was trees. All the mothers said, what a wonderful smell, and made the kids rake.

Judith and Naomi collected leaves until their arms ached. Her father raked too, and he was much faster. When they had a big enough pile, they were allowed to jump on top of it and be buried. First Naomi covered Judith, until only her head stuck out, and then it was Naomi's turn. When Judith jumped up and shook herself off, there were still pieces of leaves that stuck on her sweater and in her hair. Her father didn't like it if she tramped them into the house.

Judith thought raking was stupid because the leaves kept falling and she just had to do it over again. But when there were no leaves left, that was an ugly time. The ground was brown and everything looked grey and cold. No sun, no snow, no flowers to grow, November. That's what her mother said when Judith tried to explain how she felt.

It was dark when she got home from school, and Judith raced up the street as soon as she saw the yellow squares of light in her house. The trees were so bare she could sometimes see the house while she was still on the bus. It felt good to run in from the dark and have her mother hug her with her apron on, saying: Judith, how was your day? There would be carrot and celery sticks before supper, and if she looked outside the big picture window, she saw only herself and her mother and Naomi in the kitchen. But even if she held her hand over her eyes like an Indian until she felt the edge of her palm in a line on the hard cold glass, all she saw was the shadow of the big old tree on the shadow of the sky.

Or lying in bed, late at night when everyone else was asleep, the shadows of the cars as they passed by, travelling across the walls of her room, even when the curtains were pulled until there were no cracks, the cars made those shadows go round and round.

Alef

Her last name was Rafael. Judith Rafael. Daddy was very proud of being a Rafael. The Rafaels were an old Jewish family that went back to the 1400s. Judith came from a long line of rabbis, Daddy said. Before the Nazis there was a Rafael rabbi in every town in Europe.

Daddy lost most of his family in the war. Mummy had a big family, because they came over around 1900. But Daddy had hardly anyone. Great-aunt Chenya in Israel was his only living relative from the old days.

Daddy's father was dead. He died when Judith was six. Judith still remembered him. He came over and made up funny words like Hixum-Drixum and then he pulled out presents for her from a brown paper bag. He looked just like Daddy, and Judith did too. He was called Zeide.

When Zeide got sick he lay in bed at home, and Judith had to go visit him. Zeide forgot English then and spoke to Daddy in Yiddish. Daddy said that because he was sick his brain remembered only the language he spoke when he was little. Judith didn't understand Yiddish, but she thought she should. Once Mummy took her to Zeide's house and he was lying on his bed all grey on a rubber sheet like babies have. He tried to talk to her, but Judith started screaming until Mummy took her out of the room. Mummy whispered: Zeide's sick, be nice to him, he's sick, Daddy wants you to, but Judith couldn't stop yelling, even though in the middle of it she didn't know why she was doing it. When Zeide died she felt terrible about the screaming. She knew Mummy and Daddy thought she was only six and that she did it because she was little and scared, but Judith knew inside her that wasn't the reason.

Zeide loved her specially, because she looked like a Rafael. She was one, and she was named after her grandmother who died, Zeide's wife. Zeide married her when he was fifteen and she was sixteen. Their wedding picture was in the den. Zeide wore a fur hat, and he looked very young. They had a hard life. They worked in the store all day and all night. Zeide used to go to sleep at two o'clock in the morning and get up at four o'clock to go to the market.

Zeide was an illui when he was a little boy. That meant he was a genius in Talmud, and the men of the town used to come to him and ask him questions. When Zeide came to America he didn't have a nickel in his pocket. He came to Toronto and worked at all kinds of things with his hands while his mind went to waste. That's why Daddy became a doctor, because he saw what happened to his father's mind.

Daddy and his father had a very special relationship, Mummy said. They were so close they were more like two brothers than like a son and his father. Daddy loved his father so much he did everything he could to make him proud. Mummy said that one of the reasons she married Daddy was because she saw how he treated his father.

Daddy said: I had a better father than you girls do.

Sometimes when Judith sat in the kitchen on the yellow high chair before supper, she could see Zeide high up near the ceiling as if he were there. She talked to him and told him things. He smiled at her, loving her, she could see. Everything was all right, according to him. He didn't get mad at her for anything.

Daddy said: If only Zeide could have seen you studying Torah. It would have given him such naches.

Naches was that smile Zeide had when he looked at her from the ceiling. She didn't tell Daddy about having Zeide come to the kitchen any time she thought carefully about him.

Every year before Rosh Hashanah Daddy drove out to the cemetery to visit the graves. Judith didn't want to go, but he got a very strict face on and Mummy said she had to.

They drove a long way, and then they walked up rows and rows of stones until they got to the Rafael ones. Zeide's was there, and Zeide's father, who had come to Toronto even before Zeide, and Zeide's mother too. Zeide's stone said: Jacob, son of Rav Shabtai and his wife Eva, a gentle man. Judith always thought about a gentle man. Daddy made up those words for the stone, Mummy said. She always pictured Daddy thinking up a way to put his father's life on a piece of stone, phoning up the stone company and telling them: Write a gentle man on the bottom. It made her want to cry for him.

Daddy always stood there for a little while, and walked around looking at the other stones, of his grandfather and grandmother, and then stood there for a while, and then they left. It was hot and dusty.

There weren't very many Rafael stones in the cemetery, because most of the family died in Europe. The Nazis killed them in concentration camps. One of Daddy's aunts went back to Poland in 1939 and got caught. Sometimes Judith hoped she would turn up, or that Judith would find her, but she knew it was impossible. The Nazis were too strong. They killed six million Jews, more than anyone could imagine. Judith wondered if you could count to six million in one lifetime, even if you started as soon as you could talk.

She didn't know exactly how her family died, but she read a lot of books about concentration camps. The Nazis did operations on you with no ether and you screamed in pain and sometimes you died. They took your womb out so you couldn't have babies, and made your mother stand beside you and tell you not to scream. They put you in a cage and did experiments on you, taking off pieces of your skin from one part of your body and putting them onto another until you looked like a patchwork. They put you in freezing rooms to see how cold they could make you. Then they put you in boiling water to see how hot they could make you. They shoved all the sick people straight into the ovens or into rooms which they told you were showers. Then they turned on the gas and you realised what happened but it was too late and you started clawing at the walls and the doors to get out but they choked you to death. When they opened the doors everyone was all tangled up in each other with holes in the ceiling where you tried to punch your way out.

The Nazis collected everything. They collected hair, teeth, eyeglasses, shoes, and even skin, which they made lampshades out of. Judith couldn't imagine it, but they had pictures in books of lampshades and bars of soap that used to be Jewish people.

Judith couldn't stop reading about them. Mummy and Daddy didn't know how much. She looked at pictures of dead people with no clothes on who were so skinny their bones poked through their skin. She looked at pictures of little kids with yellow stars on their clothes. There were rooms full of Jews in striped uniforms staring at you with dark eyes. Some of them might be Rafaels.

Other things Judith knew about were: The Nazis tore old men's beards out of their faces. They set Torahs on fire and made Jews pish on them. They took babies and bashed them against the wall in front of their mothers' eyes. They threw them up into the air and shot them. They tied a woman to a tree and shot her breasts off. The book didn't say if she lived after it. Judith stared at that picture. She didn't know what she would do if the Nazis came to Toronto. She thought the shower in Riva's room was the best hiding place, because it was a shower in a bathroom in a bedroom upstairs, three in one. The other place she wished she could use was the compartment inside the bottom of the desk lamp, but no person could ever fit in there.

The Nazis separated children from their mothers and husbands from their wives. They lined you up and said, to the right, to the left, and there was no way you could know beforehand which line meant you'd live and which meant they killed you right away. If you looked strong they kept you to work for them. But if you looked weak they sent you to the ovens.

All the time this was happening no one did anything about it. Haolam shatak, the world was silent while the Jews burned, that's what they learned in school. The Pope could have done something but he didn't, and the President of the United States could have done something but he wouldn't let the Jews in. Some Jews went from country to country by boat, begging to get in, but every country said no and made the boats turn around and go back to Germany. Some boats sank on the way back and all the Jews drowned. That's why the state of Israel was created, so Jews would never be homeless again, with no place to run to when anti-Semitism started.

The minute anti-Semitism started in Canada, Judith would go to Israel, she decided. She didn't want to make the same mistake that the Jews in Germany made. They said: Nothing will happen here. We're Germans too. They can't hurt us. But the Germans said: All Jews must go. If you called yourself a Christian but your great-great-grandfather was Jewish, they made you wear a yellow star and they put you in the ghetto.

The first time Judith heard the new Toronto ambulance siren she was sure the Nazis were coming. It was the same siren as in the diary of Anne Frank movie. She was standing at the bus stop after school and she looked at the other people waiting. She thought: I'm the only one who knows. I have to do something, I have to warn them, all this while the siren was going A-a-A-a-A-a. She thought: They don't know our lives are in danger. But then the bus came and the driver didn't say anything and everyone looked normal, so she waited until she got home and Mummy said: Wherever did you get that notion? It's just the new ambulance siren.

We must never forget, that's what they learned in school, and Mummy said it too. Mummy didn't buy anything that came from Germany, except a nail file by mistake once. In Israel they had lots of Volkswagens because Germany gave them out of guilt, but Judith's family would never buy one. They are the car Hitler invented. Some rich Jews drove Mercedes. Judith's Hebrew principal said: Your grandmother's teeth are in a Mercedes.

Once Mummy's Aunt Madie took a plane that had to stop in Germany. All the passengers were supposed to get out. Aunt Madie said: I have taken a vow. I will never step foot on German soil. They tried to argue with her, but she stayed on the plane until it left. Judith didn't know if she would have the guts.

Daddy said: We must be very grateful to Canada. If they hadn't let Zeide in, I would have been in Europe. He meant: I would have been killed in Europe. When Daddy grew up there was lots of anti-Semitism. Kids called him dirty Jew and beat him up. That never happened to Judith, because she went to a day school where only Jews went, and because of the state of Israel, where Jews know they can fight back.

You live in a different time, Daddy said.

TWO

"Judith, you go up and down, up and down." Her father shook his head over her. It was not good to be the kind of person she was, that was clear. Her stomach rebelled at this neat summation of her fate—a lifetime of going up and down with no controlling it, a perpetual victim of her temperament.

In her mind there were only two colours—black and white, her mother always told her. If only they were equally distributed. Unfortunately, the black periods lasted much longer than the few ecstatic moments granted to her every once in a while.

Only her friendships saved her. Because of her friends she was still alive at the age of sixteen. This she swore to her mother, who replied that her friendships were awfully intense and that when she got older she wouldn't need them anymore.

"Never," Judith declared. "I'll never not need them."

"Your father is my best friend." Her mother would smile, a silly smile.

Her mother thought Judith came from outer space. She'd hear Judith talking on the phone and say, "I never told anyone half the things you tell your friends. You must be your father's daughter."

But her father said, "You and your neurotic friends."

"Sharon's not neurotic," Judith would say triumphantly, not sure exactly what it meant but knowing she was right. Sharon was the most normal friend she had.

Sharon had come into Judith's life when they were both eight.

The third day of Grade Three a tall skinny girl with frizzy hair had been led in by the principal, looking bewildered. Judith could no longer remember how they started talking or when they figured out they lived ten minutes away from each other. One Friday night Judith's family was invited to friends for dinner and Judith got permission to sleep at Sharon's house instead of going home. Eight years of sleeping over followed.

On Saturday mornings they would wake up together to go to Junior Congregation. Saturday afternoons they would call each other up in the boredom of this slow Sabbath day when they couldn't write or ride and decide to be bored together. Judith thought this the true test of friendship. On those afternoons they'd raid Sharon's brother's closet when he wasn't home. Behind the rows of swaying ties—he was nearly bar mitsvah—was a high shelf stacked with games. They played Careers for hours, and Clue, keeping score with toothpicks instead of writing. When no one was home they played Ann Landers Talks About Sex, a game they made up after Sharon saw Ann Landers on Johnny Carson and imitated her voice ever after, standing on the upstairs landing in her blue housecoat with red buttons, proclaiming: "No kisses before the third date."

Sometimes they were forced to play outside, where they'd build a snowman in Judith's backyard until it was too cold to stand it and Judith's mother let them come in for hot chocolate. On winter Saturday nights when the Sabbath was over at five, one of their fathers would drive them to Valley View Rink for ice skating, where boys they didn't know would laugh at them, Sharon towering over Judith in her green ski jacket that was too big but that everyone expected she'd grow into any day.

Every fall they'd bike to Coles and buy stacks of new notebooks, pencil erasers, binders, reinforcements, homework books and all the bright-coloured school supplies that made them resolve to start everything over again this year. During school Judith would suffer—everyone hated her, there were gang wars and plots—and Sharon, always liked wherever she was, would meet her after school to commiserate. "Debbie thinks you're a snob and that you study more than you say you do, but she was only put in the A class because her parents forced them to take her, so just ignore her."

Of course Judith couldn't ignore her, or any of them. No matter how fiercely she clenched her fists and told herself she didn't care, she did care. She wanted to be popular. She wanted to be the one everyone wrote notes to and chose first for soccer before school and invited always to birthday parties. What good did it do to get top marks when everyone was mad at her for it? And it was all a joke anyway, copying articles out of encyclopedias for projects, copying the flaps of library books for book reviews. "I can always tell a cheater," one teacher said at the start of the year. And Judith held her breath when the first reports were given back, waiting to be found out, to be shamed in front of everyone. Then came that special smile, softened for her, and her plagiarised report was placed gently on her desk, a bright red A in the upper corner and a comment like "Well done" stamped across the top. So much for school.

In the sharp days of autumn when the sun burnt the leaves and the city was full of their smell and the sound of their crackling underfoot, Judith would wake in the morning brimming with feeling. Under that cold blue sky it was terrible to be shut up all day until nearly dark. She wanted to fly, she dreamed of running down the street so fast that her feet lifted her off the ground. Her lightness, her small self, would be the reason that only she could do this amazing thing. Sometimes she forgot it was a dream and thought it was something she knew, like playing the piano.

In spring the green smell of grass was intoxicating, and then came lawn mowers and sprinklers and long blue evenings with roses and honeysuckle. Judith and Sharon lived in the park, staying after nine until it was dark though they knew they'd get yelled at. They walked to the drugstore on the hot summer days, bought spaghetti strings of red licorice, bags of black balls that turned colour in their mouths if they remembered to take them out and check, toffee that came in three flavours, candy buttons stuck on paper in dots or strung on necklaces, Popsicles, Creamsicles and marshmallow broomsticks.

Every year something wasn't kosher, the Orthodox girls would report to the class. One year it was blue Chiclets, which Judith promptly stopped buying. One year it was Coffee Crisps, a sacrifice she wasn't willing to make. When Debbie came in and told them all that five-cent Hostess Potato Chips were kosher but tencent weren't, Judith gave up trying to keep track. Sharon wasn't as strict, about lots of things. Her parents let her watch TV whenever she liked and she was allowed to see *The Man from U.N.C.L.E.* even on weekdays, and Johnny Carson, which was on so late that Judith didn't know what he looked like.

Judith's parents told her to read. "TV's a waste of time, it's junk," her father said. He watched the worst things, cowboy movies and documentaries and Jacques Cousteau, while her mother read in the kitchen. So Judith read too.

First there were the picture books her mother chose with her every week from the old library that had once been a church and still had stained-glass windows. As soon as she could read she went herself, starting with fairy tales—*The Green Fairy Book*, *The Yellow Fairy Book*, *The Violet Fairy Book*, which wasn't the best but had the best name. Then she read magic books, *Half Magic*, *Thirteen Is Magic*, *The Ship That Flew*, *The Tree That Sat Down And The Stream That Stood Still*, and the Narnia series over and over again.

"C. S. Lewis," her mother said, "is Christian allegory."

All Judith knew was that when Lucy hid in the wardrobe she discovered a world full of wonder and delight that she could enter whenever she wished. Judith didn't care who Aslan was supposed to be, he was the greatest power for good in the world. And when the children went to a better world in *The Last Battle*, Judith fought it vigorously, reading the ending again and again hoping there'd been a mistake.

Of course there were Nancy Drews and the Hardy Boys to keep her busy. Her mother refused to buy Nancy Drews. She called them junk and couldn't understand why when Judith opened the hard yellow covers she couldn't put them down. Often she read through the evening instead of doing her homework, staying up too late, waking to read through breakfast, the bus, and any classes she could. If she had no Nancy Drews to trade, the least she could do was get them back to the owner the next day. She always did.

Judith read so quickly that she could go into Coles and read a Nancy Drew standing up in a couple of visits. "Look what you're driving me to," she'd complain. But her mother would say, "I said the same thing to my mother and she said, wait until you have daughters." Judith swore to herself that she'd never forget how awful it was.

Sharon didn't read. It was the main difference between them. When Judith came over and read cereal boxes while she ate, advertising brochures that came in the mail, *National Geographics* because they were there, Sharon was furious.

"Please stop," she'd say. "Judith."

When Judith read, nothing penetrated.

"Judith."

Judith read on.

"If you don't put that book down you can go home right now," Sharon said. "You think this is fun, watching someone read?"

Reluctantly, in a blur, Judith would part with the written word.

Sharon was lucky she didn't have to depend on books. Judith wasn't allowed to watch TV during the week, she wasn't allowed to watch *U.N.C.L.E.* ever because her father thought it was too violent, and even when the *Miss America Pageant* came on she couldn't see it because it started at ten. This was injustice, it was going too far, and Judith brooded about it.

There were other injustices. First of all, there was Sharon's brother. He thought he could be boss just because he was older. He bothered them and let his friends tease them and told them to get off the phone when they'd been on five minutes. Just as bad was Judith's sister Naomi. She was two years younger and Judith's parents always wanted her to go along. In vain Judith pleaded that Naomi was a baby, that she embarrassed them, that Sharon and Naomi didn't get along. Her parents were firm: "She's your sister." As if that alone were an argument.

They couldn't do anything about Sharon's brother or Naomi but some things were possible. One year *Miss America* was on the day Judith had to sleep over at Sharon's to finish their Iroquois Indian project. At nine-thirty Judith phoned home as she was required to do, and when her mother said, "Are you in bed?" she truthfully answered yes, lying next to Sharon in Sharon's parents' bed, the TV at their feet just waiting to be turned on. Judith squelched her guilty feelings with Sharon's assurance that she hadn't lied, and they settled in for an evening of opera singing, gymnastics and swimsuits, with elaborate somersaults of their own from one side of the double bed to the other during commercials. At five to twelve they discovered that they'd picked the winner, and Judith imitated her acceptance, sniffing imaginary tears, "I pledge to make the world a better place in which to live," while Sharon intoned, "Miss Tennessee believes that sex before marriage is all right for some girls but not for her." They laughed themselves to sleep.

Always laughing. It was their trademark. At the ballet when Nureyev came out and Judith whispered to Sharon, "That man forgot his pants." On Valentine's Day when Sharon was sick of her candy hearts and dropped them into the underwear of a mannequin, hoping a saleswoman wasn't looking, laughing and afraid they'd get arrested. On the subway, finally, after an hour of persuading their parents that they were old enough to ride it. They rode all day that Sunday, up and down until they knew every stop in order by heart, first in their class. And they were first to go shopping themselves, alone without their mothers in Eaton's, the biggest department store, riding the escalator sitting down until Sharon stayed on even when she reached the top and Judith watched her laughing face change expression as the escalator shredded her new shorts outfit and part of her behind too. Sharon's mother didn't think it was funny but they did, laughing for months afterwards at the picture Sharon had made, her sweater wrapped around her waist for the rest of that day.

It was funny, too, standing on the bus when everyone thought they were sisters, and if Sharon sat down when the bus was crowded there was always an old lady to say, "You should be ashamed of yourself making your little sister stand." Mutt and Jeff, Sharon's aunt called them. It was less funny when Sharon's body grew faster in other directions. Judith knew that sooner or later the moment of reckoning would come, and sure enough one week after the start of school when they were both thirteen Sharon walked in with those two strap lines showing through the back of her blouse. "My mother made me do it," she apologized. "She said I needed it."

There was no doubt that Sharon had something. She went straight into a double A. Judith prayed every night to be able to fit into a triple A but she was totally flat, there was absolutely

34

nothing. And she wouldn't stoop to the indignity of a trainer bra, which her mother wouldn't buy her anyway. At the first sign of anything Judith forced her mother to take her to The Young Place, where she fearfully tried all the triple A's, hissing at her mother to make the saleslady stay out until she found one small enough. She wore it under any top that was even slightly see-through or on days they had gym and thankfully left it in her drawer the rest of the time.

It was the bane of her existence, this body. Naomi, two years younger, two grades behind, looked older by far and already got calls from boys in high school. Judith's mother assured her that she had been small too, and that she hadn't looked her age till she was sixteen. Judith fervently hoped she wouldn't have to wait that long.

Then there were her glasses. She wore them like the rest of the girls in her class, slipping them on at the last minute when the teacher began writing on the board and tearing them off as soon as the bell rang to change classes. Judith's eyes were worse than anyone's, and she became very good at identifying people by gesture, by clothing, by anything but the muddled skin and hair colour that they became more than two feet away. Her mother had promised her contact lenses when she was sixteen but that looked like forever. It was bad enough that she had no friends but to look like a reject too! She cried to her mother and yelled at her, it was her fault, she hadn't asked to be born into a family that grew like retards, it didn't help that her mother had gone through it too, her mother clearly hadn't cared as much or she couldn't talk about it so calmly. Maybe she needed pills, maybe there was something wrong with her. When the family doctor examined her for her regular checkup, added a point on her growth chart and said cheerfully, "Good things come in small packages," she groaned. "Will I make five feet?" she begged him. He couldn't promise but thought she might.

She wasn't sure she would live to see the day. Sharon stuck by her when they were put in different classes, but she had her own life and couldn't understand. Sharon gave parties in her rec room and decorated the walls with paper cutouts. She wore a gold lamé paper dress and dangling earrings, and everyone danced to the Beatles and Herman's Hermits. At thirteen there were bar mitsvahs with night affairs, those mysterious parties that started at eleven when the dinner and speeches were finally over. Then the grownups danced and the girls gathered in a nonchalant mass, defying the boys on the other side of the room to dare ask one of them without the other and defying them not to.

All the dinners were the same, chicken in a basket or roast beef, ice cream with no milk in it because it was a meat meal and after-dinner mints that the boys ground into the ice cream or threw at each other. The school psychologist said that girls were more mature than boys at that age, and the differences soon became clear as the boys moved their seats to the front of the class, taking notes and answering questions while the girls barricaded their desks with stacks of books behind which they polished their nails or read magazines. If only the boys were older, if only they were normal. All day the girls stared at their backs in scorn.

By the time she was sixteen the girls at least were talking to her. After years of silence they acknowledged her existence as a human being whom they could compliment about shoes, complain to about boys, and gossip about only after school, infinitely preferable to the blank faces she'd once spent her days with. "I told you it would happen." Sharon was her usual optimistic self.

That was the problem with Sharon. She was too normal. It wasn't Sharon who'd seen her through, saved her life. That privilege, as Judith told her parents when they talked about her friends, belonged to Rachel.

Judith had met Rachel four years before at summer camp, two outcasts who proceeded to pour into each other all the passion that human beings were capable of, they were sure. Never had she known someone so interesting before. With Rachel began her obsession with talent. Did she have any? Was it too late to acquire some? How talented did she have to be? Because Rachel was unquestionably talented and Judith didn't know such gifts were possible.

Rachel played the piano the way Judith's father had always hoped to hear his daughter play. Confident, poised, she sat down on the bench the first time she visited and raised her arms over the keys like a real concert pianist. Not only were Beethoven arpeggio sequences not beyond her grasp but she could play any popular song she wanted, without sheet music or practice. Judith's father had dreamed of her having that particular kind of fun and waited from when she began at seven to see her play Gershwin or something, her friends singing around her in easy harmony. At least, that was how she imagined it, picturing him and his friends sometime in the forties, posed with mouths open, impossibly younger.

That was never to be, she realised when she met Rachel. It took having a good ear, and although Judith's two-part inventions were close to perfection after months of work, she still never knew what sounds would emerge until she brought her fingers down. Rachel was a composer. She could make up music out of a row of white and black keys. She could hear music in her mind and write it down without going near the piano. It was miraculous.

And that was just the beginning of Rachel's virtues. She sewed and designed her own clothes, she cooked for her father when her mother was out, improvising in the kitchen with Indian spices. She could do all the new dances, although no one ever asked her, she said—Judith couldn't understand why—and she brought up to camp a fabric-covered cigar box containing twenty-two different shades of lipstick with headbands to match. Judith watched her unpack in awe. She spent Friday nights having Sabbath dinner with her family while the rest of the world, it seemed, went to dances.

"They're awful," Rachel would moan. "I sit on the side and watch Patty and Colleen dance with Scott and John all night. I'm a wallflower," she'd cry. "And I have a nose like Barbra Streisand."

It always came down to her nose. Rachel was convinced that Scott McBain would love her madly if only she had a small, upturned, fine-boned nose. Judith considered herself a good judge of such matters, as she spent most of her days thinking of what she'd look like if she could be reborn. Although she wouldn't have asked God for a nose like Rachel's, she wouldn't have cried every night if she'd been given one.

She cried because she looked seven years old. The girls in her bunk assured her she was cute but she wanted to look good in a two-piece. As much as anything else, that was what she envied in Rachel. Rachel was as short as Judith, but unlike her she seemed to have missed the awkward phase. She had hips. Where Judith was straight up and down, Rachel went in and out, a delicate curve that Judith couldn't stop staring at. She looked good in everything and she looked her age.

Of course Rachel wasn't satisfied and envied Judith for things Judith found incredible.

"You can talk to people," Rachel said. "You can tell jokes and make conversation. I just freeze. With you I'm all right but in a room, in just a normal room of people, I'm a dummy, an idiot."

And yes, Judith could talk and they did, about everything—Jeremy, Rachel's first love at camp who left her the following summer for a girl who'd make out. America, where Rachel was from, and Canada, where Judith lived. The war in Vietnam and Rachel's two older brothers' angry denunciations and antiwar speeches. One night Rachel kept her up until five, battering her with statistics and descriptions that shook her to tears. And, always, Jews. What it was like for Rachel to be Jewish in a small midwestern town where there were only two Jewish boys in her class, both shorter than she. What a different language people who weren't Jewish spoke and how isolated she felt after Jewish summer camp and Judith. And yet how narrow Judith's world was, Judith who did not have a single not-Jewish friend, who spent her long days with Jews and came home to a practising Jewish house. Was Judith blessed or deprived? Neither of them was sure.

Rachel's brothers introduced her to the hippie life of Ann Arbor, and long-distance phone calls that were once about how life could be survived until Christmas vacation or summertime were now about how life could be survived at all. Rachel's brothers at college were offering her marijuana, which Judith pleaded with her, by phone, by mail, not to take. She thought it was like sex, irrevocable once you started. Rachel laughed at her reasons, gleaned from Ontario Health for Schools pamphlets—marijuana will make you crazy, it will get you hooked, it will lead to harder stuff. Rachel called it grass, tried it a couple of times before she told Judith and then said that she had never really heard music before.

"You can't ever understand until you've done it. It's impossible to talk about in words. But it's as if I were walking through Beethoven, stepping into chords that took half an hour each to hear. I stood inside Beethoven! And Blood, Sweat and Tears. Do you know their music was written to be listened to stoned?"

Judith didn't know. And the imagination that never failed her couldn't picture it. The next visit it was her turn to go to Rachel's, where she heard echoing through the house a song full of shivery strings and bells that took her breath away.

"That's gorgeous, Rachel. I can see why you love it."

Rachel sat cross-legged on the floor in a long pale blue skirt she'd made. Her hair, no longer set and stretched straight, swung forward as she shook her head.

"Judith, you've got to do it. You can't really feel it otherwise. I wish you'd do it with me, I'd love to see you stoned."

But Judith was committed to the evidence of her natural senses, even though she felt life hadn't yet provided her with the material to test their perception. What was she afraid of? She didn't know. She didn't want to need to be stoned to love Beethoven. Life in its real state might never look as good afterwards. Not that it looked very good right now, but she believed that if she hung on, if she took it as it was, maybe she'd be rewarded.

The summer they were fifteen, Rachel decided not to go back to camp and deserted Judith for Interlocken, a fine arts camp in Michigan whose catalogue Judith memorized. Music, art, drama, dance, and Rachel had to audition to get in. Judith went to the old place, knowing she'd be miserable without Rachel while Rachel was going on to great glories. For the first month Judith heard nothing, until finally on Parents' Day she pleaded with her father to be allowed to call. The woman at Interlocken's switchboard paused and asked Judith to hold on while she checked Rachel's whereabouts.

"You'll have to leave a message even when I locate her, you know."

"All right, all right." Judith was frantic as she watched her father's change swallowed by the black box. "Just tell me what to do."

"Hold on, ma'am." Seconds. Minutes. "It seems she's no longer at camp."

"That's impossible."

"That's what our records show. Try her at home." Click.

Judith called collect and found a subdued Rachel speaking slowly at the other end.

"Rachel, why aren't you in camp?"

"It's a long story. I couldn't write, I'm sorry. Too much happened."

"What happened?" Judith was hopping from one foot to the other. "What the hell is wrong? I've been going crazy not hearing from you."

"I've been going crazy."

Judith was cautious. Hadn't they both been, always? "So what else is new?" She tried to laugh. But Rachel was very serious.

"Judith, I don't know how to tell you this."

"Try me. Have we ever not told each other anything?"

Then Rachel was blurting it out. "Interlocken was wonderful, I was practising six hours a day and taking jazz classes and improvisation, and then we had to place for the orchestra and everyone went nuts, working in the practice rooms nine or ten hours at a time and staying up hyper for half the night and I just couldn't take it so—"

"So?"

"I swallowed a bottle of aspirin."

Silence.

"Are you kidding? You're not kidding. You couldn't joke about something like that. My God, you could have died. You could have killed yourself. What on earth would I have done? I feel like someone punched me in the stomach. How could you do it without telling me? I mean talking it over. Letting me know what was going on in your crazy brain. I mean brain. I don't know what to say—"

"You've been doing all right." Rachel was laughing. "Look, I obviously didn't really want to end it all since I called my counsellor about halfway through the bottle and got rushed to the

40

hospital to have my stomach pumped. That was so bad it wouldn't be worth trying again."

"Your parents must've been ready to kill you. So to speak."

"They were all right. No better, no worse than before. I think I was hoping it would get them back together. At least that's what my shrink says."

"What back together? What shrink? See what happens when you're out of circulation for a month. What's wrong with your parents?"

"They have their problems. They're not very happy with each other. In fact, they're talking about divorce."

That was news. Judith didn't know anyone who was divorced. Her parents and all her parents' friends had the same arrangement, as far as she could tell. They got married when the women were twenty or twenty-one, they had three or four kids, and they stayed the same. Her own parents were a little behind—her mother was twenty-four and her father twenty-six when they did it—but Judith had often heard her mother say how much she'd wanted to get married and how afraid she was that she wouldn't and how not being married was a lonely life, just look at Betty Feingold, her only single friend, who'd come over for dinner and stay till all hours because single people have no one to go home to.

No wonder Rachel was shaky. Judith was unhappy but at least she could count on her family. That's what Rachel said when they compared the state of their souls.

"Your parents love you," Rachel said.

Why didn't it help? Her parents' love for her did not prevent her from getting into huge arguments with her mother about the size of her bikinis, which she was finally beginning to wear with aplomb if only her mother would leave her alone. It did not prevent her father's silent reproaches about the fact that they didn't talk to each other very much or that she'd dropped her Russian language option when he thought she should take it. And it certainly didn't help the most important area of her life—falling in love.

At sixteen Judith felt her life was behind her. Sharon had boyfriends steadily, Naomi had been going out with a boy for more than a year despite her parents' disapproval, and even Rachel had unhappily slept with someone, to Judith's resignation. She hadn't even talked it over with Judith first. Not that Judith had expected she would. Judith was worrying about meeting a boy she'd see more than once. Sleeping with a man was something to imagine in secret, like her wedding, so far off she could hardly picture it. For Rachel to do it now was hopelessness, the end without anticipation.

She gave up on camp and spent the summer in Toronto with weekends at her grandmother's cottage at Wabakiya, where thank God there were no boys at all so she didn't have to face it. Everyone she knew had been involved with someone in some way and Judith had been out five times. Five awkward times, fumbling for her glasses once the movie theatre was dark or laughing with someone who'd thought she was blond by her description of herself on the phone. She was brown. Brown mousy hair, brown eyes, dignified by "hazel" on official applications, yellow skin that she shivered in early April to tan. At sixteen she had a new friend, Anna, a tall thin daydreamer with a mane of yellow hair and great style. Anna wore plaid miniskirts with her brother's V-neck sweaters and looked fantastic. She let her hair wave naturally down to her waist at a time when Judith wouldn't go to school if the humidity curled her bangs. Anna was an artist who spent her days drawing girls who looked like her in gorgeous clothes she created, which her mother then sewed for her if they weren't too outrageous for the Orthodox Jewish community from which she came.

That year a boy in the grade above them, a swarthy lean boy with a moustache and burning eyes, stared at Anna and discovered her. He sent her a valentine, unheard of in their school, and told her she was beautiful. Anna glowed through her days, skipped classes, and spent two hours every morning getting ready. The boy wrote her poetry and worshipped her. He was romantic, debonair, and he too dressed like a dream, appearing on hot June mornings in a black shirt, white tie and fedora. They were the virgin and the gypsy, and Judith was their handmaiden, bringing messages from one to the other, her heart pounding when she approached him, for she too was madly in love with him even as she did everything she could to enable them to be together. He was not Orthodox, Anna's parents would never have tolerated it, and what tears, entreaties and pledges were exchanged over that. Anna could never hurt her parents, who had survived the concentration camps, so the boy left her letters in bushes and swept her away in his newly acquired car for secret meetings that were always too short.

Judith watched and took notes. This was what love was, this was how she looked at him and pushed her hair off her face with both hands, this was how he looked at her, like an angel whose presence blessed him, this was passion. Anna found something called Sun-In, which streaked her hair blond if she sat in the sun. By May her hair was a luminous glory, and Judith, who had just gotten contact lenses after years of sorrow, sat in front of her parents' house one Sabbath afternoon until the sun went down. When she looked in the bathroom mirror, a blond gold-skinned girl looked back.

Anna had a dream that when Judith went to camp the next summer she would find love. Judith had no hope but thought that perhaps she'd give it one last chance. Her father wanted her to sweat it out in the city, as he put it, to earn some money so that she wouldn't be spoiled and to see how the rest of the world lived. Her mother, worrying about her loneliness and probably her future marital status, suggested the counsellor-training program in New England that Judith's old summer camp sent its graduates to. Judith debated it back and forth—her father's favour or her mother's fear—and decided that for once she'd do what everyone else she knew was doing. Cool and wary, she applied to the program, ruthless in her lack of expectations. If nothing happened she could live with it. That's what she'd been doing all along.

Bet

The house stands at the end of the road behind a clump of trees at the turning. It is a two-storey house, low and squat, with dark green shutters on the upstairs windows and a screen porch that goes around the first floor. It has a screen door that doesn't fit and two lopsided steps leading up to it. Behind the screen door, her face fuzzy from the wire mesh, Judith's grandmother waits in her housedress that's the colour of the sky. On her face is her Friday afternoon welcome smile. It is the end of the week and the family is coming up to the cottage at Wabakiya for the Sabbath.

Every weekend in the summer Uncle Joel, her mother's youngest brother, drives up after work, bringing with him whichever cousins feel like coming. It is a two-hour trip from Toronto, but Uncle Joel loves to pass and on good days he can get it down to an hour forty-five door to door. Judith lies in the back seat, too scared to watch. She dreams of jumping into the river the minute they get there. Only when the first person calls out Wabakiya! does she dare pick up her head. Now he'll have to drive slowly. There are only dirt roads. They are almost there.

Twice the road curves and you think the house is around the corner, but those are false alarms. When you reach Shelton's Inn you turn right. Slow down at the marina, go a little left. Turn the car around, back up into the patch of gravel, slam the doors and jump out. This is it. Breathe deep. It is Wabakiya, the mixture of pine trees and river. The sun on the water far below the road, the boats. Turn around. Bobba is waiting at the door.

You run up and give her a big hug. She smiles like herself, soft and powdery. Hi, hi, she says, how was the drive? Uncle Joel kisses her cheek. The cousins are running all over the place, bouncing on the beds on the porch, slamming doors. Can we go swimming, where's the towels? Unpack first, Bobba says. Oh, Bobba, everyone says. She always tells you to unpack first.

Uncle Joel is first in. He makes a sound like an Indian, WHOOP, WHOOP, and races down the stairs with his hands over his head. Wait for me, it's no use, he has to beat you to it. He makes a huge leap from the dock without even feeling the water. Ah'm in, he cries, and the cousins jump in after him, scrabbling all over his slippery arms and legs, making water noises.

Judith goes in last. She sits down on the dock, feeling the wood through her bathing suit. She dangles her feet in the water. It's cold. She watches the cousins race each other across the river and sees Uncle Joel rub the soap through his hair, vigorously, washing off his workday. Come on, Judith, scattered voices, it's almost Shabbes. She stands on the dock, curling her toes over the edge. To the right up the river is Mrs. Floyd's dock and the marina far in the distance. On the other side the river opens into the lake. Pleasure boats pass back and forth. Across the way the lawns of the estate are green and rolling. An elaborate greenhouse catches all the light of the late afternoon, gold as a palace. The river is full of diamonds. Come on, lazybones.

Cool and green, the water licks her body, that's what it feels like. But there's no time to stand still. The current is strong and you have to be careful or it carries you into the lake and it's hard to get back. The cousins are good at it and unafraid. Judith has learned to love water but it's still a strange thing to her and she's careful, so she turns towards Mrs. Floyd's and slowly paddles towards the boathouse.

The river drifts from sun to shade. Where the trees bank the water, it is dark green, fingers of shadow lengthening across it into which she swims and then back into light, which now deepens to bronze, making her arms beautiful as they emerge, one after the other, rhythmic, even, to arch up towards the sun and then plunge deep into darkness, like putting on sleeves made of water.

Judith, Judith, turn around. How long have they been calling?

They're a blur on the dock. Now she hardly needs to swim, the river bears her along, past the shallows, past Mrs. Floyd's, across from the estate and she's home. The wooden ladder that Uncle Joel built was brand-new and pale last summer, but after a Canadian winter it's weathered and mossy. In a couple of years it'll probably match the dock. She climbs it quickly, shivering. Last in, last out. "Candlelighting," she hears Bobba call. Inside the porch she shakes herself, dripping, puts on her bathrobe and goes into the dining room.

The dining room is in the middle of the house and everyone's waiting for her. They all gather around Bobba as she puts the white Shabbes candles into her candlesticks, waves her hands over them three times and whispers the blessing to herself. "Ah-men," everyone cries out when it's over. "Ay-men," Uncle Joel says in his religious revival voice. "Good Shabbes, everyone."

"Now I need someone to set the table and someone to dry the milk dishes and get them out of the way," Bobba says. She looks at Judith. "And those who aren't dressed will help later." Judith runs to the back bedroom where her suitcase is. She has to move fast because there's not much light outside and she can't turn on the lamp now that they've lit candles. It's fun getting dressed in the half dark, groping for her dress in the closet, getting her shoes mixed up. Too late to dry her hair with the dryer, so it'll have to be curly. The cousins all have thick straight hair that they don't have to touch.

She takes out her nightgown and slippers for later and goes out onto the porch. There are always fights because everyone wants to sleep out here, which is the most fun and the farthest away from the grownups. Bobba makes them take turns and it is Judith's choice this time, so she takes her favourite place, the bed under the dining room window that looks out onto the side lawn.

The moon is rising over the water, a skinny crescent you can barely see. Everything's dark and quiet except for the square of bright window behind her, with the clank of silverware and Uncle Joel's humming as he finishes the prayer for welcoming the Sabbath. Before they start calling she'll go to the kitchen and see if Bobba needs help.

As she pushes the swinging door, the Shabbes food smell—warming challah and chicken and potatoes soaked in gravy and brisket and carrots—fills her up, it is so good, she can't wait. "Let's eat, let's eat."

"Miss Impatient"—Uncle Joel laughs—"where were you when the work was divvied?" He always says that. "Where were you?" she retorts.

"Now, now," Bobba says, distracted. She doesn't listen to see if it's a real fight or a joking one, she just wants peace. "I think we're ready. Is the wine out?"

The wine is out. In the light the table gleams. Old Wabakiya china, chipped and cracked, that the family's used since Judith's mother was little and came out here. Silver wine cups and big soup spoons from Queen Victoria's time, Bobba says. The challah cover that Uncle Joel chewed the embroidery off of when he was little. Everyone takes their places.

"Yom hashishi," Uncle Joel begins the kiddush. He can't carry a tune. Judith catches her cousin's eye and pinches herself. She looks at everyone standing around the table, quiet for once while Uncle Joel sings, and thinks: My cousins. My family. This is my family. It feels strange to notice them in that way when she has grown up with them and has known them all her life. Judith has eighteen first cousins. Her grandmother has five children and nineteen grandchildren counting Judith. There are five boys and fourteen girls. "My harem," Uncle Joel says. The cottage is always full on Shabbes with someone or other.

"Mikadesh hashabbat." Uncle Joel sips the wine and they all taste their own. Judith stares into her cup. The wine is sweet and purple, and if you hold your glass still, you can see the dining room light floating in it. Then the scraping of chairs on the floor as they go into the kitchen for handwashing.

Until a little while ago Wabakiya still had a pump in the kitchen, but Bobba finally decided to get hot and cold running water. Judith misses the pump, which she thinks she can remember, but as her grandmother says, she isn't the one who has to boil pot after pot of water for dishes or carry them upstairs for a bath.

Judith stands in line until it is her turn to wash. Then she fills the mug and dashes water over each hand, three times, saying the blessing as she dries her hands on the towel that's already sopping. After you've washed your hands you're not allowed to talk until the blessing on the challah, so the kitchen gets quieter and quieter as everyone finishes and goes back to the table. Whoever is the youngest says the motsi and then they all start talking and joking and Bobba goes to get the soup.

"Who wants a matsah ball?" she calls from the kitchen. "Judith, take orders."

"I do, I do," Uncle Joel says. That means he wants two. Almost everyone wants two since they're Bobba's specialty, and Bobba says, "If you have them all now there'll be none left for tomorrow's lunch," so only Uncle Joel gets two, because he's the uncle.

"When you're an uncle you'll get two too," he says to Judith.

"Ha, ha," she says back.

"The usual," she tells Bobba and carries in the bowls. Her parents always say before she leaves for Wabakiya, "Remember, don't let Bobba do all the work. Your grandmother works too hard." But it is hard to help her even if you want to because she hates fusses and thinks it's faster to do things herself than to explain how.

Now Bobba gets up to do the meat and Judith collects the soup bowls. She takes the chicken back in and Uncle Joel starts to carve. "Who wants a pulka?"—that's a drumstick. "Who wants a fliegel?"—that's a wing. Judith loves wings and luckily no one else does. The arguments are over the drumsticks. Bobba takes whatever no one wants, that's where Judith's mother gets it from. "Why make a fuss?" they both say.

There are roast brown potatoes with gravy from the gravy boat, carrots and salad and cranberry sauce. And challah to soak up the juices with, though it isn't polite. Pass the this, pass the that, everyone's making fun of themselves in their hunger. It tastes so good and pretty soon you're full, stuffed to the gills. "But there's still dessert," Bobba says. Uncle Joel moans, "Why didn't you warn me?" He's teasing, he knows that there are brownies at least and probably cake and cookies. Bobba has to make brownies when he comes because according to Uncle Joel there are two flavours in the world, chocolate and other, and he doesn't eat other.

On the sideboard are cookie plates wrapped in foil, and when the table is cleared by reluctant cousins Bobba unpeels the paper and puts down cinnamon cookies, brownies and lemon cake.

Someone takes orders for coffee and tea, and Judith has one of each dessert, they all do, it's the tradition. She licks her fingers and picks up the crumbs. At Wabakiya you can do what you want.

Then it's time for birkat hamazon, the long blessing after meals with all the tunes. Judith gets the giggles listening to Uncle Joel, and Bobba shakes her head, "Oh Judith, oh Joel," because he's winking and making funny faces as if he were still a kid. Uncle Joel goes straight to bed after supper, he's had a long day, and everyone else scatters around the house. Bobba says, "I'll just get the kitchen in order and then I'll call you for the dishes."

In the living room is a statue of Pocahontas on the wall, two rocking chairs that always feel as if they'll tip, a sofa covered with faded blue flowers and a big reading chair with lace arms. In the corner the bookcase is full of old Perry Masons and Wabakiya library books. On Bobba's desk is the 1921 dictionary she uses for crossword puzzles.

Two cousins play Anagrams, one reads in the rocker, another races up the living room stairs, jumps on the dining room chest, through the window and onto the bed on the porch. Judith picks out a Perry Mason and reads it until she gets sleepy. When she hears Bobba go up the back way to her bedroom she knows that the time clocks will turn the lights off soon and takes her book onto the porch for the morning.

The porch is pitch-black. It takes your eyes a couple of seconds to get used to it. Then slowly the shapes of the wicker chairs come clear, and the couch, and you can tiptoe past the other beds to yours, hoping you don't bump into anything. If you stand still, sometimes a car may pass by and for a minute it will be bright as day. The lights sweep from one end to the other and catch you for a second, frozen in your nightgown. Then you hurry to get under the covers and draw your knees up to your chest, head sinking into the old feather pillows, lulled by the occasional crunch of gravel, the crickets just outside the screens beside you, and from far away the faint slap of the boats going out past the point to the sea.

"When the Levys bought the cottage it was very primitive," her grandmother says. They are sitting on the porch together early in the morning before anyone else is up. Bobba has already walked into town to get the paper waiting for her at the barber shop, a standing order prepaid for the Sabbath. Judith could hear the pages rustling when she opened her eyes.

"The only thing that was better then was the side lawn. Now it's covered in waist-high weeds but in those days it was a very well-kept tennis court. There was no electricity, we used oil lamps and cooked on a kerosene stove, a big nuisance. There was no running water, only the pump outside. And of course we had no inside toilet. It wasn't any fun in the middle of the night in a thunderstorm!"

"How did you get everything done?" Judith asks. She knows the answer.

"Oh, the Levys always brought a maid who did the dishes and cleaning."

It is wonderful to imagine a maid.

"You wouldn't think so, but Wabakiya then seemed quite luxurious to me. When I met your grandfather's family they were rich but I was poor, and I certainly appreciated their invitation to the family's country place, my only outing of the summer."

"How did you get up here in those days?"

"We used to go up by train on the Canadian Pacific Railway, which left from North Toronto Station at Yonge near Dupont— it is now a brewer's warehouse—and there was a special Sunday night train back at seven o'clock for the weekenders. That was a very pleasant journey, the train filled with tanned healthy people all feeling jolly, with a stop at Burkton where we could get ice cream cones. Speaking of which, how about some breakfast, young lady?"

For breakfast there is Alphabets cereal, which only Bobba gets you because the parents think the sugar coating is bad for your teeth. Alphabets is the best cereal, and when the sweet milk is left at the bottom of the bowl you have to pour in more cereal to use it up. There is orange juice, which all the cousins drink, there's leftover challah to put as much butter on as you want, and Bobba's cinnamon buns are warming on the stove, sticky and plump, you can have as many as you like.

By now the cousins are up and everyone changes straight from pajamas into bathing suits. Judith looks at herself carefully in the bathroom mirror, trying to see if the men in the boats passing by will think she has a good figure. Probably not. She still looks too young, though she is wearing a bikini and it looks good enough for her grandmother to tell her it's a little skimpy.

"Who'll go into town for the mail?" Bobba asks. "Me," says Judith and the cousin next in line. "Me too," says the cousin after that one. They put on their thongs and beach robes and start walking to town. In Mrs. Floyd's garden her cats are stretching in the sun. The light is everywhere now, the day's warming up, but there's still enough crispness in the air for you to shiver in the shadows of the tall old trees over the road even as the air heats your hair.

They feel special walking into town in a line, the Levy grandchildren, different, Jewish. No one else in Wabakiya is. Once there were other Jewish families, Bobba says. They all got together on Saturday nights or Sunday afternoons and it was lovely. But they've moved away.

The post lady knows them and looks under L. "Nothing today."

"Thank you," they chorus and turn back. "Let's take the back road," Judith says. But the cousins want to go swimming.

Closer to noon the sun is hot on the dock and Judith lies on her towel, her head in her arms. She's dreaming of what will happen to her, a great love, countries she has never seen that she'll travel to, beauty, she will be beautiful. Looking down through the cracks of the dock, she can see tiny minnows in the shallows between the rocks. They dart back and forth from shadow to sun and she thinks of many things that dissolve and fade in her sleepiness.

The cousins are diving, showing off to each other, and they want her to join but she's lazy. Bobba comes down to swim. She's wearing one of her bathing suits with the skirts on it and she climbs in slowly at the side of the dock where you can still touch the bottom. She splashes water on her neck and arms and starts off along the shore, swimming in the direction of town until all you can see is her white bathing cap far off by the marina.

Everyone in the family is very proud of her. She has a Renaissance mind, they say. She read all of Shakespeare by the time she was twelve and she helps you with your math homework when your parents don't understand it. She has a Ph.D. in physics. She started a free Jewish day school in Toronto and she broadcast on the radio. But she acts like a grandmother. She bakes special desserts for you and worries if you go swimming and there's no one on the dock to watch.

"You have a remarkable grandmother," people are always saying to Judith, to the cousins. It is true.

Bobba emerges from the water content in herself. She takes her towel off the railing and goes inside to make lunch.

"Call me if you need help," Judith mumbles into the dock. It is a halfhearted offer. She loves the sun on her back, the full light, the way the blue of the sky and the green of trees deepen for the second after you open your eyes. She closes her eyes deliberately, often, for the pleasure of having the world spring before her again. On the river the yachts are going back and forth. The cousins assess them with an expert eye. It is their dream to be invited for a ride as one of the uncles once was when he was a boy. Not that anybody could go today, on the Sabbath. But for the younger ones it would be a real test of faith.

The older cousins don't like it here, they get bored. They complain that the river's polluted and how crowded the town has become since the new highway opened. The house is shabby, they say, and the furniture's falling apart. But they come anyway, everyone does. Bobba stays at Wabakiya all summer by herself during the week. She's never bored. She catches up on the *New Statesmans* that she hasn't had time for during the year and does crossword puzzles and does nothing, she says, smiling.

The cousins are trying to tell time by the sun.

"No later than noon."

"No way. One-thirty."

"One-fifteen."

"I'm going to check." There is a scurrying sound up the steps. And two minutes later, "Lunchtime."

It hurts your eyes to move from the outside white air, blazing, so suddenly into the dim porch, the grey painted floorboards cool under your feet. Judith gropes for the door to the living room.

"Bobba, do we have to get dressed?"

Her voice far away in the kitchen. "Anything will do."

"Beach party Shabbes," Judith calls back. "Is Uncle Joel up yet?"

"Very funny, young lady." She jumps. He is right behind her. "Come to the side porch, I've found a surprise."

"Lunchtime," Bobba calls.

They slip around the front porch towards the kitchen. "Would you look at this?" Uncle Joel says. He is pointing to a hole where the floorboard has finally rotted through.

Judith squints. "I don't see anything."

He lowers his voice. "Look more closely."

There is a dark space with a shape inside it.

"That thing?" she asks him.

"That thing," he says solemnly, "has been the object of my desire for thirty years. Because of that I lost the only chance I ever had of beating your Uncle Ben, my beloved older brother who was not beloved then, at horseshoes."

"The magic shoe," Judith pronounces.

"The very one." He opens the kitchen door.

"There you are," Bobba says. "I've been looking for you everywhere, Joel. Sometimes you're as bad as the children."

"Mother." He kisses her hand. "When you hear the reason for our slight delay you'll forgive all. Follow me."

Judith and Bobba follow him. Uncle Joel goes into the dining room where the cousins are sitting and blows an imaginary trumpet.

"His majesty would like to announce—"

"—that everyone's starving," Bobba says.

"That the magic horseshoe, missing and presumed gone for thirty years, has by a miracle and a rotting board been restored to the treasury of the Levy family. Now if I could persuade one of you slugabeds to mow the side lawn, to machete it more likely, I will fish the horseshoe out of its hiding place and take on all comers any Sunday morning. And I intend to have some stern words with your Uncle Ben on my return. He never once beat me when I used the magic shoe and I always suspected that its disappearance was no accident. In fact—"

"In fact," Bobba says, "one member of this family who is old

53

enough to know better will go without his lunch if he doesn't pour the wine and say kiddush and get down to business. There'll be no afternoon left at this rate."

"Shabbes afternoon," says Uncle Joel, covering his head before the blessing, "is for sleeping."

After lunch everyone makes their way to the bedrooms, cool and dark at the back of the house even at midday. The house is empty and yawning. Judith is sitting on the porch watching her grandmother read this week's Torah portion. She reads it carefully every week, the same chapters they read in the synagogue, mouthing the Hebrew sounds to herself and following with her finger. Then she takes a second look at the paper, reads the editorials, and climbs the stairs one by one to her room, where she too rests the afternoon away.

Judith has plans. She opens the screen door quietly and leaves the house. It is the middle of the afternoon. Judith walks slowly, kicking the white dusty road. She turns at the bridge and crosses over to the other side of the river. At the edge of the town away from traffic is an old clapboard house with a swinging sign that says WABAKIYA LIBRARY.

There is no library like this in the city. It is old and hushed and smells of books and sand from the beach. Mrs. Wilcox, the librarian, helped Judith's mother find books when she was a child and still remembers what she liked. All Judith's favourites are here, even the ones she's outgrown, which she reads again for the pleasure of finding them. There are two full shelves of Nancy Drew books. The city libraries never have them. There are piles of Harlequin Romances and a paperback shelf that you don't need a card for. The books are due back the following summer if you want them during the year.

Judith walks up and down the aisles, finding books she'd forgotten, looking for J. B. Priestley or C. S. Lewis in their old cloth editions, worn, loved. She collects an armful of books and magazines and sits at one of the tables all afternoon turning pages. Sometimes Mrs. Wilcox sits beside her and catches up on the news. When she can't read by the window light any longer, Judith gets up to go.

Outside, the trees are already dark against a darkening sky.

The river holds the last of the light and she makes her way home, hurrying now because Uncle Joel will already be saying the evening prayer. She can hear his funny monotone through the screens as she gets near the house.

The cousins are impatient for havdalah, which marks the difference between Sabbath and the rest of the week. When Uncle Joel is finished, everyone gathers around the dining room table. "Eliyahu hanavi," Elijah the prophet, they sing in the dark, "let redemption come quickly in our time." Then the wicks of the braided blue and white candle flare into light, the youngest cousin holds it as high as she wants her bridegroom to be. Bobba takes the spice box out of the cupboard and fills the silver cup with wine.

"God, deliver me, I am not afraid," Uncle Joel begins. "For you are my strength and will save me. In the past there was light, joy, honouring. Let it be so for us. I raise this cup and name you blessed, creator of wine." The cup catches the light.

"Blessed, for fragrant spices." Breathe in, cloves and cinnamon.

"Blessed, Lord of Lords, king of all days, creator of firelight." Hands are outstretched towards the candle.

"You who separate the holy from what is not holy, light from dark, Israel from the peoples of the world, the seventh day from the six days of doing, you are blessed, Lord, who gives a differed holiness from every day."

Uncle Joel sips the wine and then plunges the candle into the cup. It sputters and dies in the dark quiet room, a small death, an ending, the Sabbath departing on the wings of spices. Then cries of "A good week, a good week" and the room is full of light and clamouring. "A ride into town, come on, Uncle Joel, take us to town."

"Ice cream is for babies," says Uncle Joel. He likes it more than anyone. "Sundaes at Dairy Queen?" he asks, a formality. There is one ice cream place at Wabakiya and everyone goes except Bobba.

"Run along," she says, "no, no, I'm sure I don't want any. Drive carefully, Joel, have a good time." Her face, disembodied, hovering in the porch light.

Bobba never goes for ice cream. She says she can eat ice cream just as well at home. She likes the feel of the house to herself after the stir of the day. On Saturday nights she thinks about things to do. The *Times Literary Supplement* she's behind on, the new book on physics that she has to read. So much has happened since her time, she says, that she almost has to start over again. She thinks about antimatter and black stars, how a teaspoon can weigh a million tons. She thinks about matter so dense it absorbs all its light back into itself. The universe continually expanding!

Time to get moving before half the night is gone. There are lunch dishes to put away and the pillowcases are a disgrace. But first she must take her walk along the river. A slip of a moon, blood orange, is hiding behind the trees. The air is brisk. She'll need a sweater for the wind off the water. It's quiet at night except for the slow lapping at the dock and the occasional motorboat. The crickets sound unnaturally loud in the darkness.

She will walk down the back way where the stars are low and clear, down towards the light house at the point. Soon it will be time to start thinking of closing up the place for winter. For life is not an idle oar, she thinks, I must make that cake for Joel's birthday. September, September, she thinks, comfort me with apples.

THREE

On the plane ride to New York Judith and Sharon talked about guys. Sharon knew some who'd be at camp and she hypothesized Judith's possibilities. Judith smiled but doubted. The bus to camp left from a big New York synagogue and Judith stood on the steps and waited, looking at the people. She was wearing a green print dress and her hair was straight. The girls she saw wore straight-leg faded jeans and embroidered peasant blouses. In the humid air their hair was full on their shoulders or drawn up on top of their heads to spill down their backs, and Judith felt her foreignness, glaring. Sharon was saying hello to everyone she knew. Judith watched.

On the bus she sat behind a boy with red hair. He was saying goodbye out the window to two girls with red hair who looked the same. "Take care of her for me," he said to one about the other. The girl to be taken care of looked serious and sad. The two girls stood arm in arm for a while, looking at the boy, who leaned out of the window and talked animatedly until the bus began to leave. Then both girls waved goodbye and he did too, laughing. When the bus drew away from the curb he closed the window and sat down.

Sharon was telling jokes from the summer before to people across the aisle. She drew Judith into the conversation and soon everyone was being quick and snappy. Judith began a series of three-second quizzes, a game she and Anna used to play, terrible puns to be guessed in rapid succession. Nobody was getting the answers. Some things, it seemed, were still faster in Canada.

The boy turned around. He got the first one. He got the next one. She fired a third, an impossible in-joke that only Anna would know. He answered instantly.

"Now it's your turn," he said. "Guess what I have beside me here and mind that you keep your seat while you're guessing."

"A hat," she tried. No.

"A violin." Close.

"I give up," she said.

"The love of my life," he told her and held up a guinea pig.

"You're bringing that to camp?"

"That," he said, "is Viola, and my life has no meaning without her."

"I'm sorry to hear that," Judith said.

"Are you making fun of Viola?"

"I never make fun of people I don't know," she said and looked at him. He had long red hair and a clean face. He talked to her for a while, made her laugh, then turned around again. Judith looked out the window. They were driving through small towns, passing fast food restaurants, country houses, billboards, funeral parlours.

"How long a ride is it to where we're going?" she asked Sharon.

"Another hour and a half," she said.

Judith turned back to the window. Sometimes she talked to Sharon, sometimes she talked to the boy. Sometimes she sat still, lulled by the hum of the bus and the even catch of the wheels on the road, thinking of nothing at all.

They drove past water and into a clearing surrounded by trees. The bus abruptly stopped. "All out," the driver said, and everyone got up at once, reaching for their bags in the overhead racks, wriggling under seats, swinging guitars and tennis rackets. Sharon was already moving up the aisle and Judith hurried to follow her.

When Judith got out the boy was beside her. "See you around," he said.

"Yes," she said. "What's your name?"

"Ori," he said.

"Judith."

People were being assigned to their units and Sharon was nowhere to be found. Not that it mattered. They would probably be separated, since they came from the same city. Judith was on her own.

"Rafael," she told the guy with the clipboard.

"Gimel, unit three, over to your left, cabin twenty-six."

She picked up her suitcase and started off, wondering who her senior counsellor was, who else was in the unit and how bad the kids would be. She remembered when she was thirteen years old and impossible.

There was no one in cabin twenty-six and one made bed with a sign at the foot that said MARCY. Judith chose a bed on the other side of the bunk, to distribute the authority, and sat down. It was very hot. Her dress was sticking to her back, and her hair, so carefully straightened, felt as if it were curling fast. How could she get through the summer with this hair? She never wore her hair up. She used it to hide her face. Then again, she thought, what do I care? Where has all my work on my hair gotten me so far? She put it up.

The next step was to change. She'd brought so many clothes, but she didn't like any of them. What she most felt like wearing were her old painting T-shirt and cutoff shorts. She dug them out from the bottom.

A tall dark girl bounded through the door. "Hi, I'm Marcy, you must be Judith, welcome to camp, I'm sure we'll have a wonderful summer. I can't wait for the kids to come, can you?"

"I can wait," Judith said. "But I have two weeks of counsellor training to get used to the idea."

"I brought all kinds of games and activity plans. We have thirteen thirteen-year-old girls so we'll be very busy."

Judith knew exactly what kinds of games thirteen-year-old girls liked to play, and they were usually with thirteen-year-old boys. That's what Naomi was like then and Riva was getting to that stage. Still, Marcy was friendly.

"Why don't you unpack later and go down to the dining room for some lunch," Marcy said. "It's nearly two and dinner's not until six-thirty. I'll show you the way."

"Do you want to eat?" Judith was suddenly scared.

"Thanks, I ate already. Look"—they stepped out onto the porch —"that long building down the hill. Go ahead."

Judith walked down the path feeling naked with no hair down her back, the warm wind on her bare neck, on her legs, already tanned from Saturday afternoons on her parents' lawn. What am I doing here? she thought, then straightened up and decided to keep going.

The dining room was cool. Wooden picnic tables were lined up against one wall that was all window. The other half of the room was in shadow. Judith went in quickly and for a second she couldn't see anything. A couple of tables were set up for food, and she sat down at the nearest one and slid over until she was beside the window. She studied the yellow plastic plate. Then, remembering her resolve, she raised her head and stared straight ahead, stared at Ori, sitting opposite her several tables away, with nothing and no one between them. She held his gaze for a time, unsmiling, and then began to eat.

The rest of the afternoon was meetings and arrangements. By dinnertime the light had begun to soften and the summer sky was translucent. The girl beside Judith watched her as she looked outside.

"Are you an artist?" she said.

"No," Judith told her. "Why?"

"I'm a painter," the girl said, "and there's something about the way you're focussed." She laughed. "I'm getting carried away. But I have this instinct about people and sometimes I get a flash, and it always ends up meaning that the person—oh, I can't explain it. It's a sense. You're very concentrated. I don't know. Anyway, my name's Nancy. Cabin twenty-four."

"Judith, twenty-six. We're neighbours."

They compared counsellors and by the time they looked up it was dark.

"I seem to have lost my appetite," Judith said.

"Lucky you. That's one thing that never happens to me."

Judith looked at the food on her plate, then outside again. "It's pitch-black out there. It's a good thing you're next door to me or I'd never find my cabin."

"Oh, I know this place like the back of my hand. I was a camper here. Follow me."

Nancy led her to her door. "There's an evening activity for all new staff," she said. "Israeli folk dancing, I think. Change into long pants—I know it's hot but the mosquitoes can be fierce—and go to the social hall. I'd wait for you but I'm already late. If you go past the dining room you'll find a kind of road that leads through the forest straight to the hall. You can't miss it. Besides, there'll be other people on the way. See you later."

Judith looked at her stack of sweaters. None of them seemed right. What to wear folk dancing? She didn't even know how to folk dance and was tempted to stay in the cabin. She sat down on her bed, feeling exhausted, and stood up immediately. She went into the bathroom and looked at her makeup. "You come here to be a social human being, go be one," she addressed her image sternly. It looked back at her. In the dim light of the single bulb she barely recognised herself. The hair escaping her clip was frizzy, there was no other word for it. Even clipped hair only looked good straight. She undid it. "I'm not going to spend a whole summer worrying about my hair," she said out loud. "Too bad on them."

I'm a baby, she thought. How can I counsel kids? I'm just a kid. She shook her head in the air, pushed her hair back until it grazed her waist and lifted it up in strands until it stood out around her shoulders. "No halfway measures for this girl." She put on a bright red sweater and started off in the direction of the dining room.

But camp at night was a different place. The familiar patterns seemed to have dissolved, the other bunks were not where she thought they should be, and trees loomed inexplicably in front of her or receded into a distance she didn't know was there. Within twenty steps of her bunk she was lost. A faint mist muted whatever light there was and distorted the shadows. Judith stopped because she couldn't keep going. She waited, hoping that someone would come along. But there was no one. She was late. She was probably too late for the program. By the time she got there it would be over. Or nearly over and everyone would stare at her when she walked in. Where was Sharon?

In the darkness the night sounds were very close. Crickets and rustling, the buzz of insects, and somewhere in front of her the promise of water. She turned around in a circle. Moss, leaves, earth, the smell of summer, New England, full flowering, warm on her skin.

"Lost?" someone said.

"I am." She was grateful.

It was Ori. "Follow me." He took her hand lightly. A coincidence.

He led her through the dark as if she were blind, a walk that kept going in arcs around trees, crossing roads, past a bridge. "Where are we?" she whispered.

Voices and lights from a building ahead of them ended it. "We're here," he said, taking the steps in a leap.

He was wearing denim overalls with no shirt underneath, looking compact, a muscled clown. "Got my ballroom slippers on," he said, pointing to his hiking boots.

"You folk dance?" she said.

"I love dancing." He disappeared.

Inside, it was hot and loud. Ori was already part of a line of people who were bouncing up and down on the balls of their feet to Arab-sounding music. "Debka," the girl at the record player called out, and the line began to move in tight formation that got faster and faster until the dancers were flying.

Judith sat on the stage at the back and watched them. Many of the people in the room seemed to know how to do it. But there were others who were lounging and talking, and one of them, she was relieved to see, was Sharon.

"Where have you been?" Judith asked. "It feels like a year since I last saw you."

"Can you believe that this morning we were in Toronto?" Sharon said. "This has been one long day."

"I'll say," the girl beside her agreed. "Would you look at Ori?"

Everyone turned around. Ori was in the centre of the circle, his hair all over his face, kneeling and stomping a solo to the clapping of hands.

"Ori always was a pretty good dancer," Sharon said.

"How do you know him?" Judith asked.

"Everybody knows Ori. How can you miss him?"

The music reached a high point and ended. The dancers, exhausted, cheered each other and groaned when the girl who was choosing records announced, "Hora Nirkoda." Still, they assembled for more. But Ori came running over, soaked with sweat.

"Hi, guys," he said to them.

"How's it going, Ori?" Sharon slapped his upturned palms.

"Looks like it'll be a hot camp season," he said. "If only the kids wouldn't show up. Precamp is the best part. Do you think I'm too old to be a camper?"

"I'm excited to meet my kids," Sharon said.

"Not I," said Judith.

"A girl after my own heart." Ori looked at her. "I take it all of you are staying around?"

Sharon said she was.

"I think I'll head back to my bunk. Too much exercise can destroy a person. Maybe you should go back while I do," he said to Judith, "or you might not find your way."

Judith wasn't sure. Was the evening over? Would she miss something? She could tell by the set of Sharon's shoulders that she was consciously looking away.

"All right," Judith said. "Let's go."

Again there was no one else around. Ori walked beside her and they began to play the game they'd begun on the bus.

"Would you rather be a green light or a red light?"

"Green," she said, "for going."

"Me too. Would you rather be an up escalator or a down one?"

She thought for a second.

"No thinking allowed. Instinct, instinct."

"Up then. I hate stepping out into nothing."

"Me too."

They were back in the field somehow, near two chairs. Ori sat on the arm of one, Judith on the other.

"What's the most important thing about you?" she said.

"I'm a descendant of Rashi, the medieval commentator on the Bible."

"I know who Rashi is," she said, "I went to a Jewish day school."

"Me too."

"Where are you from?" she asked him.

"New York. And you?"

"Toronto."

"My mother's from Toronto."

They were quiet.

"Say mazel tov," Ori said.

"Mazel tov."

"Thanks, my birthday's tomorrow."

"You're kidding. Did you just think that up?"

"I'm serious, my birthday's tomorrow. I'll be seventeen and I have to go back to the city to have a little chat with my draft board."

"You came here for one day?"

"Ah, that it were only a day. But no, I am giving up pizza, my stereo and Broadway for a summer in camp. Camp! How'd I get talked into this?"

"I don't know. How did you?"

"Oh well, my sister will be coming up soon. You have to meet Jessie, she's the best. She'll be in the oldest unit."

"What does she look like?"

"She looks good. She looks like me." He paused. "Those two don't necessarily go hand in hand."

"I'll keep it in mind."

Quiet again. The mist was still softening everything, unearthly.

"We could be anywhere," Judith said. "What a strange place. Kind of like—"

"—those pictures of the moon," he finished.

She nodded.

"You know, I'm really going to miss the movies." He looked around him. "We could be in one now. Maybe we are."

"Who're your favourite actors?" she asked.

"Who're yours?"

"I like the oldies. I really fall for the obvious. *Casablanca*. Those."

"I've been looking at you, kid," Ori said. "You know, your face is a perfect blend of Greta Garbo, Ingrid Bergman and Marilyn Monroe."

She looked at him. He looked back at her, serious.

She said, "It's getting late. I should get back."

"What cabin are you in?" he said.

"Twenty-six, Gimel."

"I'm in Gimel too," he said.

When Judith got in to her bunk Marcy was already asleep. She walked over to the mirror, propped up against the window where the light from the porch fell on her. A golden girl. Her

hair was spun in waves around her face, and her face was transformed. She touched her mouth. She saw what he saw. Judith did
not sleep that night. In the morning she put on her clothes with
trembling hands. Something is happening to me, she thought,
something's going to happen.

Sitting on the grass in a counsellors' meeting, Judith pulled her
hair over her face and watched the world through it. She could
feel her skin getting browner already, the sun lightening her
already light hair. She couldn't concentrate on the instructions.
When the meeting ended everyone decided to go swimming.

"Let's go out of camp," Nancy said. "Let's go to Fraser Lake."

"Where's that?" another newcomer asked.

"I'll tell you what, go back to your bunk and change, and we'll
all meet here in ten minutes."

Back in the cabin Judith debated over her bathing suits. She
had a brand-new one-piece with cutout sides that Bobba had
bought her and an old bikini of Naomi's with strings on the legs
that tied up to make the bottom even smaller. The bikini was
faded and she'd almost left it at home, but she always felt good
in it so she put it on. She would wear a T-shirt over it and if
she were too conspicuous she just wouldn't take it off.

But she hadn't reckoned on the American girls. Nancy wore
a shocking pink bikini, looking like a gypsy, dark-eyed, voluptuous, and another girl had a crocheted bathing suit the colour of
skin. Still, looking at people looking at her, she realised that the
old bikini must be all right.

Ori was not at the beach. He'd come to the meeting but left
early. Then she remembered about the draft board. Maybe he
won't be able to come back, she thought. Maybe he'll have to
stay in the city to straighten things out. It could take weeks.

She stretched out her towel on the hot sand and lay down on
her back. The sky was flawless. Around her people were playing
in the water, listening to radios, reading the paper. She was so
tired. Her eyes felt heavy from the glare and she closed them
until the sky was only a thin blue line between her eyelashes.

"Judith, Judith." Nancy was shaking her. "Don't sleep on the
beach. You'll be burnt to a crisp. Come on into the water."

Nancy pulled her up and dragged her, protesting, to the edge
of the lake.

"I don't want to get wet," Judith said.

"Come on."

It was warm on her skin and she began to swim out, facing the sun, which scorched the water ahead of her in circles of yellow. Around the lake the trees were perfectly still. Judith swam until the people on the beach were coloured smudges, keeping her head up for her hair, elated by the looseness of her body buoyed by water. Her limbs looked disconnected. No one else was out this far.

She could probably cross the lake if she kept at it. The sun blazed in the sky. She wished she knew how to tell time that way. The top of her head felt very hot. Maybe she should go back.

"Hey," she heard a voice as she got closer to shore. "Hey."

People had already collected their things. "Dinner in an hour, Judith," someone said. She shook the water off her into the sand, where it disappeared.

The day was nearly over.

Judith wanted to go to dinner in her bathing suit. She didn't want to lose the feeling she had inside her body, all of a piece, for once. But the day was caught in the trees, high up, so that the bottom branches were very dark but the crowns were still light. It was evening, earlier here than in the rest of the world because camp moved its clocks back so that the kids could fall asleep in darkness.

It was hard to believe the kids would ever come or be important in any way once they did. Time seemed to have stretched since she had arrived. The morning was past, the afternoon gone. And the night before, a dream, imagining.

At dinner Nancy called her over. "Sit down, Judith. I want you to meet a friend of mine. Gabriel, this is Judith. Judith, Gabriel."

Green eyes looked at her. Gabriel sat tall and thin, his skin pulled taut over fine bones.

"Gabriel and I have the same yoga teacher," Nancy said.

Judith couldn't stop looking at him. He held himself perfectly balanced, harmonious, refining the room around him. Nancy and he ate slowly and talked.

"I'm going to lie down," Judith finally said.

"Anything wrong?" Nancy asked her.

"Just tired."

She went back to her cabin and tried to rest. Ori's hands, touching her fingers, the sun on the water, the waning light, Ori's fingers, the way his shoulders moved while he danced, an imagined New York, his sister, her sisters. It was so long since she'd seen her parents. Alone in a new place Judith slept.

"Psst." There was scratching on the screens.

"Who is it?" She sat up, alarmed. The porch light cast an eerie film on her pillow, on her hands. They looked white.

"It's Ori. I'm back, and desolate. Can you come out?"

"What time is it?" She looked over at Marcy's bed. Empty.

"It's early. Eight o'clock. Come on out, I'm alone in the world."

"One second." She pulled her fingers through her hair and got her shawl.

Ori was standing outside, one foot on the step, one foot on the ground. He was wearing a sweat shirt that said I LIVE ON SESAME STREET and holding a bike by the handlebars.

"Where did you get that?" she said. "And what are you talking about?"

"Mom drove Jessie's things up today and brought me back. She made me send Viola home with her. Camp's no place for a guinea pig, my mother says. I'm heartbroken. The bike's my consolation. If things get too rough I can make a quick getaway."

"You're crazy."

"Crazy or not I'm taking you for a ride."

"Nothing doing."

"Coward."

Ori sat on the bike, holding it steady while she gingerly swung herself onto the bar.

"Pretend you're Katharine Ross in *Butch Cassidy*." He began to pedal furiously.

"I confess, I'm chicken," Judith cried out, but Ori was concentrating on building up speed. The wind on her face, his arms were around her, holding her on. Ori was singing in her ear, "Happy birthday to me, happy birthday to me," careening from one side of the road to the other, over the bridge.

"Where are we going?" she yelled.

"China," he said and stopped the bike.

Judith got off and massaged the back of her legs. "I'll be shaped like a bicycle," she told him.

"We're here."

They were parked in front of an empty bunk.

"Anybody home?" Ori knocked on the window.

Tires squealing, another bike appeared and on it a girl with red hair flying behind her.

"Ori, I knew it. I knew it! I had a feeling you'd be here when I got back."

"Judith, this is Jessie, my sister."

They looked like twins, and she was one of the girls from outside the bus. It was funny to see the same face on a boy and a girl. They were hugging each other in quickstep like a silent movie.

"I have to talk to you," Jessie said.

"Later," Ori told her. "We're off to the frappe stand."

Judith didn't know what he meant.

"Soon," Ori said and motioned to the bike. Judith got back on, Ori waved goodbye to Jessie and drove through the camp gates and down the highway past the lake. Cars flicked by them but Ori rode on, undaunted, and stopped at some tables at the top of the hill, very out of breath.

"Not as young as you used to be," Judith said.

"Of course not. I'm a year older now, what do you expect?" He bent over and tottered on an imaginary cane. "Dearie, you won't get much out of me."

She started to laugh. "Ori, where are we? What's going on?"

He pointed behind her to a hut set back from the road with a sign that said THE FRAPPE. ICE CREAM, FRAPPES, HOMEMADE FRENCH FRIES.

"What's a frappe?" she asked him.

He struck his forehead. "What's a frappe? Oh, a foreigner. Poor you. Never to have tasted a frappe. How old did you say you were?"

"I didn't. Sixteen."

"That you've lived sixteen years without the tang of a frosty frappe on a warm summer eve. What can I say? I feel bad for you."

"Don't pity me. Educate," she said and walked up to the counter.

"We'll have two black and whites to go," Ori said.

Black and whites were made of chocolate syrup and vanilla ice cream. "A milk shake," Judith said.

Ori shook his head. "That's where your roots are revealed. A milk shake is, logically, milk with syrup in it. A frappe adds the ice cream. But, to be frank, these rules hold true only in Massachusetts. In New York we call them milk shakes too, but I'm into this new food concept."

He finished Judith's and they began to cycle back to camp. It was still very warm and the darkness around them hummed with growing things, the beginning of corn and fluttering leaves. The air was rich and heavy.

"I don't want to go back," Judith said.

"We won't," Ori said promptly. He crossed the road and stopped in front of the beach.

Over the water a swelling moon lit the sky and exposed the beach, empty before them. They walked over to the edge of the water and sat down. Judith hugged her arms around her knees.

"This is really beautiful," she said.

"You are really beautiful." Ori took her hand.

They sat quietly for a minute and then Judith said, "I can't keep going like this."

"Like what?" Ori said.

"This." She gestured vaguely at the water, at him. "I'm not sleeping, I'm not eating."

"I'm pretty out of it myself."

"What shall we do?" she asked.

"We could make love," he said.

"No we couldn't," she said quickly.

Make love, he'd said. She had never even kissed someone. How could she make love? How could he? How could he even say it so readily? He must have done it to suggest it. He was so young. With whom? How much?

"All right," he said easily. "We won't."

"That doesn't mean—" she said.

He took her in his arms. She lay back, looking out at the sky, at the water. He was touching her, his hands on her, she could hardly breathe. It felt so good. Under his hands she had no bones, the wind through her clothes, through her skin to the edge of her fingers. She was weightless, suspended between the hands and the earth, thinking, how strange, the hands could be anyone's.

"We could start with this," he said.

It was going to happen. She wanted to tell him she didn't know how, she'd never kissed anyone. She wondered what it would feel like, she was scared, what if it was awkward, what if he could tell that she didn't know what she was doing—all this as he moved her towards him, bent over her and put his mouth on hers.

His tongue was inside her mouth, moving around like a fish. It felt squirmy. She didn't like it. She didn't like kissing, what a terrible thing. She lay on his lap, unbelieving. This is what people did. This is what people wanted to do. It was not like the movies. It was not like the novels. How would she ever get used to it?

After a while he stopped. He lifted his head and touched her cheek. He didn't seem to notice. Maybe she could get away with it.

"I have to tell you something," she said.

"What?"

"That was the first time I ever kissed anyone."

He was laughing. "I don't believe this. I do not believe this. Why are these things always happening to me?"

She wasn't these things, she was herself. But she said nothing. Then the air started to feel cold and she stood up.

"Time to go back," she announced, and they walked side by side, the bike between them, up the beach and the highway and into camp.

"See you tomorrow," he said.

She couldn't sleep all night. All night she lay in bed thinking about it. What would happen and was it love? The cracks at the edge of the screens became light and she got up in a daze.

"I am so light," she said to the mirror. Her face looked back as if she'd woken from a long rest. "Magic," she said. "This is magic."

At morning prayers she walked in casually and sat down on the first bench. Gabriel was there, his chiselled face in repose.

"How're you?" she said.

"Well." He nodded. "You?"

They sat together and she watched him arrange himself effort-lessly into yoga position. He sat taller and straighter than anyone, distinct. Ori walked in late on the other side of the room. She saw him out of the corner of her eye, talking, smiling, and fo-cussed on the service resolutely. Afterwards she walked to the door and he came up behind her.

"How are you?" he said.

"Exhausted."

"How come?"

"Couldn't sleep. I can't imagine why." She smiled at him.

"I slept like a log," he said.

Gabriel came up to Ori and they all walked to breakfast, Ori and Gabriel talking in animation, Judith feeling drugged. While they ate Judith watched them, Ori's body, Gabriel's face. She walked back to her cabin and thought about it all.

Early in the evening Ori came over.

"I have a proposal," he said.

"Already?"

He threw up his hands. "I give up. Come to the movies with me."

"Where?"

"Out of camp. In Fraser, about a mile past the lake. Are you ready?"

She felt sluggish, she felt like sitting still. There was a heavi-ness in her stomach, she didn't want to move.

"I don't know," she said.

"Come on, old lady. It'll be fun."

She sat down on the steps of her cabin. She was planning to take a shower and go to bed early. "I'm too tired," she finally told him.

"Well, I'm going. See you later." He was leaving.

"Have a good time," she called after him.

"I will," he said.

She imagined him next to some girl, maybe that dark-haired girl with the delicate face she'd noticed. She saw him smiling at her his way, touching her in the dark. She'd made a big mistake, she'd probably ruined everything. But it was too late. She did feel like an old lady, slowly taking off her clothes, and forced herself to put on her bathrobe and go to the shower house.

The hot water steamed up the mirrors, pounded into her back, loosening her muscles, and she stood under the shower for half an hour, head bowed, letting the water pour over her, watching it form and re-form in different streams down her body. She washed her hair and towelled it and untangled it with her fingers to let it dry in the air. It was wonderful to let it loose on her bare shoulders and not have to worry. She felt limp, at ease, and on the way back to her cabin she decided to get dressed instead of putting on her nightgown and take a book to read outside in the porch light. She put on her black top and combed her nearly dry hair beside the bed, taking her time. She ran the comb through it again and again until it shone against the black. She tucked her shirt into her jeans, feeling so thin, and choosing a book from the pile she'd brought, she turned off the light and opened the door.

Gabriel stood outside, so close to her he could only be waiting. He was carrying a book.

"Why don't we read together?" he said.

"How did you know?"

"I was watching you." He was watching her now. "I watched you combing your hair."

She felt her insides turn, a slow sweet weakness through her as he said that. It rose to her face and she said nothing but walked beside him towards the steps of the assembly hall, where they sat in the bright light.

He told her about Princeton, where he was accepted for the fall and where his father had gone. He told her about his younger brother, whom he loved and whom he'd just spoken to on his grandfather's birthday.

She told him about her grandmother, how unusual she was, and about her sisters and Canada.

He talked about camping, about being vegetarian, and how he'd become so involved with a guru that it became impossible to be Jewish and do yoga in the way his teacher asked of him. He said that he'd come to camp to deepen his choice of Judaism.

She talked about day school and tried to describe the boredom, day after day with the same people until nothing ever looked new or possible.

Why did she keep going back? he asked her.

She'd never thought of it. To get a Jewish education, she said. Where did he learn?

Then he told her about his Hebrew school and the group of kids he belonged to, and how he had loved someone for years and years and that just before he came to camp she'd married her adviser, a twenty-five-year-old man.

"How old is she?" Judith wanted to know.

"Eighteen."

"Older than you."

"By a year." They were quiet.

At the far end of the road the darkness was moving, it was people, their shadows stretching long ahead of them towards Judith and Gabriel.

"The movie must be over," she said.

"Yes."

"Well"—she began standing up, raising her arms over her head —"thank you for the evening."

He stayed where he was.

Ori was running up the path towards her. "Hey, stranger," he called out.

"What did you see?"

"Nothing. The movie was cancelled for lack of an audience. Camp people were the only ones there."

"So what did you do?"

"We went out for ice cream and hung out and then I came back. Here I am."

"There you are."

"Come with me to my bunk while I change into pants."

"I'll wait on your porch, thank you."

He looked at her with amusement as she walked beside him.

She could still see him through the screen door. He took off his shorts right in front of her, he was wearing no underwear, and put on his jeans leisurely. Before he was through she walked to the end of the steps so that when he came out she was standing far away.

He was carrying a blanket and they went behind the cabin through the woods to the border of camp. There was a huge field under a sky full of stars, a million constellations changing shape as she looked, a dog, a bear, Cassiopeia. She couldn't recognise any more.

"Do you know stars?" she said.

He set down the blanket and spread it out carefully, then lay down and pulled her beside him. The stars were all she could see.

"Dipper," he began. "Orion."

"Where?"

"Over there"—he pointed—"see his belt? The seven sisters."

"The seven sisters, what a wonderful name."

He turned on his side and started to kiss her.

"No," she said.

"No?" He drew back a little, then began to touch her, moving over her clothes lightly. Small shivers ran through her skin. She could feel him all the way up and down her and held perfectly still, not knowing if it was good to show him what was happening, not knowing if she was supposed to.

"Relax," he said and moved on top of her. His body was heavy, the smell of the grasses so strong all around her, and then his hardness through his jeans, she knew what it was, surprised that he let her realise it.

He moved around and then put his hand inside her shirt.

"No," she said.

He stopped for a while, then started again and she lay there not really minding. Then she felt his fingers on her throat, smoothing her neck and slowly spreading out, moving down. It was too much, it was happening so fast, if she did this much now there'd be nothing left pretty soon. She sat up.

"What's the matter?" he said.

"Enough."

"You're a strange one," he told her but stopped. "You can still lie beside me."

She did, and held his hand to her mouth.

"I never say I love you to anyone," he said.

"Why not?"

"I don't believe in it."

"Then you've never loved someone."

"That's not true."

She thought about it.

76

"I have something to tell you," he said.

"What's that?"

"I'm very confused. I don't know what I'm doing."

"About what?"

"You. Me. You and me. I thought I was in love when I came here. I still think I am, maybe. She's Jessie's best friend, she's at a different camp this summer, her idea, I told her not to do it, she hadn't written once and I just got a letter from her through Jessie and I'm so mixed up."

So that was why Jessie had looked at her in that way. "What are you mixed up about?"

"I was totally sure how I felt about her and I was even thinking of leaving camp, I was going crazy being away from her, but at the same time you were happening and that's made it so complicated."

"Why?"

"Because something very strange is going on. You keep saying what I was just about to say and I have a feeling it's going to get worse. Or better, whatever. There's too much of this in the air. Do you know what I mean?"

"I know."

"Is that all you can say?"

"What do you expect me to say? I think this is something you might have thought of telling me before you got me into all this."

"I thought. I thought. But it was too late, from the beginning on the bus it was too late."

She remembered the bus. "Does she have red hair?"

"How do you know?"

"I saw you say goodbye to her."

"This is giving me a headache."

"Poor boy. Maybe you should leave."

He wasn't leaving. "There's no point fighting this," he said.

"It's bigger than both of us," they both said and started to laugh.

"We'll have to improvise." He pulled her up, folded the blanket over his shoulder and walked her back to her cabin.

She lay in bed thinking of Ori and Jessie and the girl. On the one hand it mattered terribly and on the other it made no difference. She would win, she knew that. It would be harder or easier, he would realise it right away or take his time. She felt sorry for her. They shouldn't have split up for the summer. She wondered if the girl was really in love with him. Clearly he thought he was in love with her. He would learn.

So that was the beginning. Every day before the kids came Judith woke up, put on her bathing suit, went to the first meeting of the day and skipped the rest. Ori and she biked over to the lake and spent their mornings swimming, lying in the sun, playing elaborate water games that they invented, crossing the lake on the inflatable pillow that Ori had brought her back from his day in New York. They turned very brown. Soon Judith came to meals in her bikini, frowned upon by her supervisors, to whom she paid no attention. At night after the evening activity they took their blanket or Ori's sleeping bag and went into the field, Ori telling anyone who asked where they were headed that they were going to make love, of course, Judith shocked and bemused beside him.

"Well, we are, aren't we?" he'd say when she protested.

"In a manner of speaking," Judith agreed.

She had reached the point where she could take off her shirt in the dark and let him touch her. She did not like to kiss him. She did not want his hands anywhere else, or she did but she wouldn't allow him. She wondered how long he would put up with her, having already made love, been making love since he was fourteen, he said.

"Fourteen! You'll be a jaded old man when you're twenty."

"Can you see me jaded? I can't help it if a girl made it her business to help me lose my virginity."

"The man I marry," Judith said, "will be a virgin." Chuppah v'kiddushin, the hallowing of a wedding. It was what her mother had taught her and what she believed.

He thought that was very funny. "I hope you're willing to be an old maid."

She wasn't going to be. She was going to marry him. "The joke will be on you," she said now.

"Probably," he said. "Can love revirginize a person?"

She took that for agreement, though it didn't change anything. He was still writing to Jessie's best friend, he was still flirting with that dark-haired girl, and it turned out he was going to

Israel for a year right after camp. He couldn't wait, he was so excited about it.

On the last day before the weekend the kids were coming, the staff was scheduled for an overnight. Judith didn't want to go. "Mosquito bites and exhaustion, that's all you get out of it," she said. "It takes a week to recover from one. Maybe I'll stay in camp. Maybe I'll play sick. I feel sick just thinking about it."

But it was compulsory. Ori put a Frisbee in his backpack and Judith reluctantly collected her things, debating about a nightgown, did people take them. She hid her eye makeup in the bottom of the bag and started walking to the main gate to load her stuff onto the truck. They were off on a two-hour hike to the campsite and the truck would meet them there.

The hike began in the late afternoon, the wind shaking light and shadow through the forest. Judith stared at the underside of leaves, at the forest bed spongy with pine needles, stepping between patches of sun and cool darkness. Gabriel led the way, checking his map, shouldering his pack with ease. Behind her, Ori was talking and joking with everyone. The light started to slip away, moving slowly up the trees until the tree trunks were dark with a point of gold at the top. The sky turned white and the trees against it were enormous in the dusk.

By the time she had settled her sleeping bag in the clearing Gabriel was making a fire. She watched his long thin fingers carefully place twig upon twig, laced with newspapers, until he'd constructed a fragile pyramid. Then he held a match to its base and the whole structure burst into light.

"Suppertime," one of the counsellors called and began enlisting everyone's help in opening cans and dipping chicken pieces into honey mix to be barbecued. Ori was gone. Judith wandered around, restless and discontented. She didn't want to squat down in the clutter and dirt to prepare food. The wind was warm, she could feel it breathing on her face, the forest smells were so thick she felt faint. She didn't feel like eating, she wanted to find water, and as she turned to go look for it, she thought she saw Ori appear out of the trees behind her.

She was at the top of a slope and she began to move down, sliding in the leaves, her arms spread like wings. There might have been steps behind her, a rustling, she wasn't sure, and then there were hands on her waist and Ori's voice saying, "You knew I was here, didn't you? You left but you knew that I'd follow."

"I thought I was alone," she said and put her arms around him. "Isn't this amazing?"

Through the last group of trees a shimmer of water and a full moon hovering over it, multiplied in endless reflection.

"I want to make love," she said.

"In a manner of speaking?"

"I want to touch you."

"I know, this is gorgeous, but I'm starving. Let's wait until later."

"Later everyone will be around." Later she wouldn't feel as she did, poised, at the edge of it, empty, but she let him lead her back.

In the light of the fire everyone looked distorted, illuminated faces without bodies. The chicken was hot and sticky from honey and they tore off chunks and ate with their fingers until they were stuffed.

"I can't move," Ori said as they drank tea from styrofoam cups. "I'm really tired."

"I'm wide awake," Judith said.

"You know, I'm actually thinking of going to sleep."

"Go ahead. I want to sit by the fire."

"Why don't you come with me? You can watch the fire afterwards."

"I'm not tired," she said. "I'll see you tomorrow."

Other people had begun to leave for their sleeping places. The ones who were left pulled up closer to the fire, singing songs. Judith sat down on a flat rock and held her hands out to the warmth. Through the flames across from her Gabriel was staring into the light, meditating, Judith thought. She began to notice the shapes of the fire, tongues of light flicking the darkness in always changing patterns.

It took time. When she looked up, Gabriel was talking to Sharon and Nancy was moving over to join them. Judith got up and circled the fire. When she sat down next to Nancy, Gabriel smiled hello. She half listened to the conversation, Sharon, then Nancy, asking Gabriel questions, he answering in an even, thoughtful voice. It was getting very late and slowly most of the people were going. Sharon and Nancy sat on either side of Gabriel and he talked first to one, then the other. Then Nancy said she was tired and left. Judith and Sharon looked at each other and waited. Finally Judith said, watching what remained of the fire, "I have an idea. Since we're still awake, why not play hide-and-seek?"

"Not enough people," Sharon said.

"How would you play?" said Gabriel.

"You close your eyes," she said to him, staring at his face, "and we'll hide near here but far enough so that you can't see us. Whichever one of us you find first—"

"What then?"

Judith stopped. "I don't know. I guess it's stupid."

"Why not?" Gabriel said. "I'm not tired. We may as well."

Sharon looked at Judith. "I think I'm getting sleepy. I'm going to give up now."

Judith said, "If you like we'll just keep sitting here, if you want to stay."

"Thanks," Sharon said, "but I'm going. Good night, Gabriel, good night, Judith."

Judith and Gabriel watched her make her way around people sleeping until they couldn't see her anymore.

The fire was almost gone. The wind had died and the forest was very quiet.

"Look at the moon," Judith said. "It's sinking."

"False dawn," Gabriel said. "It must be close to three."

They sat opposite each other and talked about their counsellors, their classes, the weather. Then they both stopped.

"You know," Judith began.

"I know."

"Ori."

"I know."

She couldn't not look at him. She wanted to draw her finger down the lines of his cheekbones and knew she could not. Every way his head turned made him more beautiful to her.

When the moon was gone the sky began to lighten, a slight tempering of the dark until the trees started to emerge and it was just possible to see the forms of people's tents and sleeping bags scattered around.

"We should get some sleep," Gabriel said.

"I don't think I'll sleep tonight."

"Get some rest," he said. "It's better than nothing."

She looked at him and nodded.

He reached over and moved his hand once through her hair, then got up and walked quickly away.

"That wasn't fair," she said.

He didn't turn around.

By the time she was settled to sleep some people were already stirring.

Then Ori was shaking her. "Judith, Judith. Time to get up."

"What time is it?"

"A quarter to eight." That was late for camp. She sat up. Everyone had their sleeping bags rolled. She could smell eggs and coffee.

"How late were you up?" Ori said.

"Very late."

"I knew you would be," he said. He sounded funny.

"Did you go straight to sleep?"

"I left early on purpose, you know that. I was giving you a chance."

"Did you go straight to sleep?"

"I meant to," he said. "But then I got distracted."

"What means distracted?"

"I bumped into an old friend and messed around a little."

"Are you serious?"

"No, it wasn't serious. It was nothing, just something to do."

"Nothing's nothing," she said. "I can't believe this. You're impossible. Am I supposed to spend day and night with you just to keep you in line?"

"Stop it. Let's get this straight. Am I the one who stayed up very late doing who knows what?"

"Doing nothing, and you know it. That's not my style. I'm really mad at you. I don't think this is funny."

"I didn't say it was. Maybe we should think about all this. Maybe I don't want to be tied down."

"You think that's my purpose in life, to tie you down? I thought you were in this because you wanted to be, remember?"

"I was. I am. Oh, I don't know what I want."

"Well, what I don't want is your confusion. I shouldn't have to talk you into being with me."

"You don't have to. I want to be. That's what's making it so hard."

"If it's too hard for you we should take a break." She couldn't believe she was saying it.

"I think that might be worth a try. Maybe it'll help."

How could it help, she was thinking, I want you.

"Meanwhile," he said, "I'll see you at swimming. We're all having one last fling before the kids show up."

Judith sank back into her sleeping bag and tried to find her bathing suit with her toe. It was somewhere at the bottom. She fished out a pair of underwear and a T-shirt and finally the bottom of the suit. She moved her foot around from one side to the other, finding different things that couldn't be her top, and then gave up, got out in her nightgown and unzipped the bag until all her clothes lay crumpled and exposed in the sunlight. Her top was in the farthest corner. Now she had to zip up the bag, get back in and try to take off her nightgown and put on her suit while staying covered.

She looked around. No one was there. She sat on the sleeping bag and raised her arms over her head. It must be nice, she thought, never to have to wear a top. To be able to jump into the water in shorts like boys or in nothing at all.

She was alone now. She was not with Ori anymore. It was probably good for her, she decided. She hadn't talked to anyone, hadn't made a single new friend except Nancy. But she didn't feel good. Someone had scooped out her insides and taken them someplace, that's what it was like. How would Gabriel find out? She couldn't run up and tell him as if she were waiting to go from one to the other, as if he were the second-best choice once Ori wasn't around. Besides, she had no way of knowing if it would work out with Gabriel. How could she start without knowing?

She didn't want to go swimming. She didn't want to see anyone. She packed up her things and started to walk in the direction of the lake, trying to concentrate on the woods, the small things, to notice the differences for once. She didn't know the names of anything. The trees were all alike to her, the shapes of leaves, the ferns and mosses a blurred undifferentiated green. It mattered, the distinctness of each, she decided, the way one leaf was pale and veined, another curled at the tip. There were tiny blue flowers at the roots of the trees and berries and bumps of mushrooms. How did they learn it all, the ones who knew? Gabriel knew, he was a hiker. Ori knew how to camp, he said he'd done it for fun. They knew their way around, they had a sense of direction, she'd noticed it in both of them. She felt she was swimming in a haze of dusty sunlight and pine, as if she had to clear the air ahead of her in order to move. There was buzzing, insects, mosquitoes, and that tingling on her back, on her legs, that meant bites. Looking down, she saw swelling welts on her stomach. Stupid, stupid to walk in just a bathing suit. She dug her nail into the centre of one until the pain was stronger than anything else.

One night near the beginning of her time with Gabriel they were walking down a hill holding hands. Judith was thinking, why doesn't he touch me, remembering Ori, how fast everything had happened, wondering about this quiet one who could walk for an hour and not say a word, who looked at her and waited for her but said nothing. Then Gabriel turned her towards him, put both his hands behind her head and thrust his face at hers, kissing her harshly. The voice in her head said, it's the same, I'm still not here, I don't feel anything. He stopped and she thought he could hear.

"I can't do it," he said. "It doesn't feel right. It's not me, it's who you want me to be. I'm still not ready inside."

That was something to marvel at, that he would let her see that in him without being afraid. He could have kept going, she'd never have known, but instead he'd said something she could have said. He was beside her, not opposite, and her feeling for him, for the exposed heart of him, was more than her pride. She kissed his cheek and said, "We can wait."

Ori would never have done that. But Ori's flaws did not prevent her quickening when she saw him, walking outside camp, biking in the direction of Jessie's cabin. He was sleeping with a waitress and doing a lot of dope, everyone said, he was changing units, he was going out with that girl, he was leaving camp. She half hoped he'd go. She reminded herself of what she knew about him, but when she met him accidentally she couldn't talk.

When Ori and Gabriel stood talking she would look at the two of them, Ori proportioned, springy with energy, and Gabriel elongated, refined. Body and spirit, she thought, how can a person not need both?

The kids came, they were awful, thirteen-year-olds from the suburbs of Connecticut, rich and spoiled. She did what she had to with them and left the cabin the minute they were reasonably quiet. Marcy spent all her time there, read them stories, listened to their troubles, shepherded them to activities when they skipped, as they often did. But Marcy, Judith decided, had nothing else in her life.

Judith and Gabriel spent their nights in the loft above the assembly hall. They listened to folk music on Gabriel's portable record player, holding each other under a blanket and falling asleep until nearly dawn to sneak back into their cabins before they had to wake up the kids. On days off they woke early to go hiking. Gabriel put his maps and dried fruits in a rucksack and took her for walks that lasted all day through the woods at the edge of camp, to end up in small New England towns whose names she'd never heard.

Now it was midsummer. The trees were full, they covered the sky. Crab apples carpetted the grass beneath them and everyone ate them until they were sick. The sun burned the lake and Judith was deep gold. All day she did dock duty to stay near the water. On a free hour, while Gabriel worked with his kids, she'd walk out of camp to Fraser Lake with a towel under her arm and lie on the beach, dreaming, listening to the transistor radios and the cries of towny children. At night the corn in the fields swayed like an animal. And still Gabriel was undecided, she more confident than he that he loved her. He was still in mourning for the girl who'd chosen another. He wouldn't let it be over.

At the peak of summer the storms began. The sky darkened, the light suddenly disappeared, and the heat seemed to rise from the ground to sear the air.

"It's the end of the world," Judith said to Gabriel at staff dinner, staring out the dining room window.

"You don't know Massachusetts." He smiled.

Ori sat down beside her.

"What are you doing here?" she said.

"What you are," he said.

"I'm looking at the weather." The sky was almost black at six o'clock.

"Pretty fantastic."

The air in the dining room did not move. "I can't breathe in here," Judith said. "It's so hot. I need to feel something cool."

"Go swimming," Ori said.

"You can't," Gabriel said quietly. "This is an electrical storm. You could get killed."

"It won't happen for a while yet," Ori said. "Go on."

She looked down at her clothes. "But till I change—"

"Don't change," Ori said. "Just jump in. I dare you."

"Only if you do," Judith said.

Ori stood up and moved towards the door. Judith looked at Gabriel apologetically. "I have to go."

"You don't have to," Gabriel said. "You want to. I'll see you later."

Fraser Lake was unrecognisable. A purple and yellow sky loomed over the water, and the sand of the beach was pocked by footprints of people who were no longer there.

"Why is it so quiet here?" Judith asked Ori, out of breath. He had raced her from camp and won.

"No birds," he said. "Come on."

He took her hand and they tiptoed into the water.

It was hot as a bath and completely still.

"This is what it must have been like before creation," Judith said.

"V'choshekh al pnei tehom, darkness on the face of the deep."

"I'm scared," she said.

"Don't forget about ruach elohim merachefet al pnei ha-mayim."

The spirit of God hovering over the water. She looked at him. "Let's go," she said and plunged in, feeling the water fill her clothes, weight them.

"I'm sinking," Ori said, and under the water he took off his shirt and held it up, a sodden flag. "These are no good," he said. "One minute." He moved back to shore and got out. When she looked back she saw Ori standing there, outlined against the sky, his body luminous.

"Ori! Are you out of your mind?" She couldn't keep going, she was laughing too hard. "This is a public beach," she finally said. "And I'm a private person. What are you doing?"

Then he was beside her, reaching out his hand. "Give me your clothes. You don't have to get out. I'll swim them over to shore and put them with mine."

She looked at him.

"Don't worry. There's no one around. Anyone out on a day like this is crazy."

"I didn't know you were no one." She tried to undo her buttons with one hand while treading water with the other, and Ori watched her, laughing.

"Madam," he said. "May I help you?"

"No thanks," she said, wriggling and kicking.

He put his arms around her waist from behind her and held her floating in the water until her shirt and shorts were in her hands.

"Well, that's part one," she said. "We'll start with that."

The water was wonderful on her bare skin and she lay on her back in the middle of the lake and raised her fingers to drip water onto her face. The picture of herself in her mind, a girl lying in a lake in her underwear, was absurd.

Ori was back.

"I dreamt I got electrocuted in my Maidenform bra." She took his hands. "Help me," she said.

He undid the clasp and took it off.

She had never felt anything like it. Her body, looking down, was perfect to her, dissolving underwater in this peculiar light.

"You are so beautiful," Ori said quietly.

He was beautiful, suddenly, his serious face looking back at her. "What's happened to us?"

"Hey, guess what?" he said.

"What?"

"It's raining!"

The surface of the lake broke into a million pieces. The sky opened up over them and the rain drove down in grey sheets, obscuring everything.

"Hang onto me," Ori yelled and started chopping at the water. She grabbed him and paddled with her other hand, watching his head rise and fall, his hair plastered onto his head by the rain, his arms steadily in and out of the water. Above them there was sound that kept building. Just when she thought they were going around in circles she felt her feet scrape against the sand. Ori lifted her up. They struggled into their soaking clothes and ran for camp. As they went through the gate the world blew open in brilliant light and the evening turned white.

Ori and Judith stood gaping. "We could have been killed," she said.

"But we weren't," he said to her. "Enough of this. We should change."

Judith stood under the shower for a long time. She couldn't get warm. Gabriel, Ori, her mind was chanting, Gabriel, Ori. By the time she got out it was late, she'd missed the evening activity, and she went straight to sleep in her empty cabin before the kids were back.

Now it was August. Gabriel soothed her, looked after her, and worked very hard with his kids. All day he was busy, rehearsing their play, running the newspaper, organizing games. She sat on her steps and watched him across the field, the familiar lines of his back at the edge of the group, guiding, encouraging. By evening he was exhausted.

"Why do you do so much?" she asked him. "Get the kids to do it. Why do you have to be so noble?"

It was the only way he could do things, she knew that. It made him worthy in her eyes. But she was restless over his worrying, about her, about him, about love.

"Don't you know how you feel?"

He shook his head.

"I know how you feel." She was impatient. "You love me, it's obvious. And it's humiliating for me to have to tell you. It drives me crazy to ask you a question and wait half an hour before you say something. Please." She stopped. "Please," she said gently, "try to tell me what's going on in your mind when you're not saying anything."

He said nothing. Then he said, "I don't know."

"You don't know what?"

"I don't know what's going on. I think about things. I think about the question you ask. You're always so sure about everything, what you like, what you don't, what you want. Not everyone's as sure as you are."

"I'm not so sure," she said immediately. "I'm not sure about a lot of things." She wasn't sure about him.

"Give me a little more time."

Always that voice made her want to cry out for him, to hold him in her arms and comfort him.

The last day off would be Sunday and it was her birthday. She was waiting for Gabriel at the staff meeting Wednesday night and Ori came over to talk.

"What's happening?" he said.

"Zero," she told him. "I can't believe the summer's almost over."

"I know," he said. "Isn't it incredible?"

"It's strange," she said. "Here it is the middle of August and the evenings haven't started to get cold yet. It doesn't smell like the end of summer. I guess it'll come all at once."

"Speaking of endings, what are you doing for the last day off?"

"I think we're going to take it easy. Just hang around camp. What are you doing?"

"New York, New York," he started to sing. "I'm going home. I need as many fixes as I can get before I leave for Israel."

"That'll be fun," she said. She had a sudden vivid picture of Ori in New York, running up and down the streets, doing his New York things. "What are you going to do?"

"Everything. I'm going to eat pizza at the best pizza place in New York, go to the movies—"

"Movies?"

"Maybe. I could do two in an afternoon, easy. I'll have a milk shake, buy the Sunday *Times*, eat my mother's food and come back as late as I can. The next day's Tishah B'av, you know, so I've got to get all my goodies in before the fast."

"Sunday's my birthday."

"You're kidding."

"Nope. I'll be an old lady."

"Seventeen?"

"Twins. I'll finally catch up to you."

"I doubt it," he said in his frog voice. "Listen," he said in his normal one, "you can't stay in camp for your birthday. It's your only birthday of the whole year. Seventeen's great, take it from me. Make that lazy one take you someplace."

"He's exhausted. Unlike certain unnameable people, he's being responsible."

"Are you implying?"

"I am."

"I admit it, I'd rather be a kid. They get to have all the fun. I wasn't ready to give it up. I tried to persuade them in the middle of the summer that they'd made a mistake, but it was too late."

"You seem to have done all right in the fun department."

"I manage, you know me. But it's been an uphill struggle lately. That's why I can't wait for New York. It'll be just what I need. My mommy will look after me."

"Poor baby."

"Jealousy will get you nowhere. You just want to be babied too. Hey, I've got an idea. Why don't you come with me?"

"I couldn't."

"Why not?"

"I couldn't. What about what's-her-name, that girl you've been hanging around with?"

"I'll tell her I'm going with you. She wasn't going to come with me anyway."

"She won't be crazy about that."

"It doesn't matter. She trusts me."

Fool, Judith thought. "I'll talk to Gabriel, but I don't think he'll go for it."

"Nothing will happen," Ori said. "I would like you to meet my parents, though. They know all about you."

"What could they know about me? I've never met them."

"I talk about you all the time. You've been a big influence on me, don't you know that?"

"No," she said. "Why?"

"Remember when we split up?"

"If I strain my mind."

"Well, I was thinking of quitting camp after that, maybe going somewhere else, maybe going to Israel early, and my parents talked me out of it."

"On what grounds?"

"They pointed out to me that since I was mentioning your name constantly, I might not be happy at camp but I could feel worse once I'd left."

"What did you think?"

"I thought they could have something there. So I decided that I wasn't ready to cope with being with you all the time the way we had been, but I wasn't ready to kiss it goodbye either."

"I can't say I've seen you very much since then."

"I know, I know. So come on Sunday. We'll have a birthday party. We'll leave early and do everything. Tell Gabriel we'll be back Sunday night. It's only a day. He'll find something to do. Do you want me to talk to him?"

"God forbid," Judith said and walked into the meeting.

It was all she could think about. The meeting went by in a blur. She was too afraid to talk to Gabriel. She started making bargains with herself. If he tells me he loves me, I won't go, she decided. If he wants me to stay, if he makes a plan.

"I don't know," Gabriel said when she mentioned the idea. "I guess I don't have the right to ask you not to."

Ask me, ask me, she said silently. "It's my birthday," she said. "Don't you want to spend it with me?"

"I want to," he said slowly, "but I think that if you want to go to New York you should. I'm not that happy about it, but I think you should go."

You're making a mistake, she thought. "Listen, think it over. I don't have to decide until Saturday night."

"Well?" Ori said when she saw him. "Are we on?"

"I don't know," she said. "Gabriel's unclear."

"Mine said I can go if I want. She has faith in me."

"There's too much faith around here," Judith grumbled. She still hoped Gabriel would declare himself. It would be a mess otherwise. She could feel it in her bones.

"Talk to Jessie," Ori said suddenly. "She'd really like to talk to you."

Judith didn't want to talk to her. "Maybe next week," she told him.

She spent all day Friday and Saturday with Gabriel, both knowing she would go, neither admitting it. Saturday night was very hot. Judith was wearing shorts and a T-shirt to the havdalah service at the end of the Sabbath. It was the evening after the fullest moon and it was barely possible to see the darkened edge that was missing. There was a three-hour evening activity still to get through and Judith thought only of Sunday. The idea of sitting with Gabriel for another evening, sleeping another night, and only then being able to go was unbearable. When Ori showed up, late, she said to him, "Let's not wait till tomorrow, let's get out of here."

"When?" he said.

"Now."

He looked over to their supervisors. "Some people are going to be pretty mad about this."

"I'll be mad if we stay."

"It's all right with me," Ori said.

"I'll run back to the cabin to change and meet you at the gate. Should I bring anything?"

"What do we need? Just you."

Judith wandered over to the door and nonchalantly stepped outside. Then she raced back to her cabin and changed into jeans. She pulled on her black cotton shirt and wrapped herself in her shawl, ready. Walking to the gate, moon overhead, the wind, the leaves rushing in the night, she felt her body gather itself beneath her clothes, taut, anticipating something, she would not think of what.

Ori looked different in the night, darker, lean. He was wearing a black T-shirt and jeans, and the muscles of his arms caught the dim light of the bulb over the entrance to camp. His hair was wild.

"That was close," he said. "I almost got caught by Mission Patrol," their name for the adviser who checked up on attendance. "He asked me where I was going. I said I was going to meet you."

"Great. My name will be mud."

"No, everyone's given up trying to figure out what's going on with all of us."

"Gabriel doesn't even know I left."

"Why don't we just forget about the others?"

"Good plan. What do we do now?" She realised she had no idea. It was nearly ten o'clock, they were in Massachusetts and they were going to New York. "We don't even know where New York is."

"It's that way." Ori flung his hand vaguely into the air.

They walked together to the turn in the road and waited.

"What do we do now?" she whispered.

"You don't have to whisper, there's no one here," he said.

They waited for an hour. They were standing on a dirt road in the middle of nowhere. The air was ripe with the smell of the fields that lay all around them, unseen. One car approached. Ori stuck out his thumb and it picked up speed.

"We're going to sleep here," Judith said.

"Have faith. We'll get there, just give it time."

A truck full of screaming kids swerved towards them. Ori pulled her back into the ditch at the side of the road.

"What time is it?" Judith said.

"Around eleven-thirty, I think. I don't have a watch."

It was very quiet. Then from far away the lights appeared, two headlights growing closer.

"This is it," Ori said, stepping out.

The car pulled up just past them and Ori ran over. Judith ran behind him.

"New York," Ori said to the driver.

"We'll take you near the Mass Pike," the driver said.

"Get in," Ori said. The door slammed and they were off.

"I can't believe it," Judith said to him in the back. "We're really doing it."

Ori's face smiled at her in the dark. Beside her Massachusetts was rolling by, clumps of trees and water. There was no one else on the road.

She was wide awake and tingling. She was sitting in a car with strangers, travelling in an unknown direction to someplace she'd never been. Ori was beside her, looking out the window. His hair touched his shoulders, his backpack on the seat between them. She had no money, no umbrella, no map. In less than an hour she'd be seventeen years old.

The car slowed and moved to the side of the road. "This is

where I get off." The driver turned around.

"Thanks a lot," Ori said and pulled his pack out after him. Judith climbed out and the car took off.

They were on a bridge spanning a huge highway. Beneath them hundreds of lights streamed out in lines and cars followed them in every direction. There was darkness behind them and darkness ahead but on the bridge it was almost day. Judith looked at Ori and he looked at her.

"I have no idea where we are," he said.

She couldn't answer, she was suddenly filled with a sense of the night all around her, the air strangely warmer, Ori leaning against the bridge, his head against the sky. It didn't matter to her if they stayed or left, nothing made any difference.

Ori said, "If that's the Mass Turnpike it should take us pretty close. I don't know how we get over there, though."

They looked down at the tiny cars. "I guess we could try hitching from here," Ori said.

A station wagon honked behind them. Six guys with hair in ponytails were grinning. The door opened. "Hey, man, need a ride?" a voice said.

It was a very old car with a funny sharp smell.

"Dope," Ori said with delight.

"We're really gone," the guy who was driving said. "We've been smoking for hours. Just finished the last of our stuff or we'd get you high too."

Judith saw the car weaving from one side to the other, turning around and around in slow motion until it crashed into a pole.

"Stop worrying," Ori said. "Lie down over here if you're tired."

She stretched out beside him and put her head on her shawl. Lying on her stomach, she could feel the car moving beneath her and the regular sound of the wheels on the road. The guys in the front were talking about music, blasting the radio. The back was light, dark, light, dark as they rode on the highway.

Ori's hand on her back.

Ori's arms were around her.

"Lie back," he said. "Lie still. Rest."

She was wrapped in him, covered by him, lying in his arms in the middle of the night. It's my birthday, she wanted to say, but the words took too long to get to her mouth and she was asleep.

94

Then they were on an enormous freeway, glaring light. She sat up. "Where are we?" They were in Queens, nearly there, Ori said. She didn't know where that was. Nearly there, though, almost in New York.

"All right if we let you off at the subway?" the driver said.

"Sure," Ori told him. He knew how to go.

They were taking a long subway ride in a nearly empty car. Judith looked across and saw reflected in the black window her head next to Ori's, a pale gleam of face, and her hair against the darkness. It was three o'clock in the morning.

They changed trains and changed again, Judith following Ori down the long, deserted tunnels. They were on the IRT, the subway to home, Ori said, out onto Broadway, the stores grated up in a way she'd never seen, everything closed.

It was grey and quiet. Then Ori pulled her into a doorway and suddenly it could have been lunchtime. There were people standing and sitting, laughing, gesturing in conversation. Judith stood in front of a menu in a daze. The old Jewish man behind the counter teased her gently and threw in the pickles for free. Ori and she held hot roast beef sandwiches, dripping with gravy and mayonnaise that soaked through the soft white bread onto their fingers. Kosher sandwiches, open all night. It was magic.

They came out full and warm side by side. A man was lurching down the sidewalk and Ori took her hand and pulled her behind him. Judith thought she was flying. I am walking with Ori in the early morning, she was saying inside. They crossed the street and Ori pointed to a tall brown building. "That's my house, we're home."

"Is that a brownstone?" Judith said.

He laughed. "Brownstones are small. That's an apartment building." Now they were at the door and a man in a uniform opened it and smiled.

"Hey, Lenny," Ori said and took her inside. "That's Lenny, the doorman."

A doorman. They were in a lobby with marble and mirrors and then in an elevator going up and up. At fifteen it stopped and Ori said, "Can you guess which one's my house?"

In front of her was a door that said in gold letters SHALOM.

Ori turned the key in the lock and the door swung silently

open. They walked down a hall and through an arch. "To the kitchen," Ori said.

"Don't we have to be quiet? Aren't your parents asleep?"

"They're at the other end of the apartment. They can't hear anything."

She couldn't imagine an apartment that big.

"It's the Upper West Side," he said. "These apartments are really old and well built. I'll show you my room next after the kitchen. It used to be for the butler."

The kitchen was long and very narrow. "The kitchens are always small," he said, "because only the cook and the maid used them."

He opened the fridge and took out a carton. "Tropicana," he said. "In our house we guzzle orange juice. Are you thirsty?"

She was. He poured her a glass and one for himself in paper cups. "We drink so much of it my mother got sick of washing glasses."

It was all new. The city, the apartment, the kitchen, the orange juice. It had never tasted as it did now, cool and sweet in her throat.

"Good stuff," Ori said.

When they were finished Judith looked at him. "Well," she said, "what do we do now? I guess we should get some sleep."

"All right," he said, "there's Jessie's room where you'll be. But first come see mine."

He turned on the light and they were in a tiny room with a high ceiling and one window at the end. There was hardly enough space for a bed and a desk.

"Isn't it great?" Ori said. "These are my favourite posters." He gave her a tour of all his things. "And here's a picture of my mother when she graduated high school. She must've been about our age. Can you guess?"

A photograph of twenty girls in long white dresses. She searched for Ori's face, and there in the centre, Jessie's face with Ori's mouth looked back at her.

Ori sat down on the bed. "I don't know why, I'm not tired yet."

"I'm getting there," she said. She couldn't imagine ever wanting to sleep again.

"Stay for a minute," Ori said. "Sit down."

She stood.

"Not for that," he said. "I just want to talk with you."

She sat down next to him, not knowing what to say. She could hear her heart inside her.

"I just want to hold you," he said.

He lay down and she lay down beside him, his arms around her in the strange light that a room has in the middle of the night.

They lay still, a cumbersome tangle of arms and legs, and she thought, the light is on, we're only hugging, what can happen?

"I know you," Ori said. The words moved down her spine. He reached up behind him and shut off the light.

Her body in the dark moved towards him, longing flickered through her skin.

Ori's hands, one on either side of her, held her firmly still.

All over her, underneath her clothes, she wanted him.

"Let me undress you," he said. "No more than that." His quiet voice again drew a hot line down her back.

Ori's bareness, his chest delicately met her own. Ori's skin on her skin.

"You see how different it is."

She lay lightly over him.

He gathered her hair in his hand. "Open your eyes," he whispered. She did.

"Judith," he said. "I love you, Judith."

At six o'clock the window was a grey square in the dark, but all the light of spring and summer was flooding through her. It was her seventeenth birthday, and she stood before Ori, sleeping below her, in the still, small room, watching the splendour of his face.

Waking, New York was steaming, dingy, the heavy air, the grimy street, everything a declaration. On the bus, watching Ori watch her, sitting at the back of the movie, his hands all over her, eating pizza, bite after bite with him, back at his parents', the end of the day, still grey, enchanted, his mother bustling, his father kind, and Judith in a dream.

Ori's mother was laughing at her. She had cooked a wonderful meal and Judith couldn't eat.

"It must be love," his mother said, teasing.

Judith felt her body dissolve into space.

Beside Ori she slept on her way back to camp and got off the bus alone. Gabriel stood at the foot of the steps, shy, smiling as she came down.

He kissed her cheek.

He said before she could speak, "I had an amazing day. I went to the ocean. I bought you this." He held out a gold scented candle. "I bought it because it smells like you do. And I have something to tell you."

"Can it wait?" she said. "I'm not really here."

"It can't," he said. "I've been thinking of you all day. I have to tell you, I finally realised that you're right and I love you."

And Nancy said, "I had a dream that I saw you with Gabriel, years from now, and I think it will last a long time."

On Tishah B'av the camp was in mourning, everyone sitting on the floor in a room lit with candles, reading Lamentations and remembering the six million. Judith and Gabriel talked late into the night, of the destruction of the Temple in Jerusalem, a nation in sackcloth and ashes, and all the tragedies the day commemorates. The city razed, the slaughter of the Crusades, the expulsion from Spain, pogroms, the shoah, holocaust.

A day of mourning, and all day Judith could not stop thinking of Ori. Light-headed from fasting, she climbed to the top of the hill in the middle of camp. It was impossible to grieve. She watched as far below on the road Ori walked slowly towards her, not seeing her there, on his way someplace else, watched as his body became clear, its outline, the swing of his arm, his face, watched as he recognised her, felt herself move from aloneness to grace, and gave up.

"Ori, what shall we do?"

"I guess we'll have to tell them. They must suspect already. I haven't been concentrating well."

"Me neither. This is the strangest Tishah B'av I've ever had." It was a day of abstaining and she was dreaming of love. It was a time for separateness between women and men and Judith looked at Ori, straining not to reach out to him.

"I'll talk to Gabriel after sunset," she said. "Now, please, go away."

He was laughing—"Yes, ma'am"—and then sober. "I'll be glad when all this is ended."

"There is no end," she said, "don't you know that by now?"

While her kids were in one final discussion about the meaning of Tishah B'av, she washed and perfumed herself, getting ready. When it was dark she got dressed and went out. Gabriel was busy with his bunk until bedtime, so she wandered down to the lake. A group of people were sitting on the sand and the smell that was dope was in the air. Ori called her over.

"I didn't think you'd be free this early," he said. Judith saw the girl sitting beside him. "Do you want to get stoned?"

"No, you know I don't," she said.

"One minute," Ori said to the others and walked over with Judith to the edge of the water.

"Are you stoned now?" she said.

"Why?"

"Because I don't want to talk to you if you are. I can't talk to you when I know you're not seeing what I'm seeing."

"You can't tell the difference."

"Oh yes I can."

"No you can't. I've been stoned quite a lot this summer."

"When you were with me?"

Ori moved his feet. "Sometimes."

"When we were in New York?" Her voice was shaky.

"It doesn't mean anything."

"It means a lot," she said. "It means that while I was feeling so close to you, you weren't there."

"First of all, you don't know what you're talking about because you haven't tried it. And anyway, I wasn't."

"It doesn't help," she said. "I never know what's going on with you."

"Just a minute, lady. Slow down. Didn't I say I was going to be with you?"

"I don't know what to tell Gabriel. I don't know what to do."

But Gabriel knew. "Do what you have to," he said when she met him, hours later, and stumbled through her reasons. "I see the way you are together. Be with him now."

"Do you understand," she said, "that I feel the way I've always felt for you?"

"Yes. Yes, I do. Be with him now and after the summer we'll see where we're at."

Judith and Ori watched the summer end. Sitting on the steps of Ori's bunk, they saw Gabriel put on the play with his kids. They walked in the evenings and felt the bite of autumn. In the mornings they could see their breath as the sun caught the leaves of the first trees turning to fall. Over, over, everyone was starting their goodbyes, tearfully promising to write, to phone, and Judith looked at Ori as if she could drink him in, absorb him through her skin to keep him through the long winter.

One afternoon when Ori was swimming Judith found Jessie waiting for her outside the cabin.

"I want to talk to you," Jessie said.

"Sure, have a seat." Judith spread out the blanket she was carrying and stretched out.

"I wanted to tell you before the summer's over that I feel really bad that we've never had a conversation before."

"It's all right, I understand. I know it must be hard for you, because of everything."

"It's true that at the beginning I was mad at my brother about you. But it had nothing to do with you. Anyway, I can see what a difference you've made to him."

"What do you mean?"

"He's really changing. Ori never used to talk about things. But he talks about you. Talks and talks."

My brother, Judith thought. Jessie would have him forever.

Judith looked at this girl with Ori's face, told her about being lonely, how her life had been a preparation for love, about Ori, his weaknesses. Jessie knew.

When the sun was almost gone and they were shivering, Jessie got up reluctantly, kissed Judith and said, "I'll write. I'll write the minute I get home."

Judith had not even dared to ask. It was Jessie herself that she wanted to write to, she was sure, but Ori stood behind her, a shadow, and she could not know how much of him, how much of her impelled her to say, "We must keep in touch."

"I like your sister," she told Ori that evening.

"Of course you do," he said.

On the last day the kids hugged her goodbye, forgetting now

her distraction, her indifference. "You were so great," they said. "We'll miss you, we love you, it was the best summer."

They mean Marcy, she thought. But their rush of emotion was undiscriminating, and it seemed she was forgiven.

She walked to the bus between Gabriel and Ori, memorizing the feel of the path, the trees, the light. Gabriel moved ahead and Judith and Ori sat at the back, quiet. They'd arrive in New York in the afternoon, Judith would go to his house for an hour and then leave for home.

On the steps of the synagogue Judith said goodbye to Gabriel. "I'll call you this week," he said.

"Good," Judith told him. "I'll see you soon." She watched his tall straight back move with purpose to the subway.

Ori's parents were kissing her hello and she was in a cab with his mother and his suitcases, he in another with his father, at his parents' suggestion.

Don't they know, she thought, we have one afternoon. But they were parents, they couldn't know about such things.

"How far is the house?" Judith asked his mother.

"We're almost home," she said cheerfully. The cab pulled up to a big apartment building. It looked different in the day, sadder. It was starting to rain and they hurried in. The elevator stopped at fifteen. Ori and his father were waiting in the hall. Inside, his mother said, "Anybody hungry?" No one was. "Well, we'll leave you kids," she said and closed the door behind her.

Ori sat down at the piano and picked out a song. Judith stood behind him. He started to sing, tentatively, and she started to cry. She put her arms around him and he kept playing until he heard her breathing. Then her body was shaking against him. "I can't bear it," she said.

"It'll be all right." Ori was patting her awkwardly.

She stopped, made herself controlled. "Yes," she said. "I will be." But she didn't know how she would.

When his father poked his head in and saw her face, he smiled and said, "Parting is such sweet sorrow."

You don't know, she thought.

Ori walked her to the bus in the rain, holding her hand. He stood outside as the doors opened and clenched his fingers on hers until the driver said, "Lady, say goodbye." The doors closed, streaky with rain, she stared through the glass at his blurry face until she couldn't see him, even looking out through the back. Then she cried on the bus and cried on the plane, not caring what people thought.

When the lights of Toronto appeared beneath her she went to the bathroom and washed her face. She thought about her parents, what they didn't know, how she'd come to camp without even kissing anyone and now she'd almost slept with someone. She. Judith. Amazing. She frizzed out her hair and met her mother in the airport to announce, "I have a lover," and watch the expression on her face.

Gimel

Ori Ori Ori Ori Ori. When her mouth was closed she was thinking of him. It was a winter of the heart. The days grew short and she'd wake early in the dark for an hour before rising to imagine him. His mouth on her breast, his hands. Walking the streets, she'd conjure him, hoping past reason that he'd appear at her door when she got home, in her room, manifest himself. On Friday night when everyone was asleep she'd sit in the dark and close her eyes to have him before her, glorious, his physical being so filling her mind that she could taste his kisses on her tongue. All day was a mourning for him and the nights were without rest. I cannot find love, she cried within herself. My body in the west and my heart in Jerusalem. She'd follow a man's set of shoulders, a boy's rhythmic walk, seeing Ori in strangers. My light, my light. The days grew short, the hurt of leaves, bleak November, and then came the snows. White, the world was white and she was desolate. There was no comforting.

She left the day school she'd gone to all her life and changed to a public school across the road, from where, at lunch, she'd run home to open the door to the mail on the floor and read the scattered letters like a fortune. If a corner of blue could be seen, all was well, but if the letters were domestic and white, grief, a clutch at the heart, and the slow retreat behind pain, on guard, to haul the body through all the way, twenty-four hours, an evening, a night, until noon the next day.

The nakedness of her spirit she surrounded with flesh, padded herself against it. Now she could hold her stomach in handfuls, first amused, then dismayed that it did not go away. It was there every day with the heaviness inside and her private sorrows.

She told no one.

Gabriel came and left unsure. She watched him in a haze of longing. She loved him, but it was Ori's face, Ori's self she saw sitting in Gabriel's place. She listened, she thought, she knew it would not be. He wrote through the fall, fifteen, thirty pages, contemplative, philosophical letters. She read them carefully. But it was Ori's letters, every two weeks, short, saying nothing, that woke her. At Thanksgiving Gabriel wrote of a girl, he sat before a fire with her, we made love, he wrote. She felt a small gladness for him. For herself she burrowed deep into winter, emerging from her room after midnight to eat alone in the kitchen, staring at the blank black window onto the garden or listening to the summer music with earphones, alone, encased in him.

Her parents thought her impossible. She knew from their mutterings, their closed faces. They had not reckoned on this. They thought she would love like Naomi, one boyfriend each year, sober, serious, hello Mrs. Rafael, goodbye Mrs. Rafael, well behaved. Not passion, not grief, not slamming the door at imagined injury, not dancing, wild dancing in the living room to her music whenever the house was free. Not walking the city in the rain until midnight, not snapping at her sisters, crying to her parents, you don't understand, you don't understand my feelings. She dared not name it love to them for they would say, there are other boys, look around, they would say, surely. But she searched for someone to erase him and only those shaped like him drew her, and none was Ori.

If she never said his name, if she never wrote to him of love, if she concentrated when she went to bed, while walking on the street, if she thought Jerusalem and pictured him, if she prayed that they might meet, if she vividly enough imagined it.

She dreamt a waking dream that Ori was living in Israel and she came to see him there, unknown to him, to walk up the pathway to his house, knock on his door and be received by him, his girlfriend of the time beside him, and Judith laughing because, still, she knew it was all in her hands.

She saw, one hundred years ago, she and he just born, their parents shaking their heads over cradles, sighing, smiling, shaking hands, his father and hers, and over a glass of wine determining: Your daughter and my son, swiftly, in our time, let it come to pass.

And Jessie, a separate love so bound to him. She answered Jessie's first letter the day it came, and then they wrote once a week, twice a week, nearly every day. In the middle of winter she went to New York, stayed in his house, ate his food, did what he would have done, her love for Jessie grown to great capacity, apart from Ori, loving her, a girl whose light illuminated the ones around her and sheltered them, who stood, stocky, grounded, and yet a natural dancer flying down the streets.

Wings, they gave each other wings, she and Jessie. And yet how strange in a certain cast of light to lean over to kiss the girl and find her brother's mouth upon her face.

In February Sharon came over one day to tell Judith of a trip she'd heard about, a two-week tour of Israel for three hundred dollars, all inclusive. Sharon was going, so was another girl they both knew, her parents were willing and did Judith think she could come.

Judith knew she could not. A two-week trip in the middle of the school year, her parents would never allow it. She didn't even ask. Clearly they would find it suspect, who's sponsoring it, who's supervising, and why should her first trip to Israel not be a long stay in the summer, with time to travel around. It was an extravagance.

In the kitchen she talked to her mother about it while she was making supper. Her mother's back to her at the chopping board, Judith tentatively set it forth.

"In the middle of the school year?" her mother said.

"Yes, her parents are letting her. Besides, part of the time is Easter vacation."

"It's a little short notice, isn't it? How do they know it's reliable?"

"Sharon's father phoned the Zionist centre and it turns out they're subsidizing it. He thinks it's all right."

Her mother's arm up and down, the scrape of the knife on the board. Her mother's hand over the stove, the sizzle of oil.

"I don't suppose," Judith began, "that you and Daddy would consider it."

"Well, dear"—her mother half turned—"it does seem awfully fast."

Well, dear, her mother had said in her hesitating voice that was not final.

"I know, but I think they can only do it because it's an off-season before Passover."

Judith sat quite still.

"It sounds like a nice idea and I'm sure Sharon will enjoy it, but three hundred dollars is still three hundred dollars and two weeks isn't very long."

"I guess not. Though I know a couple of kids who are going too. I bet it will be fun."

Her mother at the sink, rinsing the pot. Moving to the dishwasher, back to the sink, then over to the counter again.

Judith got up, about to leave.

"I don't know, dear," her mother said. "What would you do about shoes?"

What would you do about shoes! What would you do about shoes! Judith's mind careening in triumph. It meant: If you go. It meant: How will you get ready to go? She ran out of the kitchen before she could ruin it and sat in her room saying to herself, calm down. Give her time for the idea to grow. Don't say anything.

After supper her father called her in.

"Your mother tells me," he said, "that Sharon's going on a trip to Israel and you're interested in going."

"I'm interested," Judith said carefully.

"You know, two weeks away is a very short trip, and we're a little concerned that you might not see the country the way you'd want to for your first time. There are also people to visit—your Great-aunt Chenya, most important. How do you feel?"

"I know it's short, but Sharon says they have a very intensive touring program. I'd get to all the places and I'll go back many times anyway. It might be nicer to go when it's not as crowded."

Her father's head tilted to one side, his listening look. "Well, Judith," he finally said, "as I've told you, this isn't my ideal plan for your first trip, but your mother thinks it would be a good idea and I go along with your mother."

Judith didn't know what to do. Stand up, sit down, jump around, yell. "Oh, Daddy, thank you, thank you. I know it'll be great. And you won't have to worry about me. I'll have Sharon and we have friends there and it is a tour. I can't believe it. I'm going to call Sharon right now."

"One last thing," her father said. "I know you may resent an intrusive daddy's questions, but I want you to think about this. Are you sure that your decision isn't somewhat influenced by the presence of that boy—"

"Ori," her mother filled in.

"Ori," her father continued, "and that it won't be just a visit to see your American friends? Because that would be a shame."

Her heart exploding. "There are people that I want to see, but I've wanted to go to Israel all my life and finally meet Chenya after years of letters and see Jerusalem." She prayed she meant it.

He smiled. "I hope you have a wonderful time."

She ran up and hugged him, kissed her mother, and left them looking at her fondly to hurry upstairs and phone Sharon.

Then came the delicious debate. How to tell him. She considered the possibilities day after day as the trip got closer. Write him a letter. Tell Jessie, not him, and let him find out through her. Write him a letter with hints but don't tell. Write him a postcard when she got there that said, "See you in a couple of days." Not tell Jessie till she got to the airport in New York, on her way, and let him find out when he phoned home and wonder when she'd turn up. Have him find out from other people who knew, but not through her. Not tell him at all.

That was most radical and tempting. But then she thought, what about his girlfriend. She knew he had one, though she'd never ask, from Jessie's deliberate silence on the subject. And the coldest thought. What if he isn't there. It was the month of Passover vacation for students in Israel and he could easily do what most Americans there did, go to Greece or Italy for the break.

She wrote him a letter but she didn't mail it. She phoned Jessie to tell her but the line was busy. The other girl's parents changed their minds and Sharon phoned her in tears. Her parents wouldn't let her go unless she knew two other people going and now she only knew one. The Friday night before the trip began Judith found out she was going alone. She walked from her house to downtown Toronto, wandering all night, amazed. She was going to Israel. She was going to see Ori. No one knew her and she knew no one. When she got home her mother was sitting in the den in her nightgown, shaking with angry worry. Judith was immune.

At the airport in New York she called Jessie and told her, listening to her gasp and her silence. Then she burst out in speech, laughter, encouragement. She knew the implications, all of them, but she said only, it will be good. On the plane were the fifty members of the tour, a mixture of old people and fifteen-year-old boys and girls who lay on top of each other for the ride or kissed under airline blankets, oblivious to the other passengers. Judith sat at the window and looked at the sky that grew into morning as they crossed the Atlantic. It was early on Thursday and they had already been travelling since six o'clock the morning before. Six hours by bus from Toronto to Montreal with a wait at the airport. An hour to New York with a long delay. Then to London overnight. She didn't sleep at all. In London they waited and then flew to Paris. In Paris they waited and then flew to Athens. In Athens they were held over for hours. It had been dark and light and dark and light. Finally they were up in the air, the city receding in twilight and stars, over the dusk of the Mediterranean. "Yam hatikhon," she whispered the Hebrew name. And then, looking down as the music came on the plane, "heveinu shalom aleikhem," welcome, welcome, the coastline whose shape she'd known since childhood, the curve of the land in a line of lights, eretz yisrael, the holy land, Israel, Israel, and the plane touched earth.

Judith walked out into the balmy night. It was nearly summer there. She knelt at the foot of the metal staircase and kissed the ground, the concrete scraping her mouth, feeling, despite the din of the plane, the glare of the lights, one with the centuries of Jews who had longed for Zion. She looked up at the sky, a different sky, saw the just-born moon and thought, I am under the same sky as he. The moon that is shining on him shines on me. It had begun and would proceed to its fulfillment now.

The road to Tel Aviv in the dark was scented with jasmine and oranges. A perfumed land, her body languorous for love, the Hebrew on the driver's radio so familiar there was no foreignness. A homecoming, that was all. Nothing was strange, not Tel Aviv with its hotels and the lapping of the sea, not the drive up the coast the next day to Rosh Hanikra, the closest point to Lebanon. Not the Hebrew signs, the groves or the palm trees. Everything was recognised from a life she hadn't yet lived, everything known in her blood. For her parents, for her conscience, she promised herself to go with the tour to the north for the first part of the trip and travel with them to Jerusalem, then see what would happen.

On the third day she woke up at six and knew this could not be. She was on Ayelet Hashachar, the kibbutz of the dawn star. It was still cool. She rose and washed her hair, sitting outside in the fragrant air, sorting the strands in the sun. She could not wait anymore, could not be in Israel and not see Jerusalem. While the tour was at breakfast she left a note and went out to the parking lot. A van was pulling out.

"Bo'i iti." The driver smiled at her. Come with me, a browned face with green eyes, a soldier.

"L'yerushalayim?" she asked.

Yes, to Jerusalem.

All day they drove south along the Jordan. Past the fields of kibbutzim and dusty bus stations, past Arabs in long coats and kaffiyehs, past orchards and hills and ditches of wild flowers. In the noon heat he drove her to a hidden waterfall that only the soldiers knew about. He played with her, he bought her soft drinks, she swam in her clothes and threw herself down on the grass, he laughing over her. He had been up for forty-eight hours, straight from the front, and was driving back to his family, his mother and sleep. He was beautiful. He was in love with her. She laughed at him now. No, he was serious, he said. He would marry her tomorrow, he said, his eyes crinkling at the corners. He took her picture. He tried to kiss her. Any other time, she was thinking, looking at the shape of his face, perhaps something would have come of this. But at the end of the day was an evening she could not imagine. At the end of the day something would be resolved, one way or the other.

"Stay over," he said, "at a friend's house on the way. He has a little baby you will like. His wife will give us supper. Then in the morning, when you're not tired, we can go to Jerusalem."

"I can't wait till tomorrow," she said. "I must be in Jerusalem tonight."

He gave in graciously. "I told you I'd take you, didn't I," he said, "and I will."

In the late afternoon when the light was long they were climbing the Judean hills.

"Me'al pisgat har hatsofim," she sang softly. From the top of Mount Scopus I greet you, Jerusalem. He joined her and they sang every old Zionist song she'd learned, one after another, peeling the oranges they'd picked at the side of the road. "For a hundred generations I've dreamed of facing you, earning your light, Jerusalem. Shine on your children, Jerusalem, and we will raise and exalt you."

When the lights of the city approached it was dark, the air of the mountains cold, and she shivered in her shorts and sleeveless shirt, still wet from swimming. "I have to go to the hotel the tour's at," she said, "to change my clothes."

"I'll wait for you there and we can go out."

"Not tonight," she said gently. "I can't tonight."

"Lamah lo?" Why not.

"I have family, mishpachah."

Ah, he knew about Americans and their families. Reunions and kisses and long, sad stories. He understood. Maybe tomorrow.

She took off her clothes and put new ones on. Black shirt on bare skin and perfume between her breasts. Her face behind the veil of her hair, her lips shaped red. She was brown from the sun and lovely.

Mount Scopus. French Hill.

"Excuse me," she asked the guard at the gate, "but can you tell me where I might find French Hill on Mount Scopus where the students live."

"The number nine bus," he said, "but it's late. They may have stopped running by now."

"How else can I find my way there," she asked.

He shrugged. "Try the desk. Maybe they know."

They did not. I'll walk the streets of the city all night, I won't sleep till I find him, she thought.

The soldiers patrolling the city demanded, "Where are you going."

She told them, "I'm looking for my friend." They laughed.

The night was cool, the shadows gone. She was looking for him but she could not find him.

"Please," she said to some girls on the street, "if you can tell me where the students live."

They clustered around her, they ran after her. "That way, no, that way," they cried.

She turned and a man in a silver car with purple seats and a gold floor was motioning to her. Around him were soldiers, friends of his, holding their guns at their ease.

"What are you looking for, girl," he asked.

"I'm looking for a friend of mine in the place where the students live."

"I'm going that way," he said. "Get in."

The windows were open and on the wind came the scent of gardens, saffron and cinnamon. She felt half asleep but her heart was awake, saying, I'm coming, I'm coming, my lover, my one.

"What is in this friend so important," the man teased. "Why choose him over another."

She could not sit up to answer him, leaning against the back of the seat, faint with love. She thought of him, unlike any other, drew him in her mind, his thick weight of hair, his eyes like jewels, his skin.

How much longer would it be, circling the mountains, the climbing cedars, the cypresses.

Outside, the orchards, released after winter, the end of the rains, flowering and the singing night birds.

The car slowed and stopped before a locked gate. "Here he is," the man said, drove away.

She put her hand on the lock of the door, her heart stirred for him. She stood on tiptoe to open it, her hands slipping with perfume still, but there was no one there. Her hair flung behind her, she walked on the road till she came to an arch and, among many names, his name.

Then her love awoke in her, a well, a spring, deep, deep, a thundering.

A small house before her, the music of strings, a guitar, a voice singing inside. She peered through the windows but could not see. She walked to the back. There was nothing.

In front of the door she raised her hand and knocked.

"Who is it that waits at the door," a voice said. Not his.

Then she thought, what if I don't know him now. What if a stranger appears that is he.

The door let in light and a not-known boy looked at her, puzzled, a wondering face.

"Ori." She uttered the name.

The boy nodded and pointed to the back.

Down a hall she walked in a dream, thinking as she moved, this is the last point at which anything can happen, every step now is a limiting.

At the last door she paused, the boy waiting patiently in the dimness behind her. She did not breathe. She knocked at the door. The music stopped. A voice said, yes. She opened the door and stepped in.

If her mouth were full of song like the sea and her tongue rejoicing like the rushing waves and on her lips praise like the breath of heaven, her eyes the sun, the moon, her arms outspread like the sky eagles, her feet delicate as gazelles, still it would not be enough to hold what happened then. The multitude of light! From Ori's face the light streamed, struck her so that her hands flung themselves to her face and she thought, I cannot stand before him and live.

It burned, it burned continually from him as she looked at him now, he was white, the girl fled, the boy messenger gone, and still rays of light that would not be contained. She saw before her the same face and yet another, transformed by her appointing him. There were many many things she wanted to say, and she was dumb.

A young prince over water. And she had split the sea to find him, wandered over the face of the water, and now, drowning in him, had come to rest.

"How?" he said.

"Come with me. Let's go outside, show me Jerusalem, and I'll tell you the story."

"You need a coat," he said.

"I've taken off my coat. I'm ready."

Then he ran with her down the paths of the hill, the air tearing her lungs, clambering over rocks and boundaries until they reached a ledge in a wall.

"Now," he said. "I can't wait anymore."

They were sitting on top of a wall of stone. Beneath them Jerusalem lay at peace. She could begin.

From her childhood she told it to him, how all her life, and she gave him the signs, had readied her for this. Then he told her his own, his obscurity until he too was recognised. She cried for the small boy he'd been. She wanted to know him from the day of his birth, to have grown up in his house and see him grow. She wanted every bruise, every pain, every love he'd had before her. Nothing alien. Nothing strange. To be exactly the same. Loneliness transformed, early or late, into delight.

Beside him she descended into the city, wandering the deserted marketplace. Through twisted alleys and leaning walls he led her, deeper and deeper. It was very dark. All the stalls were covered in metal slats, grey walls, grey earth. An ancient chill emanated from these pits. He was not afraid. He turned her around a corner.

The rough stairs, slabs of stone, gullies, channels, dirt hollows, opened under electric light into one even white plane. Surrounded by the heaps of the Old City, they were standing on a new flat space. It slanted gradually towards the foot of a wall, the wall that Judith knew. Enormous crusts of stone, cracked, tufted with moss, it was the Wailing Wall, the western wall of the Temple courtyard, all that remained of the glory of Solomon and the work of Israelite hands. Centuries of Jewish tears had fallen unheeded before it, Rome, Turkey and England had not honoured it, and now once more in Jewish hands it was curiously naked, empty for once, not even one praying person shadowed against it, so that it looked from the distance at which they stood smaller, reduced, and she felt a disappointment. It was only a wall.

Ori was triumphant to have instrumented her first time there.

She thought that if she approached it, if she kissed the stones as she'd long ago planned to do, if she saw the notes she knew were stuffed into its crevices, prayers of beseeching and supplication that Jewish women had placed there over so much time, it would touch her. But beside her Ori was breathing, and she trembling at his nearness. Her heart knocking inside her, unguarded, how could she not be overcome?

Then it was up and up to leave the weight of stone, into air, into light, winding around the city in layers, higher and higher on Mount Scopus until they were on the rough grass of the hillside near his house. The air was so full, raw earth and jasmine, the donkeys and goats that ran wild in the day and now were tethered somewhere in darkness. Jerusalem slept.

"That way's Lebanon"—Ori raised his hand—"and that way's Jordan. There's the Mediterranean, you can't see it from here. We're surrounded by the seven hills. Come inside," he said.

I have entered his house, she thought, stooping under the low arch of the gate. He locked it behind him. There was a small garden, the flowers closed for the night, their white skins luminous. The wind in the trees sounded like water. Everywhere spices. The vines on the house were not open yet.

"Come with me," Ori said.

He led her into his room. He took off his sandals. He knelt at her feet.

"I want to kiss you all over," he said.

She took off her clothes deliberately, one thing at a time. She was naked before him.

"How beautiful you are," Ori said. "Your eyes. Your mouth. Your hair." She lifted her hair. "Your neck. Your shoulders. You are unflawed."

She stood still.

"Late in the afternoon," he said, "near the beginning of the year I went walking in the north away from the city. I saw terraces of stone and vineyards inside them. Clusters of grapes hung ripe from curling stems. It was hot in the fields, the sun still in the sky, but over me were the hills of Lebanon, white with snow.

"Your breasts are so pale," Ori said. "We'll go where the

114

Jordan begins and you can lie in the sun and turn brown everywhere. Even here"—he circled her breasts with his hands. "Even here"—he drew a line down.

He was kissing her in the place that had no name. Ah, cried a voice from inside her. A terrible pleasure, exquisite. All of her being gathered to one point. Arched under him she was nothing. Separateness, her boundaries, what she was, collapsed into that meeting place. At the very centre of her only him, only him.

When he kissed her mouth she tasted herself on his tongue. Ori in her and she in him. His left hand was under her head and his right arm held her. What could parallel his gift to her?

If he were her sister she would know what to do. If he were her child she could shelter him. But he was another. Who would teach her hands to move in ways that would please him? To be within him, to know, stamped in the flesh, the mystery of manness.

Her arm reaching out to him was a bridge and her hand spanning his wrist supported him. He lay on his side and she looked at him in his fullness, unequalled, excellent. There were soft places on his body that she knew well. Her fingers remembered the cool part of his arm and the hollow of his back where her head rested. But the essence was hardness and that was strange. Her hands approached cautiously.

Now he made his own sounds as she began. An ornament of her fingers around him that moved up and up. Tracing him, straining against her palms. She licked her hands. They slid over him, a circular stair, spiralling. Waves of fingers cleft by him, rising, rising. She could not enclose him. His heart ragged against her, ribs lifted, falling.

Her hands were a goblet and she poured him over her, coated herself in him, a new skin.

Who was like her beloved, chosen over all others?

Before him she was nothing and when he was gone she returned to nothing. He created her, granted her beauty, and all she wanted was to walk in his light, to cleave to him all her days. She wanted to be inside him. She wanted his life.

A rage of love, unquenchable. She would seal him into a tower, a jewelled wall, board him in cedar. A sea of love, she would wash him in light, anoint him with air, with water.

When she was little and had no breasts she did not know. Now all her body was praise and her being exulting, holy, holy, holy, who enabled her to reach this day.

FOUR

Nothing was satisfactory, she complained to her mother in the kitchen sometime near midnight.

"What is it, Judith?" Her mother rubbed her eyes. It was very late and she looked tired. Judith felt bad but she couldn't stop talking.

"First of all, I hate the University of Toronto. It's so stupid, it's just like high school. I go there, sit through my classes and come home. There are no interesting people in the whole place."

"Judith"—her mother turned around, the sponge in her hand—"you've been there three weeks. Give it a chance. It takes time to meet people."

"I'll never meet anyone," she grumbled. "It's Toronto. All the good people leave."

"You're here, and if you're here there must be other people."

"I'm a fluke. I shouldn't be here. I should be going away to school." Like Rachel, she thought, packing up her clothes right now to move to a dorm at the University of Michigan. Like Jessie, poring over the catalogues trying to decide which of the thousands of wonderful colleges she'd apply to. Small or big, isolated or in the middle of the city, green campus or snow in New England, there were so many choices.

Her mother came over and sat down. "We're breaking our rule of no serious conversation after midnight."

"It's five to twelve and I never agreed to that rule. Daddy made it."

"Only because you were staying up until two o'clock talking

to us, and when you're overtired you can't think clearly. As for going away to school, Dad explained to you that American universities cost over five thousand dollars for just one year, and that doesn't include extras like bringing you home for the holidays. Why should we spend five thousand dollars when you can get a perfectly good education for five hundred dollars right here?"

Judith couldn't answer that.

"I understand that you're eager to get away," her mother went on, "but we're happy to let you travel, as we've told you before. We've always let you visit Rachel or go wherever you like."

That was true. She'd been allowed to travel before any of her friends. But that was only vacation and she had the rest of her life to worry about.

"Judith, I'd like to talk longer but we both have to wake up tomorrow to go to shul."

"I'm not going. I hate shul."

"It's Rosh Hashanah, you have to go to shul on Rosh Hashanah."

Judith would have argued with her but her heart wasn't in it. She knew she had to go to shul because if she didn't go on the big holidays she'd never go at all. She'd stopped going on Shabbes a long time ago when she realised that all the guys were Naomi's age or even Riva's. No one to stare at across the low wall that separated the men and women. Besides, she didn't think it was fair that the men got to do everything and the women just sat there. And the rabbi gave sermons against changing any aspect of anything. Women's rights and anti-Semitism were indicted in one breath.

"Why do they vote people like him in?" Judith cried. "It's the death of the Jewish community."

Her mother thought that was an exaggeration.

"I've seen you wince," Judith would say. "You know you're embarrassed when he opens his mouth. How about the time he compared God's love to radiation—it touches every living thing?"

"I admit he isn't inspiring," her mother said, "but I hear he's very good about visiting people in hospital and making shivah calls."

"Great." Judith gestured emphatically with one hand and cut

herself some cake with the other. "Proves my point exactly. A rabbi whose specialty is sickness and death. I'm not sick, no one I know is dying, thank God, and I consider it a waste of time to sit through one of his sermons." In fact, most of the younger kids left in a mad rush after the Torah was put back in the ark, and there was even a club of the shul big shots who brazenly walked out before the rabbi started talking to have herring and schnapps in the cantor's room in the basement.

"Religious life here is a farce," she went on. "There is no imagination."

"I said the same things when I was your age," her mother told her. "I thought Toronto was full of old fogies, I thought my parents were so naïve. The first year I lived in New York, I was much older than you, of course, I didn't even want to come home. But by the third year I was ready. And when your father asked me, I was happy to go back."

Judith didn't want to hear that story again, though she thought her mother would probably tell it despite the hour, if only to end on an optimistic note. The idea that when she finally managed to get out she'd end up in Toronto, married to someone from Toronto, especially after she'd bad-mouthed the city for years, was an irony too painful to consider. She could only pray it wouldn't happen. When her mother undid her apron and hung it on the cupboard door, Judith let her go.

Late at night the house was finally still. Everyone was in bed, Naomi went right after supper to get her beauty sleep for the boys at shul, her father slept in front of the TV until her mother woke him to go upstairs, and only Riva was up watching old movies on the basement TV. She wouldn't come up until the late show was over and that could be three-thirty.

Judith shut the door between the kitchen and upstairs and swung the dining room door closed. She opened the blind that her father had pulled down and looked at the window where the garden was. There was no light out there at this hour. She set up the week's papers and magazines on the table, took out challah, butter and peanut butter and slowly ate as she read all the entertainment sections and women's pages. When she was done with them she unwrapped the cake again and cut small slices, hoping it wouldn't show. Then she couldn't fall asleep, thinking about how she'd have to starve herself the next day.

Sometimes if she stayed up late enough she and Riva would meet in the kitchen and watch each other eat and laugh. "This is it," they'd say, knowing it wasn't it and that as often as they declared with each other as witnesses, "Tomorrow is day one," they'd meet again, same place, same time.

It wasn't fair. Naomi was skinny and gorgeous. Of course, everyone thought Judith was skinny too, but she knew the truth. Beneath her thin exterior, underneath her clothes, rolls of fat were waiting to reveal themselves if she sat the wrong way or tucked in a tight shirt. Small rolls, but rolls just the same. She couldn't get rid of them. She wasn't used to having to think about things like that. She never had before.

Riva was gorgeous too. She was four years younger than Judith but she looked the same age. Riva ate like Judith but she had a system. She ate as much as she wanted one day and didn't eat anything the next. Riva's every-other-day approach was quite disruptive of family life. Before dinner someone had to figure out if she was on or off food. Riva was ruthless about it, and if an off day came on Friday she'd sit at the Shabbes table and not eat anything, driving her mother crazy. "It's not in ruach shabbat," her mother would plead, it was against the Shabbes atmosphere. Riva didn't care. She had a boyfriend already, she wore miniskirts with tight-laced boots and she had to look good.

Naomi looked like the girls in *Seventeen* magazine. She had shiny hair that always fell right and sparkly eyes that looked big with makeup on. She was the tallest of the three of them and thin-boned, so that even when she wore jeans and an old sweater it seemed planned and perfect. She stood in front of the mirror for hours finding imaginary flaws in her face. Then she got mad if Judith said she was beautiful.

Riva was the opposite. She was voluptuous and lush, like a Renoir woman, Judith told her. Riva didn't want to look like that, she thought it was an insult because Renoir women were fat, but Judith meant that Riva could never look fat, she just got more and more womanly. Riva was very sexy, there was something about her, she always had been, even when she was a little girl. Uncles were always giving her love pats and she had lots of friends who were boys, just as Naomi had many boyfriends. Naomi dressed very carefully before she went out, but when a boy dropped by to see Riva she would come down in her old housecoat with her glasses on. It didn't seem to make any difference.

Judith thought that now that she had Ori she would be beautiful all the time and everyone would know that she was someone to be reckoned with. That was why she was so mad that nothing had changed. Her mother didn't like Ori, Judith knew, though she didn't say so. Her father said, "The chemistry isn't right," and probably said many worse things when he talked to her mother behind closed doors.

When Ori had come to visit in the summer Judith was very nervous. She wanted her parents to like him so much, but something inside her knew that they wouldn't. He had long hair and thought he might become a rabbi. Before he came Judith tried to describe him, to explain what she liked about him without going overboard to put them off. It was very hard, because the things she loved in him weren't what her parents would find important and she knew it. She told them about laughing, how funny he was and what a great attitude towards life he had. It made him sound irresponsible and she scared herself because she wasn't absolutely sure he wasn't.

"He comes from a good family," her parents reassured themselves before he arrived. Judith met him at the airport. He looked younger than in Israel, carrying his suitcase and wearing a jacket. He looked like a normal person except for his hair, which was very long. Oh, oh, said a voice in Judith's head. But she tried to be confident. She wanted to say, please put your hair behind your ears, please be serious when you meet them. He joked about it but he was nervous and a little defiant. How can they not like me, I'm me! was what he acted like, but Judith, who agreed with him completely, felt her insides plummet. They wouldn't. On the bus to her house she stroked him without talking, trying to build up a reserve of love to withstand what was coming.

Ori shook hands with her father and said, "Nice to meet you," to her mother, grinning from ear to ear. Then he put his suitcase on the floor and bent down, unzipped it and fumbled through his clothes for a while until he came up with two small white packages. For his housewarming gift to Judith's parents Ori brought yo-yos, personally inscribed, Morton and Madge. Her parents were in shock. Judith thought it was the greatest present she'd ever seen, but watching her father's rigid face as he bounced Morton up and down, she knew it was death. "Can't you at least admit it was funny? You laughed when he gave it to you," she accused her mother afterwards. Her mother was diplomatically silent.

Ori was awkward in her house. He didn't fit. Her mother was friendly but Judith never felt it was enough. Her father stayed in the den most of the time. Her sisters were nice but they didn't know what to do. They weren't used to seeing her with someone. Thank God Riva thought he was hilarious. On Shabbes afternoon when her parents were sleeping the three of them laughed until they couldn't stifle it anymore and had to go to the basement to shriek and snort as Ori piled joke upon joke so that they were lying on the floor in a stupor. "Stop, Ori," Judith said weakly. He looked pleased with himself.

Judith and Ori took long walks in the neighbourhood where she'd grown up. She wanted to walk all the lonely routes with him and permanently banish that girl. She felt like skywriting "I have a boyfriend" all over the city. But no matter how often she ran away from the house with him, he was a stranger in Toronto and sometimes strange to her. She didn't know the city as he did New York. She couldn't pretend it was a place she liked. She didn't have a life there. That was the imbalance, he could love New York without her, and even with him she felt strangled in the city of her birth.

Sharon had a party and they walked from Judith's house past every tree and building that she knew by heart. Judith waited to feel different, to lose the emptiness that sucked away at her no matter what weather or season. But in Sharon's rec room she was exactly the same. She still felt funny at parties and Ori looked out of place instead of above everyone. Walking home in the light rain of summer, Judith stopped at a bush of purple flowers, the tiny blossoms gaping open from the water. She pried a handful loose and put them in her hair. He did not kiss her.

And very late at night when everything was quiet she lay beside him in her room, touching him desperately. "Don't worry," he whispered. "It's really all right. I like your parents. I like your family." Then she cried. The ease was gone and couldn't be recaptured, this was life, they said, that intensity couldn't last forever and she didn't know why not. She tested him by wearing green army shirts that hid her body. She put her hair up. She showed him old slides. "Can you believe how ugly I was?" she said. It didn't seem to bother him. He didn't understand how growing up could have been so bad, he'd forgotten, put it out of his mind. How can I be so lonely? she asked herself, lying in his arms, hoping the bed wouldn't creak, scared that her mother, her father would get up for some reason, her sisters would want something.

When he was gone she was so mad at her parents she couldn't talk. How could they not like the person she'd chosen? How could they not have faith in her? Couldn't they realise that it was significant that she'd waited this long to find someone? Would someone who'd had no one for seventeen years suddenly fall for any slob on the street? She was afraid that if she said something it would be worse. Behind all the conversations past midnight were these reproaches.

Sitting in shul next to Naomi, Judith wondered when life would look the way she wanted it to. When would she travel, travel around the world? How could a person who was Jewish the way she was blend into many countries? And how, if she married Ori as she hoped and prayed would happen, would she have many passionate loves?

"I expect that when my husband and I are married ten years one of us will have an affair," she said to her mother one day. Her mother's reaction was predictable but Judith persevered. "How could we not? I can't picture living with someone for such a long time and not getting tired of him." Actually she thought Ori would have an affair, he found it hard to resist the women around him every day. She was toughening up for the future. Always she conducted imaginary conversations with him in which she defended herself, outlined for him the ways in which she was different from anyone else.

Not that he'd done anything. But Ori made it clear to her that he was an attractive commodity. Women in New York were falling all over him, the way he talked. She was sure it was true. There was nobody like him. And at the University of

Toronto she couldn't even make him jealous. Ori in New York was going to concerts and plays. Judith was waiting.

Jessie said, "You should have met five years later." It was very hard. They couldn't be together except for vacations and they could never end it because it was the real thing. Judith's mother had told her for years that sex was wonderful within the sanctity of marriage, and Judith agreed with her. But five years seemed like a very long time and she'd done everything else already. Her mother didn't understand what life was like. No one went out with someone for years without sleeping with him. In her mother's day people dated, saw each other every week for months and never did more than kiss. That's what Judith's mother expected of her. Judith wanted to say, it is impossible for that to happen now. She was one of the only girls, except for the Orthodox, who wasn't sleeping with her boyfriend. And even the Orthodox girls were doing all the things she was. Judith felt terrible about it but she wouldn't stop. First of all she would lose him and second of all she didn't want to. She thought being desired was one of the best things in the world. What did you do from fifteen to twenty-four? she wanted to yell at her mother. Of course, her mother did nothing. Judith wanted so much to talk to her about it, to say, Mom, it isn't reasonable to expect what you do. Now that the subject wasn't theoretical they couldn't have long discussions about it the way they had when she was thirteen. She was so afraid she'd give something away.

Her mother was very naïve. And her father didn't talk at all. It was a whole other life, and Judith was on her own. Naomi had probably been struggling for years, she was so used to being attacked for going steady too young and not doing her homework because of boys that she'd learned to lock away her private life from everyone's eyes and heart. Naomi did not talk.

Riva thought it was all very funny. Already at fourteen she had no intention of letting anyone rule her life. She wanted to be an actress and if she had to stop keeping Shabbes in order to do it she said she'd accept it. Judith hoped she was bluffing. It was hard to tell with Riva what was bravado and what was true. But even to say it made it possible, and that was frightening.

When people complimented her mother on her daughters she

always said, "Yes, but they're still young." She meant that right now they were all right but when they got older they could change. Judith wanted to cry: Mom, we'll always be good. Her mother said a lot depended on whom they married. She meant Jewishly. Judith hoped that within five years they would come to appreciate Ori. After all her mother's preaching about how important it was to marry someone committed to Judaism, here she'd found someone who might even be a rabbi and it wasn't enough.

"Both of you give double messages," Judith said to her parents. "You tell us that you want us not to be afraid the way you were, growing up in the Depression"—she turned to her father—"and then you get mad when we don't appreciate what it was like to grow up in the Depression. And you"—to her mother—"tell us that Judaism is the highest value when you really want us all to marry doctors or lawyers."

"I do not," her mother said. "Though security doesn't hurt."

"They're hypocrites," Judith railed at Sharon.

"No, that's just what they taught them in parent school."

Sharon and Judith invented the bootstrap academy, where both their fathers learned to believe that everyone could do anything if they only applied themselves and pulled themselves up by their bootstraps. Their mothers, they decided, went to doormat training to be taught to agree with their fathers in all public debate.

"You should be something," Judith said to her mother.

"I was a teacher for many years and I was glad to stop so that I could have you."

"But your mind. It's being wasted."

"Judith, I'm perfectly happy the way I am."

If her father was passing by he said, "Are you trying to persuade your mother she's not happy again?"

"You can't convince me," Judith would say when he'd gone, "that when you went to guidance in high school they said, my dear, we think the perfect profession for you is housewife. You don't even like it," she concluded.

"I don't mind it," her mother said mildly. "I was never ambitious."

Judith didn't know what she'd be when she grew up but she

was determined to be something. She was taking five different subjects at the university, hoping one of them would be what she liked. So far none of them did anything for her. If only there were a list of all the professions in the world so that she could narrow it down. As it was, there were things she had no way of knowing about. Psychology, archeology, anthropology, she'd never taken them in high school. And what if none of them was it? Maybe she'd never find out. Her tombstone would read: She had great potential. People would shake their heads over it, teachers she'd had in elementary school, saying, what a tragedy, what a waste.

Nothing was gripping enough. There were many kinds of things she thought she should be doing, picking apples in the country, bicycling across Canada, finding quaint unknown neighbourhoods in Toronto, open-air markets, something European. Art students and actors hung out in places downtown, drinking beer and dancing. She didn't know where they were. Judith wished she could hate things a little more. She didn't especially like the Judaism she kept, she did it mostly out of guilt, she felt, rather than love and conviction, but she couldn't throw it away. Everything was in the middle.

What she was most afraid of was that she and Ori would break up, she'd spend years in mourning, and then when she was twenty-four and about to give up she'd meet someone nice enough, good enough, Jewish enough to marry and she'd think it was the best she could do. After a couple of years she'd meet her real love, the one she was meant to marry, and then it would be too late. She saw herself and Ori staring at each other in anguish, a knowledge they could never act on.

The next thing she was afraid of was that she'd have a boring life. Except for one summer it was pretty boring so far. That's why Ori was so important. It was clear he'd always do interesting things and know interesting people, and as long as she was with him she would too. When she pictured Jessie and Ori in New York, just the way they spent their everyday time, it seemed so much more vitally interesting than anything she'd ever done. She thought of their scorn for anyone born outside Manhattan who dared call himself a New Yorker. They really believed they lived in the centre of the universe.

When she went to visit them on Thanksgiving she ate turkey and sweet potato at their parents' house and then they all went out to a Broadway play. Judith sat between Ori and Jessie, feeling fine. She was with the two people she loved most in the world. For the first night of her visit Jessie wanted her to stay at her parents' house and Ori wanted her to come to his apartment. She knew that it was the way of the world for her to go with him, his parents thought it was natural and were annoyed at Jessie for getting in the way.

Ori said, "I got the whole place ready for you. I cleaned up, I have some new music."

Judith said, "It's only one night. And it's not fair. All last year when you were away I came to visit Jessie and we had a wonderful time. Now that you're back, how can I suddenly tell her, you come second. It's the same when we walk down the street. I don't like holding hands with you when the three of us are together. It leaves her out."

"You're crazy," he said. "That's how it always is."

"Listen, for years and years I was a third and I remember exactly how it feels. I swore I wouldn't do that when I was on the other side, and I won't."

"But I bought doughnuts. They're waiting in a bag on the kitchen table."

That was it. She saw him trudging to the store and buying food for her. It was so sad. He left her no choice. She stayed with him and it was lonely. His apartment was empty. She liked it at his parents' house, where people were always coming in and out, where being alone with him was a secret and a treat, sneaking into his room late at night or up to the roof if it was warm enough, to look down over Manhattan, two bridges of light over two waters and the moon over one of them, thin or full. There he would kiss her and she would slip off most of her summer dress to be bare at the top of the world.

Now winter was coming, it was early this year, the leaves mostly gone and the cold bit through her clothes. The next day they were back at his parents'. Judith was very embarrassed. She didn't feel as old as she was acting and she felt despicable because of Jessie.

Jessie was second in the family and in life, she thought. She didn't see herself. The first time Judith had visited her the year before, they'd gone to Jessie's school, where Judith met all the talented gorgeous friends to whom Jessie compared herself and found herself wanting. She introduced them proudly. This one was a painter and that a dancer. This one was sleeping with the drama teacher. Judith looked at these girls, rich, confident in their antique clothing and suede boots, and fell under their spell immediately. To be so poised, so cocky at an age younger than hers. If she lived a hundred years she wouldn't feel the way they looked.

As for Jessie, she was of a different magnitude. Jessie had something she herself didn't know about. She exploded anything she touched into life. Judith, who collected interesting people even if she wasn't sure she liked them, was totally sure she'd never met anyone like Jessie. Taking in a television set for repairs was more fun with her than anything with anyone else. Judith loved to go to the supermarket, to school, to the bank, to the doctor's, she loved doing whatever Jessie did.

Judith worshipped beauty and still she found Jessie beautiful. The girls who looked like models seemed pallid, uninteresting, when Jessie was in the room. Jessie had big bones and a big solid body and when she held out her arms it was as if she were saying, let me protect you forever, do not be afraid. Jessie's letters in her odd writing that made every word look as if it came from a different hand were missives from heaven. Each one said, there is no one like you. Each one was unconditional love. Jessie liked the self Judith most wanted to be. She was sure about Judith, that she would be successful, that she would have a happy life, that someday it would all come together. Judith believed the same thing for her. They had fed each other with those beliefs all year long.

On a perfect day with Jessie, and there was no other kind, they woke up next to each other in the big bedroom at the end of the hall. The window beside them was always light, and framed by tall New York buildings, the river, beautiful, was a bright blue stripe under a paler sky. Morning in New York. They both jumped up immediately.

While Judith took a bath Jessie sat on the hamper and talked to her. They talked all day, in fact, and this was the start. Then it was Jessie's turn and they switched places, Judith wrapped in one of the huge towels that always hung from the bathroom door. It was time to get dressed for school. Jessie wore costumes, a pink chiffon skirt with spangles and a purple leotard, or black toreador pants and a satin jacket from the forties. Jessie had old suits with splashy red flowers, polka-dot chemises, lace undershirts, a corduroy milkmaid jumper with three petticoats, her aunt's wedding dress dyed maroon, a Western Union delivery uniform, a plaid cape lined with men's shirting. Her closets were stuffed with racks of clothes and ribbons, belts and beaded bags stuck out when she tried to close the door. Judith wore whatever was too small for Jessie.

Jessie went to a private high school for girls on the Upper West Side. Judith had been there so often that everyone knew who she was. She sat in the back and watched Jessie and her friends in classes Judith had never taken, Spanish, art appreciation, figure drawing. After that they went shopping. Judith always had a mental list of the clothes she needed, and they trekked from store to store, Jessie infinitely patient with Judith's search for the perfect black crepe shirt, the perfect print skirt, whatever.

Judith thought Jessie was amazing. She knew where to stand in every subway station so that the train door opened at their feet. She knew the best place to get cannoli and gave Judith her first taste. Paradise. She knew how to get tickets for shows that were sold out, exactly when to get in line for movies on the East Side, and how to call Port Authority and not get a busy signal. She met Judith at the door with flowers. She took her Israeli folk dancing. She rented a harp. She went to midnight concerts and took the subway home. Nothing went wrong when Jessie was around, and if it did it made no difference.

After supper they went to the movies, revivals at the Thalia. They wore leotards and jeans. They wore hats. Then they came back to sit in the kitchen late at night, drinking coffee and talking straight into bed, where they lay awake in the dark watching television, the oldest, most romantic movies they could find. Only on these visits could Judith fall asleep easily, in peace, Jessie beside her waiting to make sure before she let herself sleep too.

And now with one decision, by staying with Ori, Judith had betrayed her. A year of affirmation undone by her cowardice.

Jessie was quite understanding but Judith knew what she was understanding about: Ori won everything. And he didn't even know what had happened. There were ways in which he was quite obtuse. Judith defended her friendship with Jessie against the accusations of parents and the world. As she saw it, she, Ori and Jessie had a deal. Ori would give her what lovers give and Jessie would give her the rest. Ori didn't want to talk psychology, he didn't want to analyse things. Judith wanted to undo everything down to the core so that she could understand it all, what love was, was it good to be with someone like her or better to be with someone opposite, what kind of people had mad romances and what kind of people were doomed. She talked about it with Jessie all the time.

The most unfailing conversation, the most important question, was what was the real difference between men and women. Judith and Jessie were absolute believers in the androgynous mind. At least, as Judith said, the world had to proceed on the assumption that there was no difference between men and women, because the old differences were clearly at the expense of women and the true differences would never emerge until the old myths were eliminated. They hated the men-are-active, women-are-passive one. Or men are rational, women are intuitive. "Beware of the man who praises your instincts," Judith said. "He's telling you you don't know how to think."

Judith thought about her synagogue in Toronto. The women sat there docilely while the men had the honours.

"Don't you think it's crazy that arbitrarily half a people is excluded from participating in any way just because they happen to be women?" she said. "It's as if someone said, all people with blond hair can open the ark, all people with dark hair, sit behind a curtain."

Jessie told her that a group of women in New York had gotten together to study the issues in Jewish law that prevented women from taking part in communal life. They were finding that a lot of the restrictions were only custom and they were doing services themselves rather than going to places where women were left out.

"Toronto is dead," Judith moaned. "There's nothing like that

132

there. The most radical service in the whole city has women and men sitting separately but with no barrier. That's the great innovation, the scandalous controversy. The women get no more rights than they ever did, they can't go up to the Torah or be counted as part of the minyan, but now they're allowed to watch themselves be excluded. Big deal."

Jessie said things would change. People were starting to talk about it and she believed it would happen.

"Not in my lifetime," Judith said. "You think the Orthodox are going to change?"

"Maybe not the Orthodox, but the Conservative and Reform. They'll have to. They brought us up to think we could do anything, they gave us the same education as the boys, they're not going to be able to turn back."

"I don't know. The people I went to school with are just like their parents and always will be." Her family always would be.

Jessie saw no reason why she couldn't be a rabbi. Neither did Judith when she thought about it. But the family expected that of Ori.

Ori didn't know what he wanted to be if he weren't a rabbi. Maybe an actor, maybe a farmer.

"Maybe a baby," Judith said. She didn't know if he'd ever get serious. Ori loved her but he loved a million other things. If he read about a monastery in Ceylon he decided to go. If he heard that someone rode a camel across the Sahara he thought he would. Judith was sure he'd do them all. But there was no room for her in the plans.

"What are you going to do," she said, "put us in deep freeze for a couple of years while you traipse around?"

Ori shrugged. He wanted both and he didn't worry ahead of time how it would happen. Life arranged itself.

Judith felt that only if she worried enough about something would she earn it. She was thinking about marriage now to get it over with. If only she could know life ahead of time. She wanted adventures, she was terrified of not having them, but she also wanted everything to stay exactly the same. It was impossible.

There was so much to worry about that she was always tired. Rachel was mad because Judith didn't have enough time for her.

"I make all the overtures," she said. "I call you, I came to visit you twice and you keep promising. You just don't give as much. What does this friendship mean to you anyway?"

"It means a lot to me, Rachel, you know that." Judith's fingers were clenched around the phone. "But I only have a certain amount of time off, and last vacation I had to see Ori. Besides, you never remember things right. You came here last time, but the time before I went to you and I call you just as often. You forget."

Rachel conceded that sometimes she forgot. "But," she continued, "we aren't spending summers together anymore, and calls and visits are all we have. It takes work, it takes effort to keep a friendship going. It's not going to happen by itself."

The spectre of their friendship dying had haunted them all the years when they were too young to call by themselves, when visits depended utterly on the whim of parents. To hear it spoken of as a possibility frightened both of them immediately. Inside Judith was the knowledge that she didn't miss Rachel as much as she used to, that they always argued when they were together, although the arguments seemed important. She sighed. "I'll try to come at Christmas," she said.

How she would explain to Ori that she hadn't seen him since Thanksgiving but she couldn't see him until Reading Week in February was something she didn't want to think about. And not seeing Jessie for that long would be even harder. Rachel in the Midwest lived so far away from everything. And she didn't understand about boyfriends, that if you had one and he didn't live in your city and you didn't see him during vacations you wouldn't have one. It wasn't like friendship, where you could swear undying love and when you got together after a year it would be exactly the same. Judith knew that even if she and Sharon didn't see each other for twenty years they would be laughing within five minutes once they met again. The problem was, Rachel wasn't and had never been an ordinary friendship.

Worst of all, Rachel was very upset about Ori. "It changes everything," she said. "You'll see." She wouldn't spell out what everything was but Judith knew it was their friendship. It was shocking for Rachel even to imply it, it was against the rules.

"I thought we both couldn't wait to fall in love," Judith argued.

"I was always very happy for you when you got interested in someone." When you were sleeping with someone, Judith meant. "All we ever did was talk about love. And besides, I'm the same person, I still need women friends just as much. More. There are so many things I don't have with Ori and I know it."

"It's not the same." Rachel was in tears. "I am happy for you, but it's different. None of mine was ever really serious. That's why they broke up. My friendship with you was always more important than any of them."

Well, that was wrong, Judith wanted to say but she didn't. Rachel was right, it was the way they had thought.

"You talk about marrying him," Rachel said.

"I'm eighteen years old, Rachel. I'm not about to marry anyone."

"You told me it was destiny."

Judith was silent. She had the same problem with her parents. On the one hand she wanted to convince them they were overreacting, that she had years and years ahead of her and it was only puppy love so they should relax. On the other she wanted them to accept the fact that it was grand passion, in the stars, and they should take it dead seriously. In which case, as her father said, they had a right to worry about what Ori would be when he grew up. Why wasn't love like the movies, easy and straightforward? It had taken so long to find him, and it still didn't solve anything.

On the train on the way to Rachel's Judith knew she didn't want to go. She had compromised, five days with Rachel, five with Ori, and both of them felt slighted. It took seven hours to get to where Rachel lived and Judith hadn't slept most of the night worrying about getting to the 6:45 train. Of course it was still dark, one of those freezing mornings, and Judith gulped down a cup of cocoa before anyone was up, struggling out to catch the bus to the station in the middle of a blizzard. Union Station, which she usually loved, was an impersonal cavern scattered with yawning people and screaming kids. Judith bought a bag of shortbread cookies and finished them before the train even started to move.

All she could think on the train was, I hope I can get through this, I can't let her know how I feel.

Rachel was so excited to see her and drive them home herself with her newly acquired licence. It was strange to see Rachel check the mirror like an expert and move quickly into traffic.

"Ready for the traditional welcome?" she said. "Uncle Dan's for ice cream."

"It's too cold for ice cream."

"We'll get hot chocolate too, don't you remember, it's what we always do. Takes the edge off, you always say. No need to give up ice cream just because it's icy."

"I had hot chocolate this morning." Judith knew she was being a baby but all she wanted to do was sleep, preferably right through the five days.

Rachel turned the car around and said nothing. Staring at her stony face, Judith felt like crying. "Rachel, I'm sorry. I just finished exams and I'm exhausted. Really."

The car pulled over to the side of the road and stopped. "I have exams right after the holidays and I'm practising six hours a day," Rachel said. "I don't really have time for this visit but I made time because it's important. I debated until the last minute whether I should let you come."

"Let me come! Good of you. After I went to all that trouble to squeeze in this time." And got into trouble with Ori for a visit I'm only making on principle, Judith thought.

"Don't do me favours," Rachel said. "If you think I should get down on my knees and be grateful that you agreed to see me out of the goodness of your heart—"

"Oh, shut up."

"You shut up."

They glared at each other and started laughing. It was a typical fight.

"Let's discuss this over some chocolate, hot and cold," Judith said. She'd worry about her diet tomorrow. Somehow she'd have to be a good guest at Rachel's and still not be too fat for Ori. She'd wanted so much to be very thin when she went to New York so that she could eat as much as she wanted there but she'd already blown it with the bag of shortbreads and she and Rachel always stayed inside talking at the kitchen table day and night so it was hopeless.

"How's college life?" Judith asked while they were waiting for their orders.

"Pretty awful," Rachel said. "In fact, I hate it. My dorm is huge and impersonal, I still don't know anyone on my floor. People aren't very friendly, they seem to stick with their cliques from high school and I don't have any friends from high school here. You have to be on a meal plan and there's no vegetarian food."

"Rachel, you turned vegetarian and didn't tell me."

"I told you, I must have told you. It was near the beginning of the year."

"You never did. What's it like? What made you decide?"

"Well, I started reading about India and Hinduism and I decided I really want to go. Next semester I'm going to take a course in Sanskrit if I can fit it in with the music school. Hinduism is amazing, it really shows you what a mockery this place is. They call this a university. They actually think that what goes on here is learning. Knowledge, facts, maybe. But for wisdom I think the West is bankrupt."

"I don't know what you're talking about. Where did you get this from?"

"I'm telling you, I've been doing a lot of reading. This is an oppressive institution. It's elitist, it forces you to compete with everyone else who goes here and to look down on the rest of the world."

"What does that have to do with Hinduism?"

"Hinduism would say that you can never know what people here think they know, and understanding that is the only knowledge. This isn't reality, it's just one of the infinite number of ways that reality hides itself. It's all a curtain, all their divisions, all this academic garbage."

"Is music part of the garbage?"

"As we know it, yes." Rachel nodded emphatically. "Isn't it absurd that for six to eight hours every single day I sit in front of a black machine and move my fingers up and down, hating every minute? Is it bringing me one bit closer to enlightenment, all these years of scales and Beethoven?"

"No, but it might be bringing you closer to being a pianist, which is what you said you wanted."

"That's it!" Rachel exclaimed. "Want, desire, don't you see that those are the very things that bring such misery? It's wanting to be a pianist that makes me sit at the piano and hate it. My ego, my need to be complimented, to think I'm great, that's what keeps tripping me up. If I could let go of that—"

"You'd be a vegetable," Judith said. "If people didn't want, they wouldn't do anything."

"And what," said Rachel, "would be so terrible about that?"

"Nothing would ever happen," Judith said. "We'd all just sit around."

"So?"

"Oh, come on, Rachel, you can't be serious. You have to live in the world. What are you going to do, lie at home and stare at the walls?"

"You can learn a lot from walls."

Judith looked around.

Rachel smiled. "I mean it. I've been meditating too, and that's the only time I feel any possibility for tranquillity."

"We're not put on the earth for tranquillity. We're put on the earth for action. India, how can you talk about India? Do you think you'll find peace of mind while children with swollen stomachs are clambering all over you?"

"Don't be melodramatic. I know that argument, but what are you doing about starving children? Probably no more than I am. I'm not going to pretend they're not there, I'll accept them as part of the world. There is pain in the world."

"Nice of you to acknowledge it. But there can be more or less pain, depending on what people do about it."

"Do you really believe that?"

"Rachel, of course I believe it. You know what Judaism says, we're supposed to seek justice, it's our responsibility, to guard and keep the earth, which means not abusing anything with life in it."

"I was wondering how long it would take for Judaism to come up." Rachel looked at Judith. "Just teasing. I still consider myself a Jew and I always will. I'm very proud of being Jewish. But right now these are the kinds of things that interest me, and as you would say, they're not particularly Jewish."

138

"I was restraining myself," Judith said.

"Don't bother. I agree with you. That's why I have to look outside."

"But Judaism has a lot to say about this. You shouldn't turn to another religion before you study your own. There's a lot you don't know. There's a lot I don't know. I can't answer your questions, but someone must be able to."

Rachel shook her head. "The rabbi at home can't pronounce Hinduism and the Hillel rabbi told me it was idol worship. A useful comment, don't you think?"

"That's two people in the whole United States. Have you looked in the library? Have you tried the bookstores?"

"Baby, there ain't no books in the bookstores. I found one on how to keep kosher, no longer a consideration for me, and one on how Jews have suffered through history, a real inspiration. Oh, and there was a little pamphlet by some ultra-Orthodox guy about the laws of family purity and how you bring disgrace on the house of Israel if you sleep with your husband at the wrong time of month."

Judith grimaced. "That's not representative and you know it."

"I know it, Judith, but it doesn't help."

Judith couldn't think of anything. It was at times like this that she felt most inadequate. Her Judaism was left over from childhood and had not grown since then. All she knew were the same old arguments.

Rachel saw her struggling. "Look, Judith"—her voice was gentle—"it works for you and that's great. But you have a family to support you and friends who are into it. I don't have any of that, and I'm not sure it would satisfy me if I did. That's not a reflection on Judaism."

Judith couldn't discuss her own dilemmas because she knew Rachel would say, why keep doing it if you don't believe it, but stepping outside wasn't an option for her. She was afraid that if she stopped keeping kosher or Shabbes she'd never start again. As for Rachel, it was hard to tell what was behind her talk. Ever since Judith had known her, Rachel had hated practising. She argued it back and forth. Sometimes she would practise eight hours a day every single day for a month and then she'd crack and cry and swear that it was too much, that she didn't want her life dominated by a black monster, that she had no time for fun, for movies, for just hanging out like normal people. But then after a little while she'd go crazy away from her music and one day Judith would get an ecstatic phone call. "I'm back at it! I'll never stay away again. It's far more torturous to be deprived. Bless Beethoven, bless Bach. They're my real love." So it went.

They didn't talk about Ori because Judith didn't know what to say. There was a lot that was confusing to her about him and a lot she was scared about, but she knew that Rachel wouldn't understand since she wasn't in love and never really had been. Rachel thought having someone solved so much that it was grudging to complain, it was false modesty. And Judith didn't say much about Jessie because she felt guilty about how much she loved her, how even in the middle of her visit to Rachel she couldn't wait to see her. One night, lying awake as usual, she sat up in a panic. What if, her mind was saying, you love Jessie only as a way to get to Ori? What if you're using her? Using her, using her, the voice knocking around in her head, she couldn't shake it. She tried to remember how much she loved being with Jessie, how great it was to talk to her, how she lived for her letters. But tired in this room so late at night, she wasn't sure anymore. Had she made it all up, talked herself into it? Maybe the people who thought it was weird were right. Oh, it was awful, you are awful, said the voice that wouldn't stop inside her head. To do that to someone like Jessie, who had suffered so much from people who did that to her. Now she remembered Jessie's stories of Ori's girlfriends who befriended her only as long as they were together or the girl who spent day and night with Jessie and then never talked to her once Ori started getting interested. You're just like all the others, the voice said, you're one of them.

"Judith, what's the matter?" Rachel must have felt her moving around.

"I can't sleep," Judith whispered. She couldn't even open her mouth.

Rachel sat up too. "But what's the matter?"

She wanted to say it out loud but she was so sure it was true that if she let the words into the air they would never go away.

At the same time she felt the secretness building up inside her until she thought she would choke.

"I don't feel well," she said.

"Are you nervous about going to New York?" Rachel said.

Judith was surprised that Rachel realised she was going.

"A little," she said.

"Is it Ori?"

"Somewhat. But"—she took a deep breath—"it's more Jessie." There. It was done.

"What about her?" Rachel said. Her voice was quite soft.

"Rachel, do you think it's possible to love someone and then suddenly realise that you only think you do but you don't?"

At first Rachel didn't say anything. She was thinking it out.

"It seems to me," she said slowly, "that if you think you love someone, then you do. There's no other way of knowing."

"Yes, but what if you love them for the wrong reasons and you're actually bad for them?" Judith was shivering.

"Love is not bad," Rachel said firmly.

Love is not bad, Judith said to herself.

They both were quiet.

"From everything I've heard," Rachel said, "you love Jessie very much. I guess it must be hard to juggle her with her brother sometimes, but it's very logical that if you love one person in a family and they're very close to another person you'd love the other person too. Why should you have to make choices? Baby, love 'em all," Rachel said, "you know what the guru says, love is all there is."

"Thank God for the guru," Judith said. They laughed for so long that Judith was in pain. Rachel leaned over and put her arms around her.

"If you hadn't gotten depressed," she said, "we never would have had a good time."

There was no one like Rachel, Judith thought when she left. What would she do without her? All the problems were worth it. No one stimulated her mind the way Rachel did. Whatever it was, from their first conversations about the draft to the latest on India, Rachel was provocative. Judith was deeply grateful.

The East was in the air. Ori had discovered yoga and took Jessie and Judith to a class where a man whose name used to be

Richard Cohen introduced himself as Lakshma and told the students to lie on their backs and relax their abdomens. Judith didn't dare look at Jessie.

"Could you believe that?" she said to her afterwards. They were slumped on the floor of the dressing room, weak from laughing. "And then when he said—"

"Shut up," Ori said. "If you want to laugh at what you don't understand, fine. But don't do it around me. That's the very last time I ever tell you about something that matters to me."

Judith looked at him. "Are you serious? Come on, Ori, you have to admit it was funny. It was hilarious, all those people lying on the floor, breathing through one nostril in unison—please!" Just the recollection started them off again.

"Laugh away," Ori said, "but I mean it. You say you want to know what I'm involved in, I believe you, I take you to something that's important to me to try to show you what it's about, and the two of you can't even be mature enough to wait till you get outside. I brought you here as my guests."

Every morning of the visit Ori got up at six-thirty to do yoga for an hour before breakfast. Judith couldn't believe it. Ori, who hadn't been able to open an eye before eleven, was stretching and grunting and hanging himself upside down before the sun was up. She loved him for being able to change, to transform himself as often as he liked into a new person. But it drove her crazy that he would not be interrupted, that he lay on his mat in the living room and no one could talk to him, including her. Now she wanted to join him, to try to understand why it was so fascinating, but of course she could never ask him after that yoga lesson. Besides, yoga felt very un-Jewish to her, it was one of the troubling aspects of the place he'd taken them to. At the beginning and end of every session there was chanting in Sanskrit with invocations to Jesus and Moses in some benign tolerance that made Judith suspicious. What kind of religion was this that had room for everyone and claimed that people could be both their old religion and this one?

"It's not a religion," Ori said. "It's a way. It's a way of being in touch with your body, a kind of physical prayer that complements regular morning prayer, not contradicts it."

"But it's not in a Jewish mode," Judith said. "I'm sorry, but you can't tell me that saluting the sun and saying words in Sanskrit harmonises with our shacharit. It seems awfully close to avodah zarah to me." Avodah zarah, idol worship, was what haunted her. It was the most forbidden thing. Do not have other gods before me, the Torah said.

"There's only room for one," Judith said. "You can't try to blend them all together in some kind of spiritual porridge. Religions aren't like Tinker Toys, where the pieces are interchangeable. If you feel something's missing from Judaism, it's in Judaism that you have to look for the answer. Do you really believe that a system that's been around as long as ours hasn't been challenged this way before?"

"You don't know what you're talking about," Ori said furiously. "Do you think I haven't tried? You find me a system of meditation in Judaism. Go ahead, find me one book that gives you these kinds of exercises. Do you think I like feeling like I'm a sinner? Do you think it's fun to have rabbis look at me like I'm a crazy person?"

Judith didn't know what to think. For Rachel it was understandable, but Ori was born and bred in Judaism. Of course he said he was as committed as ever, and he probably was, but Judith was afraid that it would lead to more dangerous territory. It went against the deepest things in her. She felt all her ancestors looking down, pointing their fingers and saying: Avodah zarah, stay away or be burned.

Ori suggested that she come to an interreligious conference being organized in New York in February.

"What's the idea behind it?" she said.

"A bunch of Jews into spiritual alternatives will be talking about how other religions have affected what they do, and I'll be on the panel discussing yoga and Judaism."

"What would I do there?"

"You'll get to hear some interesting Jews"—he paused—"present company included." Ori named several people she'd never met but had heard of from magazine articles. "And you'll have an excuse to come to New York and mess around."

Judith was suspicious but curious too. "Any women on the panel?"

"Not that I know of," Ori said.

"That figures."

"Wait a minute, actually I think I remember that there will be one woman speaker. I forget what she's into. Yes, I'm almost sure there will be."

"I don't know if I'll be able to come back again so soon," she said.

"Hey, I have a great idea. I bet that's just when the Grateful Dead concert is happening. Wouldn't that be amazing? If I'm lucky maybe my friendly dope dealer can get me two tickets. It'll be incredible, all those Dead heads coming out of the woodwork."

She didn't like the Dead. "You going to wear your kippah to the concert?"

Ori touched his head. "I wear it all the time."

"Starting when?" She'd never noticed.

"Starting now. I just realised that if a Jew is supposed to cover his head before God and God is everywhere, then being bareheaded is a denial of God. Whooh, instant theology by me!"

Judith couldn't keep up. Ori was lightning fast, that was for sure, his aspects flashing before her, Ori the rock fan, Ori the spiritual leader, in such a hurry it made her dizzy.

"I never claimed to be consistent," he said.

When Judith walked into the conference there was a room full of people. She couldn't find Ori anywhere. Wandering around looking for him, she passed a man with a long beard and white clothes, a girl wearing bells, two people in orange monk robes with shaved heads, and a woman with a ring in her nose. Ori looked wonderful to her when she finally spotted him.

"What a place for a reunion," she whispered, kissing him hello. "What shall I do with my suitcase?"

"Just put it down in a corner," he said. "We're almost ready to start."

It made her uneasy to leave all her earthly possessions alone in a corner of a huge room in New York, but it was worse to suspect these religious people of wanting to steal her clothes. Not that some of them would wear her clothes, she remembered.

Ori was first. He stood up, made a few jokes and then got serious. He talked about his upbringing and what he expected Judaism to be and what was missing, and then he gave a list of the Jews he admired who were doing what he was. He put himself in good company. As she saw it, Ori was saying that though he'd had to stray from the straight and narrow so did all the other sensitive Jews he knew.

Some of them spoke after him, leaders she recognised, people from whose writing she'd learned a lot. Buddha, yoga, the East, ideas she already knew from Rachel. Some were for, some against. A chasid spoke after a Reconstructionist student. One hip Orthodox rabbi in jeans said he thought Judaism couldn't tolerate these alien concepts. There was a stir of approval and a stir of disapproval at the same time. Then a woman came to the front. She had long pale hair pulled into a braid in the back and a light face. She was wearing an Indian dress and sandals, and she stood at a distance from the other speakers and leaned towards the microphone.

"I was brought up in a traditional home and went to a day school," she said. "My parents went to the Orthodox synagogue we belonged to every week and I went too. I was observant right through college, but I began to be more and more uncomfortable with the institutional Judaism I knew. In a personal way it was still good, but I couldn't pray in my parents' synagogue. It seemed to have nothing to do with spirituality or what I thought prayer should be about. Part of the problem was that I myself didn't know what I wanted from prayer or from God."

She leaned even closer. There wasn't a sound.

"I tried to talk to my rabbi, but he treated me like a kid whose questions were very simplistic. He recommended some books that I found simplistic"—she smiled—"and then I figured that maybe rabbis weren't the answer. I started to look for books about what I was interested in. How to contemplate, how to think about God in a way that could draw me closer to Him, and what part I as a woman could play in this religion.

"By this time I was praying only at home, spending a couple of hours in the morning and evening concentrating on the siddur and trying to understand what lay behind the Hebrew. The farther I went, though, the more confused and unhappy I became. It didn't feel right. The concept of God and His involvement with us was something that grew harder and harder, and nobody I asked could help. I was also not at ease about praying so privately from a book that was meant to be used in a community."

Although her hands moved urgently when she wanted to make a point, the rest of her was quite still. Now she spoke more softly.

"I've been listening to the speakers before me, and it moves me very much to hear Jews struggling with the same issues that I have. But I do feel I'm in a different place. As a woman I didn't have the option of chasidic Judaism, which is very expressive and can be intensely spiritual for men. But I wasn't comfortable in Conservative synagogues either, although some of them gave women rights, because there was equality but no life, no heart in the buildings I saw.

"I was very lucky, though. At a time when I was really floundering and quite alone, I met an old friend who took me to see her teacher. There I met the woman who became my teacher too, and I started commuting from New York to her ashram to spend time with her. She rarely said anything, we didn't study from books or talk about issues, although at the beginning I wanted to and was very impatient. Instead I just sat in her presence and meditated, or tried to meditate. Her students would sit there all day, getting up at five and breaking only for one light meal.

"It was then that I started to discover what was involved in a spiritual life, to try to serve God and devote my life to Him. It is a life, so it's not something I ever expect to know or finish. But I feel I'm on the way, and that there are many ways. Infinite numbers, of which each of you is one," she said. "We are all part of the same great truth that shows itself in Moses, Jesus, Buddha, and millions of others whose names we don't know."

Nobody clapped. No one knew what to do. Judith hated the girl for being so calm, for leaving instead of fighting, for thinking she'd found the answer. There she stood, smiling placidly. I am not the same as you, Judith wanted to say, you are wrong. But the girl seemed so clearly happy. Judith thought that if she left it all she'd feel like a person condemned to die, sitting in a terrible prison for one, herself, while all around her Jews would be living their Jewish lives, walking to shul, celebrating holidays in each other's houses, and she could only stand apart and watch, knowing it was a richness she'd turned her back on. It would never let go of her, she was sure, even if she no longer believed in it. Nothing seemed sadder than having each day of the week the same, all foods the same, nothing making any difference. It was all worth it, even her confusion, to belong to this.

Now it was time for the audience to divide into groups. Judith hoped Ori had arranged for them to be together, she was tired of sitting with people she didn't know, but when she got to her group she didn't recognise a single person there. Everyone sat in chairs in a circle, coughing or staring at the ceiling. Right across from her was an old man with sidecurls and a long black coat, the real thing. He was looking at her in a kindly way and Judith felt his eyes saying, you look like a nice girl, why do you have to wear jeans and dress like that? She couldn't imagine what he was doing here. One woman introduced herself as the leader and suggested that they tell what their religious background was and why they were at the conference. Judith didn't want to talk about her parents and her family in front of strangers, but the person beside her stopped and she had to begin.

"My name is—"

"Could you talk louder?" someone said. "We can't hear you at this end."

Judith cleared her throat. "My name is Judith Rafael and I'm from Toronto," she said. Suddenly everything was coming out. She was talking straight at the old man, who was wavery through her tears. "I come from a long line of scholars and rabbis. For hundreds of years there's been a Rafael rabbi in every generation. I inherited centuries of Jewish blood, and my sisters and I can't even pass on our family name. I'm sick of hearing about how women have a different spirituality. I'm sick of being taught how important it is to put on a tallis and tefillin every morning and then to be told that women don't need concrete symbols because they have some magical female ability to sanctify themselves. You don't expect women to bring Shabbes in just by thinking about it. You expect them to light candles. Why should it change for other prayers? Sure, a woman can daven every morning if she chooses. But the physical act of wrapping yourself in a tallis, of reciting the blessing for tefillin, knowing that for centuries Jews have expressed their bond with God in just this way—

there is no substitute. A man who davens every day with tefillin knows his prayer is incomplete without it, but a woman's prayer has nothing physical, actual, to say: I am here."

She couldn't stop. "I went to a day school where both boys and girls learned boys' Judaism. My teachers told the whole class that to go up to the Torah, to be counted in a minyan were great Jewish privileges, and I believed them. Later those boys told me: Aren't you lucky? You don't have to go to shul every week, you don't have to be on time in case they need you to be counted. Wait a minute, I say to myself, I sat in that class. Nobody told me then that for men among themselves going up to the Torah was an honour but for men talking to women it was suddenly a burden. And why have Jewish men fought throughout history to hang onto this burden? The ignorant Jewish woman with her naïve piety who inspired her husband and sons to the ways of Torah is no more a model for me than for any Jewish man who has studied. Judaism is a religion that loves knowledge, and women who are untrained have nothing.

"Nothing, nothing, nothing." She was so mad at the old man. "So don't walk around bemoaning the loss of Jews to assimilation. Yes, if you give women equal rights it will change Judaism. But it needs changing. People are starving for an inner life, and if they can't find it in Jewish life they'll find it someplace else.

"We are losing Jews." Her voice was trembling. "You heard that woman downstairs. No Jew should allow another to be turned away."

She was crying so hard she couldn't talk. Someone handed her a tissue and another girl put her arms around her. Judith couldn't help it, deep ugly sobs that hurt her chest. She bit her lip to stop making those noises and the leader went on to the next person. After the meeting was over she wanted to run out of the room. They must think she was crazy, acting like that. What if they told people?

As Judith hurried to the door the old man beckoned to her. Everyone else left. They were the only ones there.

"I'm sorry," she began. "I didn't mean anything against you."

"Shh," he said. "You are hurt. It is understandable. So you are a Rafael," he said. "For some people it is harder not to do than to do. You are davenen with tefillin already?" She shook her head. "So you will. I can see that you will. It is important to listen to the heart. When I see a young maidele crying, crying" —he spoke very slowly—"it is for the heart. You must go do what you have to do."

The voice that she'd never expected to hear, the door that was closed, had sounded, had opened, turned into a blessing. She could begin, that's what he was saying. That's what she explained to Ori as they walked down the street after it was all over. "It's the past I never had, sanctioning me." There was so much, Torah, Talmud, thousands of years. The unknown faces of the sages passed before her. Bearded men, older and older, tefillin knotted on their brow, and she among them. Judith was chosen, distinguished. All the resources were in her, she felt, frightening and exhilarating. She hoped she could live up to it. Right now the sun was low between the huge skyscrapers that floated into the clear air. The wind spun through her, if it could lift her in space, it would. Ori was trying to talk to her but she was unapproachable. Never mundane again, she thought, how could she talk of movies, of dinner, when such greatness was waiting, such a bigger world than this. Ori looked so small, even love was small in the face of it.

Unfortunately it couldn't be sustained. Even the next day it had left her somewhat and she could invoke it only by concentrating. The urgency for prayer, for study, was lessened and the worrying crept in to take its place. Nothing was resolved after all. At home it was after a thaw and winter was back. Back in March to boots and slush and grey Toronto streets.

"Why does it last so long?" Judith complained to her mother.

"And here I feel that I've had no time for anything this winter," her mother exclaimed. "Between my classes and your father's schedule and planning the hospital party."

"It'll never end. I want to be on a South Sea island, I want to lie in the sun and not think about anything."

"You'd be back in a week."

"I would not." She really didn't think she would be. She could feel the hot sun lulling her to sleep even now.

"When we went to the Bahamas we were going to stay for two weeks, but your father was so stir crazy we came back after one."

"Well, that's the difference. Daddy would actually rather work than stay home. I like staying home. I like doing nothing. I think I could do it for a living."

"If you can find someone to pay you for doing nothing, go right ahead. You have my blessing."

Judith knew why she was sitting in the kitchen talking to her mother. She had exams in four days and she'd do anything rather than study. "In two weeks it will be over," her mother kept saying. Objectively that was true but it was impossible to believe.

"Why bother learning all those facts when you can look them up," Judith told her. "I want oblivion. I want out."

"I want you to go back to your studying," her mother said. "I think you'll feel a lot better once it's done."

"It never is done, that's the problem." Judith was heading for the stairs. "If it were a doable task it wouldn't be so terrible." I'd still leave it for the last minute, she thought, knowing me. She'd started every essay this year at midnight and worked until seven, sitting at the kitchen table drinking coffee, leaning over reference books and typing with the door closed all night.

The world looked very different after midnight. There were many nights when Judith couldn't sleep. She'd lie down at eleven-thirty and tell herself to be calm and then feel the half hours creeping by until it was too late to get a good night's sleep. Don't get up, she'd say to herself. If you turn on the light you'll just stay up longer. But it was maddening to be in bed thinking about nothing, thinking about how awful she'd feel in the morning. Don't get out of bed, she'd say, turning on the light. But she felt too tired to read and her stomach would make her head weak. You're not hungry, she'd lecture herself, you only think you're hungry. But after a while she was sure she was hungry, she was sure that if she had just a little snack she'd feel full and it would be all right.

Of course she didn't stop. Then she'd lie in bed and watch the room get light around the shades, get up, really exhausted now, to write a note to her mother not to wake her, and skip her first class to get five or six hours' sleep. What a life.

Her next trip to New York wasn't until Purim, which was late this year. Ori loved Purim but Judith didn't like it at all. Everyone was supposed to get dressed up in costumes to read the story of Queen Esther and drink until they couldn't tell the difference between night and day. There was something un-Jewish about it even though it was completely traditional. People always acted silly during the reading, and the little kids screamed and wouldn't stop whirling their noisemakers even when Haman's name wasn't being said. Purim was about the triumph of the Jews over their enemies in ancient Persia, of whom Haman was the biggest. But it was hard to take seriously with all the joking around. Ori and Jessie would wear great costumes, they always did, and do skits that would make everyone laugh. She loved it when Ori was funny but she dreaded Purim.

What would become of them, that was what she wanted to know. They weren't writing letters anymore because they could call, but they couldn't call that much because it was expensive. They saw each other often, but not often enough to feel as if they were together, and even when they were together she still didn't know what was going to be. She loved him, she wanted to marry him, but she didn't see how they could have a life together. Sometimes when she looked at his face she didn't feel anything. It was terrifying to find him plain or even ugly. How would she live with him for the rest of her life? What if he saw her that way?

Riva was cold-blooded. She said: Always go out with a good-looking man. Then if you're mad at each other at least you can walk down the street with him and stare at his face. Her mother said: When you love someone he looks beautiful to you and when you don't like someone even if he's gorgeous you can't see it.

But Ori's face wasn't enchanted anymore. She herself didn't feel the way she'd looked that summer. Another summer was coming up and she didn't want to go back to camp. She couldn't bear to walk in the same fields and swim in the lake when it wouldn't be, could never be the way it was. Everything would look older, uglier. Places that had once held such mystery would be just cottages and cabins like anywhere else. It would be humiliating. She hoped Ori would think up a plan.

There were other things on her mind. Sometimes on Saturday nights, watching Naomi go out, or at rallies, events in big public places where she met everyone she knew, she would have given anything for a boyfriend in the same city, an arm around her in the dark. Every once in a while she would go to a concert with Sharon or meet Anna for coffee downtown, but everything was with girls, she was always with girls. She loved her friends but it was hard not to feel like an outcast, to keep saying to herself as she walked alone around the campus, between classes, staring at couples who seemed to be in every corner now that spring was coming, I have a boyfriend too, he's just not here. She always reminded herself what Ori was, why she was with him and not anyone else, about Jewishness and magic and New York, her key words that she recited to herself to summon before her the remembrance of what they had and how it had all begun.

It was harder for Ori. He wasn't living at home, he could do what he wanted, he was always attracted to people, she knew, and there was no end to the long-distanceness. Judith wanted to feel really beautiful at Purim, ready for spring and for love. If she could get through exams and the next little while, maybe it would be all right.

Jessie was disturbed about her frame of mind. She wanted Judith and Ori to work out, she was sure that someday they would, but for now she advised seeing other people. Maybe it's what you both need, she said.

Judith was passionately against it. "That's not a solution." There was no way they could go out with other people and get together afterwards as if nothing had happened. At least she couldn't. "I can't turn it off and on," she said to Jessie. It frightened her that Jessie could consider it so coolly. Maybe she had inside information. Maybe Ori wanted to but wouldn't tell her. Judith didn't ask.

By Purim it should have been spring but it wasn't. Judith, who wore spring clothes anyway, shivered on the way in from the airport. She was late and the reading was already under way. They were up to the part where Esther's uncle puts her in the harem of the king in the hope that she can save the Jews. The kids were going crazy every time Haman's name came up, flinging their noisemakers about in the air and stamping their feet. Ori and Jessie waved to her from the other side of the room. He was dressed as an ape and Jessie wore a frilly white dress with live flowers in her hair.

"King Kong," Ori said, bowing to her when she reached him. He put on his gorilla mask and looked like a monster. "I'd hug you," he said, "but I'd rip you to shreds." He held up his claws.

"Call me Fay," Jessie said and kissed her.

They looked fabulous.

"I don't know which one of you to look at first," Judith said. "Have I missed a lot?"

"The best is yet to come," Ori said. "A spectacular party at yours truly's apartment. Wine, women and song. You're the woman," he said, looking at Judith. "Or are you the song?" He turned to Jessie. "Boy, am I out of it."

Judith had a faint suspicion. "Are you stoned?" she said.

"What?"

The noise was unbelievable. Judith gestured a cigarette. Ori laughed.

"How could you do that, Ori?" she wailed.

He couldn't hear a word.

"I said, what's the matter with you? Why didn't you wait till I got here? We were supposed to have a good time together tonight. That's what you promised."

Her face was getting through to him and he walked out into the hall.

"All I did was smoke a little dope, what's wrong with you? I didn't know when you'd show up."

"It takes you away. You're not here when you're stoned. I knew this would happen."

"What are you talking about? You knew what would happen? You're making a big deal out of nothing."

"It isn't nothing. I don't like you when you're stoned and I've told you so often enough. You did it on purpose."

"You are crazy. Would you get rational?" His hands were on her shoulders. "Do you want to ruin Purim for everyone?"

"You ruined it first."

"Oh my God. I'm going back in right now. You're welcome to join me."

"I'm not joining you and I'm not going to your party if all you're going to do is become more and more mindless before my eyes."

"And what"—Ori's voice was quiet and sweet—"does madame

propose to do for her first evening in New York?"

"Don't be sarcastic. I'll spend the evening talking to Jessie, something I probably wouldn't get to do the rest of the visit anyway."

"Suit yourself," said Ori and disappeared.

Jessie came out almost immediately. "What's the matter?"

"I hate Purim."

"Me too. But what's with Ori? He looks upset but he wouldn't talk to me."

Judith sat on the stairs and told her. "I know I shouldn't be telling you this."

"It's all right," Jessie said. "I've heard it before and worse."

"There are times I just can't stand him. How can I marry someone I can't stand?"

Jessie stood over her looking quite stern. "You're not marrying anyone in that frame of mind. You two are killing each other. I don't want to hear you talking about marriage until you're absolutely sure. I want to hear your voice radiantly happy, then you can announce it to me. This is not the way a person who's going to get married even in a few years is supposed to sound. I'd rather you split up altogether than sound this way."

Judith started to cry. "But, Jessie, how can I not marry him? I love him. There's no one else for me, you know that."

"Nobody who's as unhappy as you sound," Jessie said firmly, "should get married."

Judith knew she was right but didn't know what to do about it. "We can't break up. It would be the end."

"I'm not saying you should break up"—Jessie was gentle—"though people can be apart for years and then get back together. But you clearly have a way to go before you're ready, that's all. Now don't worry," she said, "dry them tears, lady. Dust yerself off." Jessie waved an imaginary rag over Judith's shoulders and knees. "Everything's going to be fine."

"Jessie, promise me you won't let me do anything that's a mistake."

"I promise," she said. "Now let's go to the party and have a good time."

"I hate parties," Judith said but followed her in. She didn't want not to see Ori all night.

Judith couldn't wake up the next day. She wanted to talk to Ori but he was gone very early to arrange his credits at school. When he got back they had to go out right away to the movies. Waiting for the subway, Judith said, "Ori, we have to have a serious conversation."

"Here?" Ori said.

The train rumbled in. "Not here," Judith said, swinging from the metal strap inside the car. "But soon."

"About what?"

"You know what." She was annoyed. "About us. About the summer."

"What about the summer? It's all arranged."

"What's arranged?"

"Oh, I must have forgotten to mention it." Ori was smiling. "Guess where we're going this summer?"

"Just tell me."

"No, you have to guess. I'll give you a hint. California, here I come," he started to sing.

"Oh, Ori." She threw her arms around him. Everyone on the subway looked around. "You're incredible. I love you, I love you, I love you."

"We're going to be counsellors in a Jewish camp out there. At least, you'll be a counsellor and I'll be a camping instructor."

"But you barely know how to camp. You've only done it for fun."

"I'll fake it." He shrugged. "Besides, I swore I'd never be a counsellor again. I think I'll be able to swing it."

"But how will we get there? The plane ride costs a fortune."

It was time to get off. "I can't believe I have to go to the movies now," Judith said. "I won't be able to sit still. This is so great." She remembered her question. "I can't ask my parents for all that money."

"Never fear." Ori gave a flourish. "We're on scholarship. They want us because of our superb training."

Judith tried to forget that she didn't like being a counsellor.

"Besides, it's an excuse to go to California," Ori said.

That was certainly true. They linked arms to go into the movie.

❖   ❖   ❖

On the phone when she was back in Toronto, Judith and Ori decided to go out with other people until the summer.

"Maybe that'll get it out of my system," Ori said.

"Maybe I'll fall madly in love with someone and forget who you are," Judith said.

"I just feel we both need a change. A little refreshment. Jessie agrees."

"I know what she thinks."

There was a pause.

"Well, what else is there to say?" Judith said. "Have a good life and I'll talk to you in June."

"Don't be ridiculous. I'll call you next week. Maybe neither of us will find someone," Ori said hopefully.

"Maybe." Judith knew he'd find someone tomorrow.

By Passover Ori was going out with a gorgeous girl in Jessie's class. Judith knew about it because Ori told her. It was nothing, he said, just filling in time. Judith, to her own surprise, was seeing someone too. A friend of a friend had started calling her up. He was nice and she was awkward. She liked him enough but she felt guilty every time she saw him because he had no reason not to hope something could happen but she knew it was impossible. She let it fade and spent the rest of spring alone. Ori kept going until the week before Judith was due in New York.

"How are you going to end it?" Judith asked him on the phone.

"She knows the whole situation. She knows it'll be over when you get here."

Judith thought no one could carry off that situation. And Ori was so bad at ending things, he said that he let all his girlfriends break up with him because it was easier. "They feel they made the decision and I don't need to feel guilty about it because it was their idea," was how he put it. Judith suspected it would happen that way for her too someday and she was determined not to be the first to crack. Still, she was a little nervous, coming into New York, that Ori would have forgotten to bring it up with the girl and that she'd have to spend the first few days of her visit persuading him to make the phone call.

All was well, though. The path was clear. But Ori was more shaken up than he thought he'd be. When she came into his room the first night, he was sitting up in the dark.

"We have to talk," he said.

"Why? You knew I was coming."

"I know and I'm happy you're here. It's me that's the problem. I'm finding it hard to switch gears."

Judith's voice was chilly. "I don't think the situations are exactly analogous. You're comparing someone you went out with for a couple of months to someone you've been involved with for a couple of years."

Ori groaned. "I know. And I wasn't in love with her. But still."

"Of course it's not easy," she softened. "You couldn't not care about her. You spent time with her, you did things together, it must be difficult to have to shut it off all at once."

"I guess so," he said. "Come here." He held out his arms.

She hugged him and he groaned again. "I can't do it. I'm not ready yet."

Now she was getting alarmed. She didn't know how she felt about him but she knew exactly how she expected him to feel about her. She wanted a grand reunion, all the more passionate for having been apart for this time.

Ori kissed her but his heart wasn't in it. "I think I'll become a monk," he said.

Judith stirred herself. "You wouldn't last a week."

"I'm serious. I'm thinking of trying celibacy for a while."

"Thanks a lot."

"You always told me I didn't know what it was all about and now I believe you. I thought I could do anything but I can't handle sleeping with someone last week—"

Judith didn't hear the rest of the sentence. Of course Ori was sleeping with that girl. How could she have expected he wouldn't? Out of their relationship he was back to his old self. Judith was thinking fast. She would never let him know how naïve she'd been.

"Judith?"

She wanted nothing to do with him.

"What do you think?"

"I think it's the best idea I've heard yet," she said.

"Stop it."

She didn't know what really to say.

"You're mad, aren't you?"

"No, I'm not mad that I planned to come to New York and be with you and spend the summer with you, and now that I get here you tell me you've changed your mind. Why would I be mad about something like that?"

"I get the impression you're mad. Look, I still love you and I want to be with you and I know we'll have a great time in California. I just need some thinking time."

"I feel sick."

"Me too," Ori said.

"What are we going to do now? How can we go to California? Come to think of it, how are we going to California? Did you make reservations?"

"I decided not to go by plane."

"What do you want to do, walk?"

"Hitchhike." He watched her face. "Now don't reject it out of hand."

"I'm not hitchhiking. It's dangerous."

"I'll protect you."

"You're doing a great job so far."

"Come on, Judith, it'll be wonderful. We'll have such a good time."

"Where will we stay?"

"We'll camp out," Ori said.

"I don't know how."

"Me neither. This'll be my training for the job."

"I don't even have any stuff."

"We'll buy it this week. I've looked into it. You can get it secondhand in an army surplus store. I've checked it out already."

Judith looked at him sceptically. "How long have you had this up your sleeve?"

"Awhile."

"You might have mentioned it."

"If I would have called you up and asked you, you would've said no, wouldn't you?"

"Yes," she had to admit.

"So I just skipped that part."

"I've always envied those hitchhiking couples I see at the side of the road," Judith confessed.

"Here's your chance."

"But we're not even a couple anymore."

"The cars won't know. Besides, we get along all right. Maybe we'll change our minds."

"I'm not changing my mind. This is it." She was bluffing. "Absolutely. We've been through this too many times."

"You know I could get you back if I wanted to," Ori said.

"Nothing doing." Her fist slammed into her palm.

"Yes I could," Ori said, "but why argue?"

"You. Could. Not."

"Call it a draw," Ori said generously.

Judith cried herself to sleep.

Dalet

America. On a road in the middle of Wisconsin, early in the morning, clean light on the rolling land, clear wind, and over it all a breathing sky, the very beginning of the day.

It was so quiet, except for the wind in the grasses, except for Ori, standing in the centre of the road, impatient, watching for cars.

The road was blank, a strip dividing dark fields from light, curving through the low hills to disappear up near the horizon, still faintly blue with what was left of night.

The jumbled land was very small under that sky. Through the thin air the light spread itself transparently, without substance, until the sun, radiant, emerged from the hills to turn the air white. The blinding white air collected over the earth, bursting the shade into green and trembling blue. It was going to be a good day.

Ori's thumb stabbed the air. His back strained inside his shirt, his calves knotted and eased as he shifted his weight, first to one foot, then to the other.

She yawned. Far away a glitter moved towards them, turned into a car. It was Sunday morning.

Curled into the back seat between the packs, she saw the light flickering, two narrow crescents of green and gold through her closing eyes. The wind brushed continually against her face, the open window sent forth the fragrant world. She slept.

It was very hot. The car drew in the growing heat of the sun. Nothing was muted, everything plain and glaring under the raw sky. Ori was murmuring in the front seat, the driver's sudden voice startling her. He was explaining to Ori about ROTC. The back of his neck was pink, and bristly hair stood straight out from his head.

Outside in the fields there were cows. She couldn't stop watching them lumbering by. Real cows!

Ori was checking his map book. Then they were standing on the road again, the wind lifting her hair, her legs wobbly. Over her head a sign said 151.

Bob in a red car was going home to Nebraska and would drive till he got there. He sang straight through Iowa and showed them the Mississippi River, a wide sluggish band of water that looked nothing like Stephen Foster songs this far north. Still, it was the Mississippi. She had never expected to see it. Bob wore a work shirt stamped with roses and a yellow suede jacket whose fringes made flapping sounds as he moved his arms on the wheel. They passed Waterloo, Fort Dodge and Sioux City, and Bob's voice rose as he got closer.

It was strange weather. On one side of the car the air was full of light, while the other was suddenly black, all black but lit from below by a thin gold rim that hugged the earth. It was sunny and rainy as they drove.

Nebraska was flatter than Wisconsin, and gas cost twenty-nine and a half cents a gallon. When Bob walked over to the men's room, his bell-bottom pants, last year's style, shook in the wind. Behind the pumps was a bar where he and his friends used to get drunk every Saturday night. There was nothing else to do, he was apologetic.

She thought his hometown would be grim, a dry dusty place that the young people left. But Norfolk, Nebraska, was beautiful, with small clapboard houses and old trees leaning over. Bob drove down Main Street twice, calling hello to everyone he saw, other guys his age in cars, mothers scurrying under the awnings. The rain spattered his outstretched arm but he didn't care. He was so glad to be back.

The sky was still divided when they got out of the car. They were waiting in sunlight where two roads met as the dark side of the world started sounding. Out of the darkness a van pulled up, painted blue and green with a yellow sun on its door, winking a lazy eye. As they slammed the door shut a tapping began on the roof, occasional clicks with no rhythm at first that soon became one dense roar. It was hailing in the middle of the summer.

India print bedspreads covered the windows and a poster of Grace Slick hid the driver. It was very dark. Beside them sitting on a crate was a girl with blond hair, smiling and offering them a cigarette. The van bounced up and down and the light from the match the girl held darted crazily in the darkness.

When it was over an enormous quiet rested. They emerged from the van blinking. It was not night at all. A pale light softened the grey road and unseen birds began rustling. They were just outside Columbus, five minutes from a city park that Ori had picked out in the map book.

It was civilised, a mowed green square with pruned trees. The board at its entrance said PARK CLOSED 10 P.M. to 8 A.M., and she was disappointed. Camping was acres of wild land and the scamper of animals, and a lake no one else had found. But the unfamiliar pull of the pack and her damp legs persuaded her.

Ori got water and unfolded the tent. A shapeless mass of orange plastic lay crumpled on the floor. He found the corners and the top seam and showed her how to stretch it out, edge by edge, staking the end loops to the ground, pulling out the flaps, making the sheets of plastic taut until they turned into a triangle with overhanging sides, neat and tight with a door to unzip and a screen window at the back.

When they crawled in they were sitting in an orange space, the first of the evening rain overhead, snug and warm and safe. They ate crackers with honey and dried fruit as the rain poured down. Outside the window the world grew darker, but the sky flamed yellow in the last flare of sun and they were full and hugging each other to the sound of the rain and the prospect of good sleep. So that was the end of the first day.

She woke in the morning to a green world and a sky green with leaves. Up before Ori, she wandered around between bushes and the backs of trees, listening to the dripping chirping world.

A truck driver in a wrinkled grey shirt took them to a café and two hippies with gold chains on their necks drove them to Kearney. A Lincoln Continental rode so smoothly that they both fell promptly asleep. There was a Florida vacuum cleaner saleswoman on her way to a convention and a girl named Jay Sue who drove too fast.

Then they were on a plain in Nebraska X'd by highways, a hot dry wind blowing back and forth without relief. It was the kind of noon when the right thing to do was to strip off their clothes and jump into water, but instead of a sea there were waves of tall grasses, brittle and yellowy in the crackling air. When she pressed her palms to her thighs, the heat of her burnt skin rose and her fingers left white ghost hands that welled red as she watched. No cars would stop and she wanted to leave, so they ran clumsily across the concrete, over yards of parking lot to a faded white building shaped like a chef's hat, a bulb planted preposterously in the middle of nowhere.

It was a freezing drive-in restaurant, and they sat in the booth with their packs crowding them, gulping iced tea made from a package and coconut cream pie. She phoned home collect from Miss Kol B'seder, everything's fine, in Hebrew. But the operator couldn't say it right and her parents were confused. They accepted the charges and she had to lie, the bus was leaving any minute, she told them, annoyed. She was sick of Nebraska.

A truck that was endless clambered over to the side of the road and the driver motioned them in. He wore a fresh white shirt and his dark eyes shone in his brown face. Jim lived in a tiny town in Colorado in a tiny house with two rooms. His wife and his son were waiting for him to come back after twenty-two days on the road. That was the usual length of a trip, he said. He showed them where truckers slept, the space between the seats and the van made of a mattress that you could order, queen, king or deluxe. More comfortable than a hotel, he told them, and she could believe it, she liked being so high, looking down on the world to the steady hum of the labouring wheels and the great mass of truck behind her.

Jim asked lots of questions about religion. He was once going to be a priest. He knew about Buddhism and the Sufis and Jews, he found Judaism quite interesting. His mother was a white witch in California, he said, and after that anything was easy. He invited them home to break bread with Maggie and Brian. They protested—what about the reunion?—but he insisted they would honour him by sharing his food. Then he would put them to sleep in the truck and when he left, at three in the morning, they'd be in the Rockies when they woke up. He wouldn't take no for an answer.

The town had a circle of houses and Jim's was the last. It was like a dollhouse, the furniture shrunk to fit, and Jim towered over his small pretty wife and the boy who clung to his leg, staring at them. They sat at the little green table and Maggie brought white bread still hot from the oven and clots of fresh butter and jam. She fried Jim some eggs and warmed up some milk and they all talked and laughed, except for Brian. Maggie was sorry and tried to console him, but he kept crying and running from the room.

They left for a walk, out past the houses along a back road that was quiet at the beginning of evening. Around them the open fields lay in the dusk, peaceful and empty after the working day. People were resting, and from far away the faint sound of dishes and TVs carried, barely heard. The air was cooling and smelled of unseen water somewhere nearby. As they turned slowly to go back, Brian came running up to them, his hair unruly, throwing from his small clenched hands hard-edged stones that pricked their bare arms and legs, not quite hurting. His face twisted in concentration, he aimed one after another until his hands lay empty against his stomach and he fled.

It was strange to settle herself in the truck knowing that when she got up it would be morning in a different place. At four-thirty there was a great lurch, and Jim touched her gently and asked if they wanted some breakfast. Ori was sitting up, rubbing his face with his hands.

In the restaurant Jim greeted the waitress by name and she teased him back. It was an all-night diner especially for truckers, though right now it was empty except for the three of them. The waitress gave them doughnuts and hot chocolate for free, and Jim drank three coffees to keep himself up.

When they stepped out, the sky, dark when they'd entered and sprinkled with stars, was a pale pink, flaming to rose where the clouds streaked across it. Everywhere she looked the horizon blazed, a circle of red that fired the dark earth and washed the pale sky with light that grew and faded in a false dawn. The cocoa had made her sluggish but now she was suddenly wide awake, as if whatever was bringing in day was bringing her life too. She turned round and round, dancing a prayer for the morning, light as a child as she jumped and spun to Jim's applause. Back in the truck she couldn't sleep, astonished by the beauty of the world at an unaccustomed time. She watched every change of light as Ori lay beside her, one arm flung over his face.

At seven o'clock they were sitting in a coffee shop eating toast and eggs. It was a glorious day in Loveland, Colorado, and she insisted they stop here because of the name. Breakfast in Loveland, the American dream. They were the only outsiders in the place, listening to the familiar exchanges of people coming in and out who'd known each other for years and eaten breakfast like this every morning, the sun brightening the room slowly, catching the metal edge of the counter, the glasses whose water drops were small suns themselves, momentarily blinding. It was time to go.

Rocky Mountain National Park had every kind of weather. Up through the gorge she saw layers of pine that peaked into clouds, while before her a lake, centuries old, was perfectly set in a shelf of the mountain to capture the blue of the sky. It was hot when they sat down to rest, and they stripped off their jeans and packed them away, climbing higher and higher until everything shifted, changing beneath them, the mountain stark and copper, the sky no longer a blue crown to the land but suddenly most of the world. It was white with snow that never melted, all year, and took people's lives in accidents that were not avoidable. Forty degrees and she was shivering, the cars speeding by, windows rolled up, reluctant to stop and confront the cold's omnipotence at the height of summer. No one would pick them up. Even with her sweater on she could not stop shaking. She saw two skeletal hands poking out of a mound of snow, found next spring, her flesh eaten away, the help that never came, no one would stop.

One half hour later a van full of hippies pulled up. It was almost full but they all squeezed together and welcomed the two of them, laughing. Colorado was a bad state for hitchhiking, that's why no one had picked them up, they said. It was illegal. The cops would throw you into jail and not let you out until someone else came in. There was nothing you could do about it. They had heard of one guy who sat behind bars for thirty days until the cops were in the mood to get rid of him. Walk backwards on the road if you want a ride, they said, driving past grazing fields patterned with sun, but never stick your thumb out. That's what they can get you for.

The van dropped them on a side road away from the main highway, where no one would notice they were camping before the season started. And stay away from rednecks, the hippies said. On the Fourth of July rednecks in Colorado went wild. Last year at the park a drunken towny stuck his shotgun out his car window and killed three people they knew because he didn't like their hair. Ori grimaced.

But where they were now felt very safe. There was one family trailer at the far end of the clearing and otherwise it was quiet. The family was barbecuing meat, and the smell drifting over reminded them of dinner and peacefulness. They could set up camp with nothing more to worry about. High above them on the side of the mountain was a spring, whose clear water was good for drinking. Ori climbed and she decided to follow him up the steep incline, her legs and arms contorted from having to place careful feet in small places, clinging to rocks with aching fingers. There was no choice. At the top she was breathless and triumphant.

The water was icy and she drank and drank, feeling the cold spread from her throat down her arms and legs, a map of coldness tracking her. The air was pure and thin, it made her head spin to look down at the forest, deepening green that swayed in the half light of dusk. Ori was slapping himself, the sharp claps returning in seconds, muted by leaves. Mosquitoes surrounded them in halos and they scrambled down to set up the tent and escape. They put on jeans, socks and shoes, and zipped up their hoods till they looked like spacemen, covering every open place except for a strip of their eyes. And still the mosquitoes hummed and circled, the air was dark with them. She sat on a stone bridge overhanging a creek to see the night come in the mountains, brushing her gloved hands continually over her face.

There were some things she just didn't know. She crawled into her sleeping bag in a T-shirt, as the manuals said, but nothing prepared her for what happens in mountains at nighttime. She woke in the early hours of morning, her body frozen, locked in coldness. She was whimpering. When Ori woke up he opened his sleeping bag and helped her get in. She was hoping they could warm each other, she'd read about it in accounts of plane crashes, but the reign of cold was impenetrable and she fell asleep shuddering against him.

The sun of the day was weak and inconstant. It wasn't yet over the mountains and the tent was soaking. She collected her things with knotted fingers and walked over to the family to ask for a ride. There was no room. Now they were stranded in the Rockies, jumping up and down just to keep moving, praying that someone would for some reason want to see this campsite at eight in the morning.

Three fishermen drinking beer came bouncing along in a truck, looking miraculous. They were off for a day with the boys and let down the back of the truck for them to get in with the gear. Along the dirt roads they twisted and sped, Ori and she perched on the floor among boxes of bait and reels. The wind that blew in was a warm wind, they had a long ride, the fields were green in a turquoise sky as the road grew behind them and the sun grew strong overhead. She took out oranges and chocolate for breakfast and everything tasted so good. It was a wonderful day.

In Wyoming huge ranches ran without fences for miles and miles. They passed no one, no cars, no dogs, nothing. A VW from Texas drove them to Laramie, with warnings about snakes and cowboys. Laramie was a cowboy town. Everything was closed except for one dirty café. The bars looked mean and the women looked cheap. People scowled as they passed, the sun was hostile, and the dust covered their skin in a thin choking layer.

For no reason a white car began backing up from far away on the ramp of the highway, backwards on a one-way street until it screeched to a halt right in front of them. Hey missus, a man called out, where ya headed? He insisted she sit beside him and her husband could stay in the back. When she climbed in, the floor was so full of beer bottles there was no room for her pack. Popeye was headed for Salt Lake City, exactly where they wanted to go if they'd live to see it. He had blue eyes that were faded to white and rotten teeth, and he had to make frequent stops to go to the rest room, he called it, moving a little ways from the car and turning his back. Popeye meant well but he had trouble staying on the right side of the line. The sky was full of colours that preluded night, yellow, navy and red, and it was getting harder to see the road. Popeye had driven four hundred miles, pausing only to pick up some six-packs, and he didn't know if he'd make the next hundred, he was so tired.

She was terrified. She wouldn't admit it, they needed the ride, why was it the crazies always turned up when they were too desperate to say no? The bands of colour withdrew and a soft grey evening settled on the mountains. They couldn't camp here in the wilderness and the snakes, so they kept Popeye talking, she first, then Ori, asking about his kids, his age, his house, his habits. Salt Lake City beckoned like paradise across the expanse of darkness. They would splurge on a motel.

The AAA strip had no vacancies and sent them to Ruth's. Popeye assured them it was no trouble and took them over himself. But Ruth's was full too and then Popeye drew himself up, motioned them in, and drove them royally to Bob's Welkum Inn, halfway across the city. It was his pleasure, he thanked them with dignity, to help out some fellow travellers.

A shower, clean sheets, soft pillows, a door, she luxuriated in all of it while Ori checked in. There was even a television with the same old programs. For the first ten minutes she could only stare at it blankly, so bone-tired that undoing her shirt seemed too much work. She forced herself into the shower and by the time she got out, scrubbed over and over, Ori was almost asleep. A pile of clothes was waiting to be washed but she'd never manage it. Ori reached out to kiss her by instinct and she sank into his arms.

Babies were squalling and Ori was watching cartoons when she woke, slow as molasses. She couldn't get up. On the street people were friendly, smiling and stopping to say good morning. They ate apples and headed for the centre, the sweet feeling of the shower soon gone in the still, sticky air. But she walked along easily in the heat, sipping orange juice from a can, the pack that had burdened her at the start now part of her body. They were going to check out the Mormons, beginning with a view of the temple.

A temple in the middle of America. It was raised on a man-made hill and looked quite lovely in the sun, but towering over it, leaning into the sky, were neon billboards and a huge apartment building piled in ramshackle blocks until it ran out of room. No outsiders were allowed in the temple, a young man out of the fifties told them kindly, but they were welcome in the visitors' lounge where all questions would be answered and they could see a movie.

God is flesh and blood, the tour said, and eternal life is just as we are now. There were murals of scenes depicting our sins, and the movie showed what heaven was like. The Mormon Tabernacle Choir lived there, singing gloriously on clouds of dry ice. It was a very literal religion, and she didn't know what they did about divorces. What if you were married twice, which husband would you be with in eternal life? And would you be the age you were when you died or could you choose? The Mormons kept track. Under the earth in caverns miles long they stored genealogical information on everyone they could. It was useful in case of nuclear war but its real importance was to preserve the purity of the line. In an instant, thanks to computers, they could know if you'd been properly baptised or if your great-grandfather had been.

All the Mormons were nice. They were eager to explain their church and she was ashamed of her unease. But it was too much, the earnest young men, the single way, and when a car blasting the Stones stopped at the outskirts of the city she was relieved to be going.

Ori was so excited to hear music that he sang the rest of the songs he knew after the tape was over, beating out the rhythm on the back of the seat as the guys in the front improvised guitar in falsetto. She sang along feeling stupid, zipping through Utah on rock music, passing as a hippie girl. Mike and Dave didn't know, though, and treated her with the offhand chivalry that hip men have for a girl who is one of the gang.

The desert was going by, naked and brown with splotches of cactus and dwarf trees. Her eyes were gritty with the sand that flew in and she closed them for a few minutes, she told Ori, just to rest. It was one o'clock in the morning when she woke up. Far away where the land met the sky a couple of enormous stars were stuck in the dark. They started to grow, to split and expand, and soon a swimming sea of lights, closer and closer, was banishing the darkness. She thought it was a natural wonder, southern lights, once a year at midsummer, perhaps, after midnight.

It was Las Vegas. Broad daylight with thousands of people milling about. There were twenty-four-hour weddings and funerals to order. In neon letters that poked into the sky Johnny Carson, Trini Lopez, and Carroll O'Connor were flashing hot pink, red and gold. STARDUST, CIRCUS, INTERNATIONAL, meet the stars, the signs said. We need a motel with a pool, Dave said, nothing else will do. They cruised up to the Capri and Mike took a double. Split four ways, sixteen dollars was a bargain. They celebrated Dave's birthday coming up in November and Ori's future adventures. They went out to breakfast on coupons. Free eggs, one restaurant offered, free coffee, free toast. They table-hopped. She borrowed Mike's Day-Glo shirt and they slipped into a casino to play the slots, standing beside old ladies with blue hair and toreador pants who were poised before the whirling machines, watching the silver pour into their styrofoam cups. A man took her picture in front of a million dollars. The colour TV had movies till dawn and they all fell asleep in the two double beds to the radio, TV and the lights.

She was sleeping beside two strangers and it was so hot. Morning in Las Vegas was quite a different story. There wasn't a soul on the street except for a couple of housewives, who actually lived here, on their way to the supermarket in kerchiefs and dark glasses. Wedged between the aisles of food were slot machines. She bent over the frozen foods with Ori until they were numb, said goodbye to the boys and caught a ride with a fat black sergeant to Lake Mead.

Oleander trees, pink, white and red, were clustered in front of a lake. But what should have been grass was concrete, and the trees sprung from clay pots, set at symmetrical intervals in the parking lot. Tiny patches of lawn were crammed with tents, and Ori squeezed theirs onto a spot near an artificial creek. Lake Mead, it turned out, was an artificial lake, with a little sand shipped in to make it look like a beach. All the girls were mahogany-coloured in bikinis that looked glued on. She felt fat. The air was so still and the sun unrelenting. After an hour her bathing suit was outlines on her skin. It could only get worse but there was no shelter. She bought lotion from a man under an umbrella and smeared it all over, guzzling orange juice from

Ori's canteen, trudging from the hot sticky tent to the water, waiting for the day to be over. Evening was such a relief. The sun plunged and a steady wind came in from the mountains. The day people left and the campers sat around with guitars, singing folk songs in the dark.

Her legs were moving or something was moving on them, tiny fingers tickling her, she turned over. Behind her knees were little shivers. She looked down and yelled. The floor was swimming with ants. Ori, Ori, they were everywhere, all over the food and inside her clothes, ants assembling and dissolving in formation. Ori turned the tent inside out and myriads fell, she and Ori shook out what could be shaken and still the black dots clung to everything. Against her will a massacre was called for, and she refused to let Ori be the sole murderer. She crushed and stomped at any speck, the sand and the ants indistinguishable in her frenzy. Finally the surfaces were still, the invasion was halted. As they were folding up the tent Dave sauntered over. He'd been driving around after Las Vegas and here he was. They all grinned at each other and Dave said, you must see the Grand Canyon.

The trucker who drove them there stopped for lunch and invited them in. He ordered a plate piled high with biscuits and soaked them with butter that melted in yellow streams over brown-toasted backs to pool on the plate. He split one in half and dabbed the soft ends into sugar. That's how you do it, he said, help yourselves. The trucker wouldn't let them pay. All over the country were people like him, it amazed her, the bountiful kindness.

The postcards were frauds. Only eyes, only a person standing at the lip in late afternoon, outlined in sun, could record it. It was a wedding. The Grand Canyon shifted and collided beneath its rock skin, through which blends of gold, of violet, came forth to turn into air and return. Where rock became air it was impossible to tell. Veils of rock and beneath them veils, a weight distilled into the great chasm of air that hung inverted in the canyon to be absorbed again. The earth was a mouth of praise. Its offerings were the colours of heaven, seen only here, one time, on this day.

It wasn't fair, she was crying. To be able to stay for an hour in a place that demanded many days to see every change of colour and light, to engrave each one, to carry it away bound to the heart. You'll be back, Ori said, trying to comfort. He would be back, certainly, he was free in his life to promise himself what he chose. But she despaired, because she did not know what portions life would allow her and whether returning to loved places was one of them.

They would not sleep until California. Outside a city somewhere in Nevada the moon was a full pregnant orange, bulging low over mountains in a purple night sky, a great and perfect circle whose weight was too much for itself to bear, while the opposite sky was clearing for morning, luminous blue whitening by degree, the light before dawn that signified sun. It was the evening and morning of the same day.

Elizabeth Taylor weighing two hundred pounds in stretch pants seemed to be the next driver. Hop in, she said, and when they did there was a plastic leg lying on the back seat. My husband lost his in the war, she told them. His birthday was last week and I made him a pink and blue cake with rifles on it. Don't get me wrong, she said, he's no dainty but he did like that cake.

San Francisco was pink and blue, houses the colour of seashells, delicate, that rose from bridges suspended in the sky. A creation inclined to water, and at last on the far side from a high place she faced the Pacific. Behind her the city was dissolving in mist and the ocean was unformed. A spirit of wind hovered over the water. Soon Ori would be here but not quite yet, as she stood at the edge looking at the new world.

FIVE

"Girls, after supper your father wants to have a talk with you."

"I'm going out after supper, Mom," Riva said. "Tell him to tell us now."

"I have a ton of homework, I can't," Naomi said.

"Tell him not to be a baby," said Judith. "I hate this big buildup. What is it, a hair dryer?" That was the reason they'd been assembled the last time.

"It's more important than a hair dryer," her mother said. "You know your father. This is how he wants to do it."

"At least tell us if it's good or bad," Judith said.

"Good," said her mother.

After supper the three of them sat on the couch waiting for their father to come out of the den.

"All right." He smiled, looking at them. "I guess you're wondering why I called you here today."

"Daddy!" they said.

He looked at their mother. "I suppose there's no use keeping you in suspense. How would you like to spend a year in England?"

"No," Riva said. "I wouldn't."

"Starting when?" Naomi said. "Next year or just some time in the future?"

"Judith?" her father said.

"I'd love it." She would. It would solve a lot of problems. Get her out of Toronto, get her away from not being with Ori but not being able to be with anyone else. Maybe she'd fall in love.

"I'm glad that at least one of you has something positive to say. Because—and this isn't official yet so I don't want you to tell anyone—if everything is cleared I will be starting my sabbatical in October and we'll be on our way to London."

"This October, I won't. I can't go, Daddy, what about my friends, what about my life? What about school?" Riva added hopefully. Judith and Naomi looked at each other. They knew that Riva was madly in love but there was no point even bringing it up as a reason.

"Your mother has been writing a lot of letters and we think we've solved the problem of school for all of you. Naomi and Riva can go to what we hear is an excellent school for girls in the neighbourhood we want to live in. Judith's situation is a little more difficult, but I think an arrangement will be possible at the University of London, where I'll be a visiting professor."

"School for girls," Riva said. "Does that mean no boys? I'll kill myself."

"Riva, for heaven's sake," her mother said.

"Naomi, how can we go to a school with only girls?"

Naomi didn't know. "When are we allowed to tell people?" She was trying to figure out a way to tell her boyfriend.

"In three weeks I'll be sure," her father said. "But until then I want your word."

As soon as it was over Riva and Naomi phoned their boyfriends. Judith knew because she saw them conferring beforehand. It felt funny talking to Ori knowing she'd be going away. A year in England would certainly help get rid of the five years they figured they needed until they were ready to be together for good. A whole year in which she wouldn't have to talk to Ori and wonder about his love life or figure out how she'd visit Jessie and deal with him.

They packed the whole house, dismantling their lives into boxes they stored one on top of the other in closets in the basement. They said goodbye to Bobba and Uncle Joel and the cousins. "I'd love to stay," Judith told them, "but I'm afraid I'm off to London tonight." Her mother and father were already there, finding a house and setting things up.

At the airport they stood in a sea of suitcases with people around staring at them.

"They probably think we're spoiled rich kids off on vacation in the middle of the school year," Naomi explained.

Riva looked down at the luggage and said in a very loud voice, "Do you think this is enough for two weeks?" and they all got the giggles.

I'm going to live in a new place, Judith was thinking, I'm starting everything over again and this time I'll do it right. No more wasting time, she was determined. She'd make each day an adventure, get to know every nook and cranny of London, have English friends and enjoy every minute. And forget Ori, put him in suspended animation for a year. Maybe this is the last thought I'll ever have about him, she said to herself, watching the clouds slowly lighten as they flew into morning.

England was much smaller than Canada. The houses looked like toys and there was so much more sky than she was used to. Their house was very light, with a loft that looked out over Hampstead Heath and piles of English clouds. Against her sisters' protests Judith claimed it for her own, using her different schedule and anything else she could think of to be able to live in this great white space.

Everywhere there were gardens, tiny plots of roses that bloomed now in October and for most of the year, they were told. Neighbours on both sides brought cakes and blankets and whatever they needed until the rest of their stuff arrived. In her whole life in Toronto Judith had said not much more than hello to the people on their street, and here were kisses and invitations, who said the English were cold? She was bursting with new things to tell but there was no one to call. The telephone stayed quiet day after day in a house with all the girls home. It was unnatural, their parents teased. And although the post, as they called the mail here, came twice every morning, it was too early still to expect anything. After a week Judith felt it had been a life.

Riva and Naomi started school but Judith had time. She took the train into town every day and wandered around. She went to museums and galleries, churches and bookstores and matinees. She looked at the girls in their dolly makeup and platform shoes and listened to accents she could hardly understand. Apron meant pinafore and pinafore meant jumper and jumper meant sweater, it was confusing. What she loved were the parks, Regent's and St. James's with their ponds and fountains, rolling for miles, safe, free to walk in, dotted only by birds and old ladies with baby carriages.

But her greatest discovery was the Heath. In the mornings she'd take a Victorian novel and walk down Bishops Avenue past mansions bigger than any she'd seen, until she reached the great gates. Along paths of moss and leaves, she ambled down through the tended wild that slowly gave way to gardens, brilliant flowers sheltered by greens from which rose Ken Wood House. She walked from the woods into rooms that were ordered in mellow age. The glass shone, the wood shone, the paintings on the walls, Gainsborough, Reynolds, showed the men and women who'd sat and supped and made love in rooms like these. Someone who loved light had given the back wall to windows. Along the length of the house they ran, with doors opening onto a lawn that began at her feet to slope gently down at just the right pitch to a lake. The lake had ducks and lilies and a bridge that became an illusion only when you knew where to look. On the lawns of Hampstead Heath she read for hours, the sky, the pouring light and the sounds of the birds her only company. Sometimes she ate lunch in the tea garden, watercress sandwiches and cups of cream tea, sitting with her book and brimming with the beauty of the autumn day. If only she had someone to share it with.

There were no men. Young English Jews were most peculiar. During the High Holidays the Rafael sisters met many at meals and teas to which they were invited. They all seemed to be twenty-two-year-old tycoons who made their money selling Rolls-Royces in places like New Zealand and Peru. They travelled a lot. They gave out their cards. They wore dark formal suits to shul and were Orthodox, but in their bachelor pads in the city they led a wild life. They talked only about sports and business. Judith had nothing to say to them whatsoever. It seemed that in England there were no Jews in the middle, nothing between Orthodox and Liberal, no one like them.

On the second day of university Judith got the flu from walking in the rain without a coat. While her father went to work and her sisters were at school she lay in bed with a fever that wouldn't go down. Too weak to do anything, she watched English television wrapped in blankets or sat up for half an hour at a time to write letters to her friends. Finally letters started to come to her, and so it began, the process she knew, figuring out how long each one took and how long the reply, writing eager questions to her friends, whose answers would be out of date when she got them.

Jessie wrote faithfully, almost every day. Judith missed her so much sometimes she couldn't stand it. It was unbearable not to just pick up the phone and call. Her longing was so acute that she waited for the knock on the door, not believing that such intensity of feeling would not take material form, would not convert into some magic transport bringing Jessie in from New York.

Sharon wrote from Israel, where she was studying at Hebrew University. Why not come to Israel for Passover, Sharon said. Judith started to work on it while she was home anyway. It was never too early for a plan, and she reminded her mother that they had no Pesach dishes in England and no family to invite and think how lonely it would be while Great-aunt Chenya was waiting for them in Israel, and it was so much closer from London than from Toronto. We should all be in Jerusalem for Pesach, Judith said, and her mother talked it over with her father.

Anna was going to teachers' college, the only school her parents would agree to, but her real plan was art school at night, where finally she'd get some training. She hoped to take painting and sculpture and design and see as much art as she could. Being an Orthodox artist was not easy. People thought her work was a hobby and that once she was married it would pass. You're lucky to be away, Anna wrote, Toronto is worse than ever.

Rachel was in love, she thought, with an Indian man. He was a Parsee, a sect a lot like the Jews, Rachel said, and she was learning Gujarati and Indian music and thought that this might be it. When he finished his training he was going back to India and she was moving with him. She didn't know what would happen but it would be years, at least, before she returned, and she was shipping her books and her clothes. She had tried and tried to get a flight through London but they couldn't arrange it, so she was leaving in a couple of weeks and here was her address, care of his parents. Judith was not surprised. Rachel was always drawn to the most exotic, the circumstances least like her own. She thought other was better and would cross the world to find it. I don't think it's an accident, Judith wrote, that you and I are happier in foreign places.

Judith was not happier, actually. It just took longer for her same old self to reappear. When she got out of bed from the flu the feeling of belonging in London was gone. At the university everyone hurried from class to class in the cold stone rooms, walking with friends they knew from private school, talking in a slang Judith didn't understand. The University of London, she was sorry to realise, was the same as the University of Toronto. In fact, Toronto was modelled on London, and the college she'd gone to there was built from the same set of plans. Old grey halls and cavernous basements, classrooms whose heaters sputtered and steamed, never warm enough, and big lecture rooms where famous professors talked urbanely about books they'd written, which were all missing from the library. A grand old poet was boring. The tutors were pedants. No one illuminated the Victorian novels she read on the train, in the streets, trying to catch up.

Once school had begun, the days of exploring London were over. Trudging from the train to the university and back, she found it hard to remember that she was in one of the great cities of Europe and that she should take advantage of it. The British Museum was around the corner and the National Gallery a walk away, but the day ended at four o'clock and all she wanted to do was be home in her loft and warm. It took a long time to make friends, and when the term was over she realised that the only people whose rooms she'd been to were Americans.

At Christmas vacation Judith took stock. School was not terrible but it wasn't good enough to devote herself to. She would have to find something else or the year would end, and she would have to meet real English people or the true London would not reveal itself. She'd been to the galleries and museums, she'd tried on clothes at Harrod's and Liberty's, and she'd seen most of the good plays, but she still had the feeling that the essence of England was somewhere else. It was what she loved in the long English novels, that feeling she'd had in the early fall days, but the students she'd met weren't it and the Jews she'd met certainly weren't. If she were going to fall in love it wouldn't be with one of them.

Naomi had been seeing someone for months, one of the really rich ones who kept buying her tickets for concerts and taking her to great restaurants. Judith thought he was awful and didn't know how Naomi put up with him, but she knew she was jealous too, not of him but of the situation, as the car pulled up and Naomi was taken to this place and that without any arranging.

"He's very nice," Naomi said as she got ready to go after supper.

"But you don't care about him at all," Judith told her. "You're using him for his car and his money."

"I am not. I'm not in love with him but why should I be? We have a good time, he's not complaining. He's not pushing me to decide anything, so as long as he asks me I'll go. And don't act so high and mighty, it's a lot better than nothing."

Judith knew that Naomi felt guilty because she was going out and Judith wasn't. It was Riva that Judith took as her date, when she could get her to go. Riva was miserable. She hated school from the first day and would skip as often as she could to see plays, but otherwise she would do nothing. She refused to go on any family outings, she stopped seeing the neighbours for tea. All she did was sit in the kitchen and eat. Riva got fat, and the fatter she got the more upset her parents were. There was a lot of yelling in the house and most of it was about Riva.

"I was having a great time in Toronto," Riva said. "I was happy. I had my boyfriend, I had my friends, things were finally getting really good. I told them I'd hate it here, I knew it would ruin my life. I should have refused to go."

"But what would you have done?"

"I'd have stayed there without them, with Bobba, she would have had me."

"It seems crazy," Judith said. "I know you didn't have much say in the matter but now that you're here you may as well try to like it."

"I can't like it. I'm stuck in a school with English girls, how could I like it? All my friends at home are boys. I'm so lonely." Riva started to cry. "Name me one good thing about my situation, I dare you."

Judith couldn't think of any from Riva's point of view. Riva didn't want to be a martyr, she didn't see loneliness as a challenge. "The only comfort I can offer," Judith said, "is that you're taking the heat off me. For the first time I'm not the one getting yelled at. It's certainly a novelty."

That got Riva smiling. "You know I'd do anything for you," she said and pointed to her stomach.

Riva wore the same skirt every day, a long blue, green and white plaid one that was fading from being washed so much. Her parents begged her to go out and get some clothes but Riva had standards.

"I'm not spending money on this body," she said, "you'll have to take me as I am."

Judith was worried about her. For the first time her powers of persuasion weren't working. She couldn't talk Riva into anything, although her parents kept asking her to try. Riva wouldn't go out until she was thin and she wouldn't be on a diet because she never left the house anyway.

"Let me see, what shall I wear today?" Riva would say with a flourish. "Of course if it's dinner I shall wear my blue skirt, but for the theatre only my green will do. I'd love to appear in the white, you know, but I'm saving it for Shabbes."

They were all the same skirt. To show her respect for it, Riva stored it over the window.

"Skirt by day, curtain by night, one size fits all, that's people and windows," Riva proclaimed. "Think how much money you can save."

An American girl in Judith's class had a New Year's party for expatriates, and Judith was invited with her sisters. Naomi was going out, of course, and Riva backed off at the last minute. It began late and Judith was later because she didn't want to go alone and she couldn't decide what to wear. The Beach Boys were blasting from the window in the residence hall and she recognised a couple of faces on her way up the stairs. There were actually people to talk to, she must have met more than she'd realised in the term, and when midnight came and the kisses began and Happy New Year was shouted and whispered, Judith thought that maybe the year would bring good things, it was possible. She danced with people she didn't know, giving in to the music and the beer and the hour, and when she got home she went straight to bed and slept for the longest time she could remember.

Winter in London was not like Canada at all. There were roses up till December and back again in a month. The year did not die in the same way, it simply rested a little. Judith went to Kew Gardens on a January day and looked at the bare trees in the fog, lovely in their austerity. At home there was a message from the girl whose party she'd been to. Come to dinner, it said, a last fling before second term.

Across the table was someone from New Year's Eve, someone who was looking at her quite intently.

"He asked me to ask you," the American girl whispered. Judith was amazed. Here was a man she hadn't even noticed, she who was always looking, and he had noticed her enough to want to meet her.

James was English, that was the first surprise. He spoke beautifully, in a low measured voice that had hundreds of traditional years behind it. He was long and thin with black hair and white skin and a full pouting mouth. James wore a wine-coloured cape whose velvet ties his pale hands played with as he talked of poetry. He was getting his doctorate in English at Oxford and he was one of those people who clearly knew everything and didn't realise that not everyone else had assimilated the learning he took for granted. Judith looked at the Americans in her class and saw that for them too it was the colonies in the shadow of the Empire. James didn't speak often, which was just as well. His accent made her weak.

She knew he wasn't Jewish, she suspected he would call and wondered what she'd do about it. In the short time over dinner she had more to say to him than in months of toying with the tycoons. It was unnerving. She didn't want the evening to end, and when he asked her rather gravely if she cared to walk for a bit she was happy, consequences be damned.

They talked for hours and hours, slowly walking through the park, then sitting near water until even his cape around her could not keep her warm. The woman he had loved for years was now with a friend of his, and the pain in his voice woke her own pain. Under the hardness she tried to cultivate was a great unhealing, and she instinctively reached out to him. His hand met her hand between them.

Three days later a card came in the mail. On the cover was a young man in a plumed hat and a girl with fair hair waving on her shoulders. "We were the last romantics," was written beneath. Judith had that feeling she thought she'd forgotten, as if she were turning around and around. It was happening. How it would be arranged, what she'd say to her parents, why she was unable not to do it, she didn't know.

James came to London and she took the afternoon off. They went to Westminster Abbey and sat in a back pew talking about God. James was not a practising Christian but he was a believer.

"What do you mean, a believer?" She didn't understand him.

James said, "I believe that there's an order in the universe, and that it began out of nothing and is still chaos but contains in the dung heap possibilities of wonder."

"Possibilities?"

"Sometimes they manifest themselves," he said.

"Where?"

"In the flesh"—he smiled—"for one. Where do they for you?"

"In the spirit, of course. I think we've changed sides."

"It's not a war."

"No, but it has been," Judith said.

"I know it has been." He was impatient. "I read history too. In fact, I know rather a lot about Judaism, my last girlfriend was half Jewish."

"Was she observant?"

"You mean was she kosher? No, she wasn't. I don't think she did much of that."

"You probably don't know very much, then. You can't."

"I have a feeling I'll learn quite a lot."

She shook her head. "It's a different country. The most you can do is get to know the difference."

"Perhaps it will augment both our visions," James said.

He was optimistic. He had none of the terror bred into her, of crossing forbidden boundaries with no turning back. He had no secrets and her life was about to become rich with secrets.

According to her parents James was her friend. His strange

looks and his antique clothes helped. They couldn't imagine that someone of such outlandish appearance could be taken seriously. Judith didn't yet feel deceitful, the present was pretty much what it appeared to be, it was what could become of it that filled her head with dreaming and made her wander around the house, jumping when the phone rang.

Waiting for someone was another kind of time. What once seemed endless—train rides to school, long lectures—now passed in a minute as she went over their conversations in her mind or walked through the night in the park, the day in London, again and again savouring that glance, that touch on her arm, the way his hands moved over his cigarettes that made smoking graceful. But the hours between dinner and midnight were days, the clock in her head slowed to make minutes of seconds until he called. When he did, it was terrible to feel the erosion from the first tremulous hello when the whole call lay before her to the good-bye that meant waiting another day. And when he couldn't, she went to bed with such loss and emptiness she didn't sleep. It was only a phone call, and not having it one day made the next day more certainly good, but it wasn't enough. The addiction was frightening. When she got the card she wanted to see him and when she saw him she wanted to see him more. She felt drugged. Surely if she were strong she could give it up, only a week had passed, almost nothing. It was bound to be painful, it had to end, she had no right to start it, knowing the futility. Just after she spoke to him, content, it was easy to renounce. What was it but loneliness? If anyone had called and wanted to see her and looked at her in that way she'd have weakened. But the next day at school or on the way home his face was before her, no one else was like him and no one else would do.

James invited her to Oxford for a day and she decided to go. He told her exactly how to get there and waited for her at the station so that when she got off the platform his tall lean frame was so familiar and good she felt nothing could possibly be wrong. James was kind. When he moved down the footpaths through narrow archways he placed her before him and showed her where to walk.

Oxford was masses of stone, ancient colleges that closed about them or became quadrangles of lawn and winter trees until the next solidity. But over their heads the towers and spires delicately traced the sky, so lightly they seemed independent of the squat colleges that carried them. They walked for a long time, around the buildings, then through open fields to the river, where to Judith's delight young men were rowing their girlfriends through the dark water.

Over tea James told her about his friends. He had many, all entangled with each other like a Shakespearean comedy.

"But without the happy ending," James said. "Tyler's in love with Rosemary, and she loves Desmond. Desmond doesn't love her, though, he loves Laura, who's been pining for years over Willy. Willy's sweet on both Laura and Megan and can't make up his mind."

"Why not choose Megan and give Laura to Desmond?"

"It's just as well Willy hangs on to both. Megan isn't sure she loves him, since she's intermittently engaged to Pat."

"Intermittently?"

"Pat loves Megan quite a bit. But he's alcoholic and needs frequent drying out."

James knew lots of people who were drinking themselves to death. "When Pat is sober he loves Megan dearly, but when he's drunk he is mad for Tyler, which brings it full circle, do you see?"

Both of them were laughing, James ruefully. "And now that you're briefed you can meet the characters of the drama," he said. "I think there's enough time before your train to show you the house."

On the outskirts of the city was a rambling house encrusted with dormers and bays like a sea creature, and in it lived James with six of his friends as well as his once girlfriend with her new love, one floor above him, just over his head.

"And I thought my life was complicated," Judith said.

"All my friends are unhappy," said James, "but I suppose I am too." He was calm. "Everyone I know is embroiled somehow."

James's room overlooked the garden. "Exotically neglected," he called it. "None of us has a green thumb except Kitty"—that was the girlfriend—"and she's too busy these days."

The shadows were already mounting the walls. "No wonder

you're all melancholy," she said. "The light is gone by the time you get up."

"One never rises early at Oxford," James said. "Only the cats are up before noon. We stay awake until dawn poring over books to avoid completing our papers."

The books began on the floor, a double row at the base of each wall with more piled on top until they were waist-high. "It's scholarly wainscotting," James said. His bed was covered in a royal blue quilt with engravings on cream-coloured paper, unframed, hung above it. She couldn't make out what they were. The only other furniture was a stereo, and when James pressed the button the sweet voice of a woman came on low, sung to flute. It was Old English music. It was perfect.

The room was darker. They sat in silence. In the light that was left James's face moved towards hers, a ghost face, and she turned her back to the light as he kissed her.

"Before you go," he said, "come meet the others."

In the kitchen people were drinking wine, some chopping mushrooms, some breaking eggs, one girl with hair swinging down to her waist was fussing over the stove.

"Everyone, meet Judith." The faces turned.

"I wouldn't bother with the names, old boy, it simply isn't important. Let her pick them up as she goes along."

"Nonsense," James said. "Around the table, that's Tyler and Desmond and Laura and Pat. And that's Kitty at the stove."

Kitty turned around. She was wearing a satin blouse with a lace skirt and her face was vivacious and shining. Her voice was melodious when she said, "How nice to meet you," smiling.

"I can see why you loved her," Judith said as they walked to the train.

"Kitty's quite an unusual person," he said.

"Why didn't it work?"

"It worked for a time and then she fell in love with someone else. It happens."

"Not if you're really in love."

"What strange notions of love you have. Can't you imagine loving two people at once?"

Judith had to admit she could.

"She loved me first and well, then she loved me and Michael—

you didn't meet him, I'm glad to say, he's away for a time—and then she loved Michael and he wanted her without me. We still see a lot of each other. It's hard to avoid."

"Isn't Michael afraid you'll get back together while he's gone?"

"It wouldn't matter to him if he has her when he's back. But it's no longer a live issue." James reached for her hand.

"Does Kitty know who I am?"

"Of course."

So he too didn't think it was only a week and reversible. He hugged her goodbye and she felt his hands all the way home.

Then it was James's turn. He came in to London on a dismal winter Sunday. They went to the Tate Gallery far away on the embankment of the Thames for James to show her the pre-Raphaelite paintings, and she froze walking the short blocks from the train.

"This is awful," she cried. "It's so cold. How can a country be so cold?"

James was walking with an open coat. "This isn't bad at all. What happened to the hardy Canadian who suffers snow all winter? England is temperate in comparison."

"I hate Canada for its winters," Judith said. "Besides, in Canada when you go into a house it's warm. English people don't know how to live. They still think there's a war going on."

"Shall we get a cup of tea for you now? Would that help? I'm sure the gallery has a shop."

"No, no, it's all right. Once we're inside and walking around I'll feel better."

"You know, we English are trained not to think about our bodies. You should have seen the school I went to as a child. You've heard of our public schools?"

"They're infamous."

"Yes." James smiled. "You've probably read too much Dickens. I went from the age of seven and they're not bad, just rigorous. Cold showers at ungodly hours and no flinching."

"Did you go to Eton or Harrow? I'd be so impressed."

"I'll have to impress you some other way, though I did go to the next one under them. At any rate, it was quite an interesting training, perhaps not much of an education in wisdom but certainly a good preparation in how to be an English gentleman."

"Is that what your parents wanted you to be?"

"Among other things. Of course, they wanted me to learn history and languages, but they also wanted me to be able to conduct myself in a decent and befitting manner. Don't everyone's parents? You went to a private school, as you call it. What did your parents want you to be?"

"A good Jew." She thought of the anarchy in her day school where the kids did whatever they wanted when they weren't in class and sometimes when they were. "Manners weren't our strong point."

"I'm sure I'd find it refreshing."

"You'd probably find it disgusting. It wasn't very civilised."

"God, was ours civilised. We had uniforms for lessons and uniforms for games, which were more important than lessons. When we went into town we had to behave in a way to credit the school. There were always people watching."

"Weren't you lonely? You haven't really lived at home since you were a child. It must make your relationship with your parents a little strange."

"I suppose I was lonely at the start, I can hardly remember now. But one makes very good friends in that situation, many more than I'd ever have met where I come from. My parents' house is quite isolated, outside a village in the middle of the country. It was fun for me to have so many playmates. Some of them are my friends still."

"I forgot, you were only with boys. It's not just your parents then, you must think girls are strange too."

"I'm trying to make up for it by getting to know some now," James said.

"No, really, how were you for your first love?"

"My first girlfriend was at Oxford. That is a little delayed, though other boys managed."

"It must have been very intense to make up for lost time."

James laughed. "But that wasn't my first love."

It didn't take her long. "That's terrible. How can your parents put you in a situation where they know that when you're eleven you'll fall in love with another boy?"

"Believe it or not, that wasn't their primary consideration. Besides, they went through it too and they're happily married. They might even think it's safer."

Judith thought it was sick.

James looked amused. "Now that you've analysed my parents' failure to prepare me for love, would you like to see how other people looked at the subject?"

The paintings James loved were full of pale women with flowing hair and sombre eyes and young men in velvet cloaks looking wicked. They lived in dim murky light, encroached by leaves or water lilies, and their trailing clothes circled their limbs like vines. It was always autumn in those paintings. They were of broken engagements and broken hearts, of lovers who would meet only in death. It thrilled her to think of his loving them, his casting her as one of those beautiful sad women. They were so white, so pure, and the men desired them in awful despair. Doomed love. She took his arm. Beginnings were so wonderful, she'd forgotten the way she held her breath, desperately impatient and at the same time hoping it would all stand still, trying to savour every moment because, no matter what became of it, good or bad, it would never be as acutely felt as this.

At the end of February she would have three days off. She couldn't decide if she should tell him, because she still didn't know what she wanted to happen. If she stayed in London he'd never know that she could have been with him, but at the thought of escaping whatever it would mean to go to him she felt a terrible loss. It was her one chance to see him for more than a day, and afterwards she'd anguish when she wanted to be with him and couldn't be. How many times could they wander around London freezing in the winter? And how often could she skip school to take the train to Oxford? Judith stayed up late at night waiting for a sign.

The next morning, far too early, Naomi burst into her room. "Judith, Judith, wake up, you have a letter."

"You woke me up for the mail?" Judith spoke into her pillow, too tired to turn over. "I can't believe you did that. Do you know what time I got to bed?" It must have been six. She had seen dawn. "I feel awful."

"You won't when you see who it's from."

"Just tell me," Judith said. "And then get the hell out of here."

"Judith, why do you have to be such a bitch? Your letter's from goddamn Ori and I only brought it all the way up here because I was so excited for you. That's the last time I'll ever do something nice, I can tell you."

Judith sat up slowly. Her sister was crying.

"Naomi, I'm sorry. I really am. I just feel terrible."

"Well, don't take it out on me." And Naomi left.

Judith sighed. If only she could have woken up to it on her own time. It would have been so great to come downstairs at around twelve and find a letter, her only letter from Ori all year, waiting for her. She wished she could go back to sleep and try again but now she wouldn't be able to.

Ori's letter did not sound like him. He was unhappy, that was the first surprise. He was fighting with his parents about yoga and Judaism, struggling to reconcile two worlds. And for the first time in his life a girl he cared about had turned him down. He talked for pages about how he felt. I want you not to worry or regret anything, he said. I see that pain can be important.

She was full of feeling for him, glad that he was suffering, mad at the girl who turned him down, how could she? She missed the old Ori who always bounced back and never let anything bother him, even while she was so relieved that he finally seemed to be letting life touch him. Maybe he could grow up. Maybe it would all work out.

Judith took the letter to school, touched it in her pocket all day. She hoped that he really was changing, that when she got back she'd notice the difference, if they ever met again, that he wasn't just talking. Surely the fact that he'd written her a letter like that meant something. She wished she could ask Jessie about it, though Jessie was probably sure he was changing, she had infinite faith in her brother.

If everything worked out with Ori she had only half a year left. She hadn't taken advantage of England, she'd barely travelled or seen anything. Since school started she'd put it ahead of the rest of her life. Ten years from now she wouldn't remember a single lecture. It was people she'd remember. She'd probably remember James forever even if nothing else happened. James was an England she'd never get to see otherwise. She was always turning things down for the right reasons and she was sick of it. Sometimes you have to take a chance, she told herself. When James next called she mentioned that she had three days off. "Although I have work to do," she added.

"I do too. I'm putting together a magazine of poetry and letters. If you don't mind spending part of the time alone, there are lovely roads, you can take walks."

"It sounds wonderful. I'd love to get out of the house. Though I don't know what I'll tell my parents."

"Just tell them you want to explore Oxford and you have an opportunity with a native."

That was what she told them. She felt guilty but not terrible, because it was true and perhaps that was all that would happen, though her heart beat faster at the thought of more. She packed her lace nightgown.

When she left London it was raining but by Oxford it had turned to mist. The train station was hidden at the edges and James's face and hands were the only clarities. He took her suitcase quietly and she was suddenly shy. It was different from the other time. She didn't know what to say. Then he looked at her and smiled and she smiled back. She liked him very much. It would be fine.

"We're invited to a party tomorrow," James said, pushing open the door to the house. "I forgot to tell you. It's a white party. Did you bring anything white?"

"Only my nightgown."

"That wouldn't do, I don't think. You see, it's a garden party to welcome spring, to try to usher in spring, at any rate. We have it every year, a month ahead of the equinox to give the season the idea. It's actually quite stupid. We all stand around in our finery trying to look warm, drinking too much brandy and hoping the roses will show. But now it's a tradition."

"I don't want to stand out."

"Maybe you could borrow something. Someone in the house must have extra whites. Maybe Kitty does."

"I'm not wearing her clothes."

"She won't mind."

"I mind. It's perverse."

"Don't be silly, she'd be delighted. Of course, you are much smaller. But if she has a shawl or something, you could wear the nightgown underneath. It would look very romantic."

"I'd feel funny."

"You don't have to ask her. I'll ask her later. Don't worry."

"Is she coming?"

"Probably not. She never did like my literary friends. She fancies herself an actress, and the theatre crew and the poets hold each other in mutual disdain."

"Why is that?"

James sat down on the bed. "It's a long story, and in perfectly proper Oxford spirit. To sum it up, the actors find the poets lifeless and the poets find the actors inflated."

It was foreign to her.

"Are you hungry?" James said.

"No."

"Would you like something to drink? Some wine?"

"That would be nice." Maybe it would help her feel a little less strange, sitting beside him in this room in the middle of the day.

"Hang on and I'll get it."

Alone, Judith walked over to the window and looked out. The sky was still heavy and the sparse winter grass was plastered to the brown earth by the damp.

James touched her back and she turned. He held two glasses of dark red wine and she took hers, grateful to have something to do with her hands. There was plaintive music from another room as they drank.

"I'm starting to feel it," Judith said. Wine was so reliable. She loved the softening of the first few sips, the way she could feel it inside her throat, melting her arms and legs, easing the angles until her body was comfortable to her and the room grew slightly richer.

James looked beautiful now. He put down his glass and took hers.

She put her hands in her lap.

He drew her to him and kissed her, looked at her, kissed her again. She kissed him back. His mouth was very soft. His hands moved on her face. She outlined his lips with her tongue. Mm, he said.

They kissed for seven hours. They kissed until it was dark. All day she lay in his arms, his mouth on her mouth, his hands moving about her. He held her gently and talked with her. She felt his eyelids under her mouth, the hollow of his cheek, small curls of his hair. He moved her hair back over and over again. James did not hurry. He touched her as if he could spend years touching her and still not be done. Where had he learned about women and touching? To be treated as sculpture, to be loved in every part, slowly, to be savoured, to have the beginning go on and on, that was the dream of lovemaking. They went out to dinner and drank more wine, staring at each other in the dark across the table, laughing at themselves. Her body was light, her head dissolving. He grew more and more mysterious. He was a stranger. She was a dancer. They got up to go. Walking beside James, fitted to him, she understood why lovers wanted no more boundaries, chose to spin themselves into each other, she wanted it too. She wanted it under his fingers, because he was good. It frightened her, the way she felt now, it was so close and would be easy. No one would know. Nothing to stop her but the great fear, an unknown man's nakedness. He was different from Ori. She couldn't. Ori and she were in a room inside her head, carried around even now, despite his imperfectness. The dream of what could be with Ori, sacredness and the Song of Songs, made James a mockery. Reverent, attending, not a Jew.

He did not ask her. James left to work on the magazine and when he got back the room was already light. She struggled up from sleep as he got in beside her.

"I am cursed," James said, "by the training of gentleman. My entire life's been an education in delayed desire."

She felt his ponderous age, five years older than she, half a decade, weighing him down.

"You've caught me in the autumn of my years"—he laughed—"unable to persuade a maid to bed with me."

"That's not it," she said without explaining. She didn't want to tell him what his hands had done. She'd been up for hours in his bed, dreaming of his fine slender fingers.

"Go back to sleep," James said. "I'll see you when I'm back from class."

Judith was alone in the house when the telephone rang. A voice she could barely hear was asking for her.

"It's me," Judith said, "who's calling?"

"Judith, I'm so glad you're there. I need you so much. I have to see you, I'll come wherever you are, it's important."

"Rachel?"

Rachel was crying. "I have to get out of here, I'm going crazy."

"Rachel, listen, can you hear me? All right, now calm down so I can help. Where are you?"

"I'm in India."

"You're calling me from India!"

"I phoned your parents' house and they gave me this number. I'm coming to London tomorrow. I have to see you. Everything's fallen apart."

"What happened? Why are you leaving?"

"I can't talk about it now. There are people all around. I get in at six-thirty in the morning. Where should I go?"

Judith was trying to think. She had to see Rachel but she didn't want to go home.

"Rachel, I'm in Oxford. Can you come here and then we'll go back together? It'll give us some time without my parents, and there's someone I want you to meet."

"Is the someone a man? Don't talk to me about men, I don't want to see another one as long as I live."

"He's different."

Rachel groaned. "Be prepared, that's all. I'm hostile."

Judith spent the day giving James a crash course in Rachel. It was hard to summarize her. "You'll see when you meet her," Judith said. "I just hope she's not too crazy."

"It does sound as if something's happened."

Something was always happening to Rachel. Judith wanted James to understand how important Rachel was.

"Stop apologizing," he said. "It'll be fine."

Judith knew Rachel would like James, at least because he wasn't Jewish and also because he was quiet. But when Rachel arrived she barely noticed him. She sat on the bed in his room and catalogued the evils of love.

"It was a nightmare. By the time we got to New York I knew it was a mistake but I couldn't go back. We'd had a huge goodbye party and I'd finally gotten my family to understand that I had to go, and they knew it would be at least three years till I saw them again. I couldn't turn around and say I changed my mind. Even New York was horrible. It was raining and we were staying in this crummy hotel and he was supposed to have arranged the flights through a friend of his, but it fell through. Finally we were sitting on the plane and I was crying and he kept saying that once we got to India it would be wonderful. Was it a disaster!"

Rachel was vehement, her face contorted as she spoke. "Little did I know what he meant by wonderful. All the time we were together in the States I never really told my parents what our relationship was."

"What do you mean you didn't tell them? They must've known you weren't moving to India because he was a good friend."

"That's exactly what they thought. At least, that was all they'd admit to themselves. On some level they knew, but he's a lot older than I am and it was easier for them to think it was an opportunity for me to broaden my horizons than to picture their little girl making love with an Indian."

Judith started to say something but Rachel wouldn't let her.

"He was a big talker, but his family didn't know anything either. He put me up at his cousins' house while he stayed with his parents and for three months he came over in the evenings and stayed all night. Of course, I didn't see him during the day, so when he finally got there we stayed up talking. I was exhausted. The heat was so intense, I've never felt anything like it, it's not like the heat here at all. I had my music but I couldn't play, I was sick all the time, I couldn't eat the food, they made everything with curry. I pleaded with him to tell the cook to make me something plain, but he kept telling me it was impossible, even the eggs. His family was really nice and they would have liked me if only he hadn't kept blaming me when it wasn't my fault. He told me I was getting sick on purpose to ruin his life and he wouldn't believe me when I told him I needed a doctor."

"But why did things change? He must have loved you if he wanted you to go there with him."

"He loved me the whole time. He still loves me, but he also hates me. I should have known. He used to tell me about his first wife—I didn't tell you he'd been married before, I thought it would prejudice you against him."

Judith looked at James. "That's not exactly the most shocking situation these days," she said to Rachel, thinking of the people in the rooms around them.

"Anyway, I always thought it was completely her fault. I couldn't understand how he put up with her and her wild accusations. Now I know. Always pay attention to the woman before you. I wish I could talk to her now, she was onto him. He used to tell me about their fights." Rachel lowered her voice. "All night we stayed up fighting. He wouldn't let me sleep. I told him, I begged him to let me, I couldn't think, but he deliberately woke me up if he saw me start to sleep. He shook me and scratched me. I have his nail marks all over my back. I have bruises." Rachel was whispering. "We used to hit each other. I punched him out. I hit him as hard as I could. Me, can you believe it? That's what he reduced me to. I was afraid he would kill me."

James said, "I'm going to the party. I'll be back."

"This is some introduction," Rachel said to him. "I'm sorry, but I had to come, you can see why." She was shaking.

"You must be exhausted," Judith remembered. "Are you hungry? James, are you going to eat before you go?"

He shook his head. "I think that you two should have some time alone. Help yourself to any food you like"—he smiled at Rachel—"and I'll see you later."

"I hope he's not mad at me," Rachel said when he'd gone.

"Don't worry, he's not. All his friends are having problems with love."

"This isn't a problem, this is hell."

Judith was afraid Rachel would collapse or start screaming. "Come downstairs and we'll talk over lunch. You'll feel better if you eat."

"I'm not hungry," Rachel said, but she followed her down. She opened the fridge and stared. "Eggs," she said, "milk, cheese, jam. No spices, I'm in heaven, apples, what's that, noodles, good plain wonderfully American-looking food, I never thought I'd see the day."

"Have whatever you like."

"Bread. Real bread with texture and body."

"I don't know how real it is after the English have gotten through with it, but it certainly isn't seasoned with anything fancy. Want some?"

"I don't want to eat, I just want to look. I want to stand in front of this beautiful refrigerator that actually keeps food cold and feast my eyes."

"Feast away," Judith said. "You don't mind if I have something?"

"I'll watch you and relish it. Here are Rachel's three rules for travelling." She closed the fridge door and sat down. "I made them up on the plane over here."

It was good to see her laughing.

"One," said Rachel, "never try anything new. I know that travellers are encouraged to do things they don't do at home but it's a big mistake. Learn from my experience. Two, never talk to strangers. Same principle. Supposedly you'll learn about different cultures but it'll only make you unhappy."

"What's three?"

"Three's a subtle one. Three is never cross a large body of water. This rule is designed to prevent the major mistake of travellers, which is going away from home. I figure if you're limited to rivers and small lakes you can't do too much damage."

"What happened to Rachel the adventurer?"

Rachel opened Judith's sandwich, approved of the contents and took a bite. "I'm retiring. I'm sticking to middle-class Jewish boys."

"Even I'm not sticking to middle-class Jewish boys." Judith smiled.

"I hope you won't be sorry," Rachel said solemnly.

"You've met him," Judith said. "Does he look like the type who could hurt a fly?"

"That's what I thought." Rachel climbed the stairs behind her. "I only found out when I saw him in his native environment where I had no one on my side."

"Sounds like a war." Judith settled herself on the bed.

"It was torment," Rachel said. "You have to realise that we were in love. Madly. When we weren't fighting we were very passionate. I have never had lovemaking like that. I probably never will. He is such an amazing artist, he's really a genius. He loved me very much, that's why it was so hard to let go. I still love him, I just can't be with him. We were too much alike."

"You're not like him at all. I can't imagine you hitting anyone."

"You just don't know me as well," Rachel said. "We knew each other perfectly. He could read my mind. He knew exactly what I was thinking, that's why he could get me so angry."

"It doesn't sound like love to me."

"Judith, you always want everything to be nice. It wasn't nice, but it was love."

All Judith saw were Rachel's small hands ripping bloody trails in a brown back. "I know I haven't had the most placid existence, but I still believe it's possible to have peaceful love."

"Sure it's possible if what you want is security." Rachel tossed her head. "I wouldn't settle for that and I still won't. It's death, it's being like our parents. To be friends—" Rachel dismissed it. "No, I'm going to live alone for a long time. My music and my work are what I'm concentrating on. That's another thing that got me so mad. He was getting his work done. Nothing stopped him, no matter how bad it got between us. While I could feel my fingers atrophying, look how stiff they are." She held out her hands and then balled them into fists. "I had to leave so quickly that I didn't have time to pack my music. I left it all there, boxes of it. His cousins promised to send it and I only hope he doesn't think to stop them."

"You mean you didn't say goodbye to him?"

"He won't find out I've gone"—she looked at her watch—"till about three hours from now." Rachel's voice was gleeful. "He's going to be furious."

Spare me love like that, Judith thought. She wished James would come back. She wanted to talk it over with him, she wanted him to see the Rachel she loved, she wanted Rachel not to be like this.

"I can't talk anymore," Rachel said. "I absolutely have to get some sleep, I haven't slept for weeks. I hope James won't be offended but I think I should go to bed now. Do you mind?"

Judith said she didn't mind.

"I'm sorry I can't get to know him better but it isn't a good time."

"He understands."

"Just show me where to sleep."

Judith took her to the storeroom that had an extra bed. "It isn't much," she said.

"It looks wonderful. A room of one's own, that's all I ask." Rachel stripped off her clothes and crawled into her sleeping bag. "Bliss," she proclaimed. "I'll see you in the morning."

Late at night Judith went walking, following James out to the road where the houses were shuttered, motionless. The moonlight fell softly. The air was mild. There had been a turning sometime in the afternoon and the harshness of winter was gone. She and James talked quietly, circling the sleeping houses in no hurry, glad to be out in the open. It was good to take deep breaths and dream of the coming spring.

The season brought fair weather and crocuses. In their gardens the English were tending the roses, pruning and clipping as the ritual of March dictated. Judith's heart was in another climate. It was the time she had first seen Jerusalem and soon in the same weather she'd be there again. Already her parents were making arrangements, buying tickets and taking down names. Judith went to Oxford for a day to say goodbye and tried to tell James about Israel. She described her first meeting with her great-aunt Chenya. Yehudit, Chenya had called her and opened her strong loving arms.

"We talked all night," Judith told him. "We had always known each other, we just hadn't met. A formality, Chenya said. She has the most musical voice." Judith could still hear it. "She broadcasts on the radio, Kol Yisrael to Russia, poems and stories in Yiddish to give hope to the Jews there." Language was inadequate, how to explain Chenya. "We had the same blood, it was unmistakable. We were so obviously of a piece, she finished the sentences I started."

James was looking perplexed.

She tried. He had no brothers or sisters. "Isn't there someone in your family who looks like you or has your gestures?"

He shook his head.

"Who understands you before you say anything?"

"God, no. I loathe most of my family and they hate me as soundly. I have cousins who should be sent someplace where they can do no damage."

She could never talk that way, even if it were true. "They're your family, don't you have the concept of family? You know, family stick together and blood is thicker?"

James looked sorry for her. "I think it's terribly destructive. Why should you create an elaborate mythology to persuade you to care about people with whom you'd otherwise have nothing in common?"

"I have worlds in common with Chenya and it's because she's part of what I'm part of." Judith stopped in frustration.

"I know that Jews are very close-knit." James was conciliatory. "I'm sure you've had to be."

"It's not that I have to, I want to," Judith said. She wanted to walk up to that doorway again and be met by Chenya's love, abundant and ever-flowing, guaranteed no matter what. She wanted to be in that city, the setting of her greatest desire, which Ori's presence still illuminated. She'd celebrate Passover with the Rafael side of her family, freed of constraint and secrecy. Perhaps she could decide about James, perhaps she could give him up.

"Come back for the first of May," he said. "May Day in Oxford is something you'd love."

She loved his imagining it and promised she would. Then she left for Jerusalem.

Sharon was waiting at the airport, waving frantically through the glass. They had weeks together and Judith was sure they'd talk right through them. Sharon, blessed Sharon, as known as herself for so many years it wasn't worth counting. They hugged and laughed, they jumped up and down they were so excited.

"We're creating a spectacle," Judith said in her most English accent.

But this was Israel. Everyone was chattering, yelling, pushing and agitating. There was no order and no system. Officials shrugged when she asked a question.

"Your guess is as good as mine," they told her in Hebrew. Sharon found the whole family a taxi.

"Just insist long enough," she said. "Put both feet on the ground and stand still. Sooner or later you'll get what you want."

It could not be more different from England. No one knew how to line up or ask for information in a low voice. But how the streets vibrated. Everything mattered, nothing was neutral, people had opinions and she heard them exploding, uninhibited. There was no room for shyness or subtlety.

"Push," Sharon said, laughing, the first time they took a bus. "You'll never get in otherwise."

Judith left her parents to stay with Sharon until the seder. It would be a Rafael reunion at Chenya's apartment, and Sharon, almost a member of the family, would join them.

Until then they travelled the country. They went to the Galil and saw the Kinneret, dark blue in the windy spring. Farther and farther north they wandered, staying in youth hostels and kibbutsim, walking through fields of new flowers and forests, higher and higher. They hitchhiked to Tsfat to see synagogues from the sixteenth century where famous Jewish mystics had had their visions.

Tsfat was perched in the mountains, a city whose main view was air. The streets were narrow and crooked in the hillside, and all of them in the old section turned into synagogues. At the low doorway to the first shul they paused, reluctant to leave the sunlight for a tiny dark room. They peered through the window. It was empty.

"Here goes," Sharon said and pushed at the door.

It was locked. Judith, looking around, found a bell and its hard jangle made both of them jump. Nothing happened.

"This is crazy," Sharon said. "It's the middle of the day."

"It's hard to believe this was once the most vibrant community. Do you realise how much of what we love in Judaism started here? Think about it. These were the people who invented our Shabbes, they created the bride and the songs we sing to usher her in and the presence of the Shekhinah dwelling in us and the possibility of redemption."

"You know, somewhere around here are their graves, they're buried in Tsfat, the big ones. Maybe after this we'll try to find the cemetery. You'll recognise all the names."

"What should we do?" Judith said. "Try the next one?"

An old man in a grey coat slipped through the arch beside them. Shielding his eyes, he turned half away and muttered in Hebrew, "What do you want?"

"To see the shul," Sharon explained.

Judith started feeling uncomfortable.

"Look at them," the old man mumbled. "This is the way for daughters of Israel?"

Sharon and Judith looked at each other in their shorts and sleeveless tops. It was hot in Tsfat when the sun was out and they'd been sitting in cars for hours.

"All right," Sharon said. "Can you tell us how to get to the cemetery where the tsadikim are buried?"

"The old cemetery," Judith said, "with the righteous ones." She wanted to show him they were serious, that just because they were in shorts didn't mean they were ignorant.

"The cemetery?" he said. "You should go to the cemetery."

Judith watched Sharon smile uncertainly.

"You should be buried there now," he said. "Better that than to see daughters of Israel fallen."

Judith started to cry. The old man was gone. The sun ignited the cracked glass of the shul window.

"Don't pay any attention," Sharon said fiercely. "He doesn't know anything."

"What hope is there?" Judith wailed. "That's the future of the Jews, that old man guarding my decency when all I want to do is get into the shul. How was I supposed to know that you couldn't just walk in, that they'd actually have someone there in a shul no one uses just to keep us out?"

"Judith." Sharon was laughing. "You think they hired that guy and said to him: Your job is to stand around and make sure no girls in shorts get in."

"I bet they did." Judith was laughing too, but each breath came in a sobbing sound. "I want to go someplace where there are no Jews."

"Good luck."

"I mean no Orthodox Jews. I'm sick of being criticised. Let's go someplace secular, like Haifa or Tel Aviv. I want to eat in a restaurant."

"All right, all right." Sharon led her to the bus station, and they began the long descent to the coast, the dust rising through the windows to choke them, past Nahariya and Haifa, emerging perpendicular from the Mediterranean, down into the lowland heat and the market hum of Tel Aviv. They stayed one night and treated themselves to Italian food. After they'd ordered, Judith realised the restaurant wasn't kosher, still jolting to her, although Sharon had told her more weren't than were in this city, and when her meal arrived she wasn't surprised to see flecks of an unnamed pink meat floating in the cream sauce.

"This isn't the kind of secularity I had in mind," Judith said, her face grim as she struggled to explain to the waiter that she didn't eat meat with milk.

"But we have no certificate," he said. It was impossible for him to imagine that there were people who didn't check every restaurant for a document of kashrut issued by the rabbinate but who still cared that the food they ate was permitted.

"The gap between the religious and unreligious is much greater here than in America," Sharon said. "If you're not religious here, you're nothing at all, you don't know a single blessing, you've never been to a bar mitsvah, it's unbelievable."

In Chenya's house the tables were set with new Passover dishes she'd bought specially for her kosher Canadian family. She'd acquired them in great love but without understanding. Her compact body moved among the chairs in a brusque impatience that Judith remembered from the last time she was here. Finally they were alone.

"If I have to choose between feeling God before me always and performing rituals without heart, I'd choose God every time."

Judith hugged her in affectionate exasperation. It was such a Rafael way of looking at things. "Why is it that Rafaels are unable to consider that you could have both?"

Chenya shook her head. "To me the worst sin is not to feel. My soul knows"—she put her hand on her heart—"that God is listening. I don't need to go anywhere or do anything. I can sit in my house and He's there."

"Of course," Judith said.

"I can read poetry in my room late at night and hear the God shining through the poet's voice. Not that I don't go to shul sometimes when I need to." She looked at Judith sternly. "There are times and there are times. So"—she patted the couch and sat Judith down—"the table can wait. People before tables. Tell me everything."

"I don't know where to start," Judith said. She knew what she wanted to talk about.

"It doesn't matter. What is important will come out." One of Chenya's tiny hands clasped Judith's and the other touched her hair. "Wonderful," she murmured, "such soft hair."

Judith felt the tears coming. "I want to tell you something but you have to promise you won't tell my parents, not a word."

"Shah," Chenya said, "what are you saying? You think you need to ask this of me? It's understood of itself, don't even spend time on it. So who is he?"

Chenya had done it again. The story came out in a rush, all Judith's questions and confusion, and Chenya absorbed it in silence.

"Now I don't know what to do," Judith concluded. "I know it will end in June and I shouldn't be in it at all, but he's a wonderful person, he really is."

"If you care for him, he must be," Chenya said.

"But it's a terrible thing to do, don't you think?"

"Terrible, not terrible, these aren't words you apply to love."

"I don't want to love him," Judith said.

"That's not up to you," Chenya answered her quietly. "You think it is in your hands to decide yes, no, chik-chak." She slapped her hands neatly. "Let me tell you a story. I had a sister who was lost to the Germans, may their names be erased." Judith remembered. "Her name was Miryam and she was very beautiful. She had many loves, what a life she had, a remarkable life. And the life in her. I worshipped her. Anyway, long after the war, fifteen years, maybe, one evening I hear a knock at the door. Who's there? I say." And Chenya moved to the middle of the room to show it, the rich timbre of her voice deepening. "No answer. Who's there? I say again. I'm starting to get frightened. Here I know my neighbours. A friend, a man's voice says. Into my house walks a man, old but refined, a delicate lined face, thin, and dignified"—her hands went up—"he was still handsome. I must see you, he says, he is trembling, I've been looking for you for twenty years. Me? I do not know him. Why? Because of these, he says, and takes out of the pocket of his suit some letters. I can see that they're letters but they've been opened and read so many times that they're almost transparent. As I move closer it's my turn to tremble. They're in my sister's hand. If I would see them for the first time twenty years from now

I'd know immediately. What are you doing with those? I whisper. I loved your sister, he answers. I have a wife and children who have made me happy, but never will I love like your sister. I'll carry these to the day of my death, he said. Perhaps he still does."

"Who was he?" Judith was shaking too, the power of love over time, over life.

"A diplomat from Cuba. He came all this way. I don't know where he met her or when they loved. But you see, the force of it. Many fires cannot quench love, it says in the Song of Songs."

"I know."

"So how can I answer your questions? You'll do what you do and find your own answers."

"But I don't know the answers, that's my problem."

"That's not a problem." Chenya laughed.

"I'm tired of not knowing, I want to know everything. I want everything to stop being so confusing and hard. All I ask is tranquillity."

"Tranquillity? Tranquillity is only for the dead. I once said to my sister, you should write a book. You've had so many adventures, you should put them to paper for people to see what can happen to a woman. She just smiled at me and shook her head. Chenya, she said, when I reach a quiet shore I'll do it, but I know I never will. She didn't want quietness, and then even if she'd wanted, it was not to be."

Judith kissed her. Chenya held her close, and then she started bustling again. "I'll say only one thing, because you're a Rafael and because you're Yehudit. Remember where you come from, Yehudit."

What a seder the Rafaels had. The remnants of the family from all over the country, her father's first cousins and their children, whom Judith had never met, Judith and her sisters, Sharon sitting beside her, and Chenya, reigning reluctantly at the head of the table. It had been a long time since the Israeli branch of the family had been at a traditional seder, but for Chenya her father's table was still alive. Judith and her sisters sang the tunes to every Pesach song they knew, and when they were through reciting the haggadah they did the Hebrew songs they'd learned at camp, Israeli pioneering songs and even English folk songs because Judith's father loved them. Chenya beamed

206

and Judith knew that Chenya saw in them the living music of her brother, Judith's grandfather, and her father, who had sung together in wondrous harmonies that Judith's father had heard as a child, who'd led Rosh Hashanah and Yom Kippur davening in voices so angelic and with such love between them that the congregation listening would swear they heard the gates of repentance open.

Looking around at these faces, the line of jaw that was hers, the wide-set eyes that were a family trademark, liquid ancient eyes that carried hundreds of years of rejoicing and sorrow, Judith thought, how can James possibly know? They stayed up very late telling stories of Poland before the war and Israel in the early days, the unseen presences of the ones before them manifest in voice and inflection. This is the way your grandfather told it, said Chenya, and so it was your great-grandmother gave me the tale. Then everyone was in the room, the old bearded men from the silver-framed portraits, the sister's great beauty, the father long buried, the loving aunts. Judith felt what she'd known and forgotten, the thin line between life and unlife, the souls of those with bodies sitting now in the warm fragrant room and the souls in the spaces between, celebrating with them. It was turning to light when Judith and Sharon walked into the cool of the morning, the full moon of Nissan, the spring month, still in the sky. Zman cheruteinu, season of our freedom, Judith whispered. On this night the children of Israel were sheltered from harm.

In Jerusalem Judith looked for signs. She was waiting for something to be revealed about Ori, some indication of what was to be. But the city was not exalted. It looked very normal and everyday, and she couldn't even find the hotel the tour had stayed at or the places he'd shown her. It was as if the Jerusalem she'd known were another city, invisible in this one, that could be entered only by believers or lovers. The streets she walked always seemed about to become other streets, mysteries that stayed unsatisfied. Sharon was busy with school and friends, and Judith followed her around, trying to discern from Sharon's life how her own would be shaped. On a Friday afternoon before Shabbat, Chenya came home from work so excited.

"Lo taamini," she said, "you won't believe what happened today. I'd just finished reading my poem for Shabbat on the radio, a wonderful poem by an unknown poet, such pathos, such feeling, and I was talking to some of the people who work with me, and I was talking about you."

"Me?"

"Yes, I told them about your listening, how you listen to the stories from a life that is gone and you understand, you know. It's an instinct, I said, where did she get that soul? And then Yakov Shtern, the poet, I read his work often, said to me, there's a girl who should speak Yiddish. I told him more about you and he wants to meet you. So," Chenya concluded, "he'll be calling soon and I'll tell you how to get to his house."

"But I don't know him. What will I say to him?"

"You know him, you just don't realise it. You'll see."

Yakov Shtern lived in an old Arab house on the most beautiful street in Jerusalem. When Judith rang the bell it sent shivery chimes into the garden where she stood, hesitating. Banks of flowers, flowering trees and vines cascaded over the whitewashed walls. At her feet too they were clustered, and the scent of growing things in the confined space made her light-headed.

"Bo'i, bo'i," a voice cried, and she pushed open the door to enter a room of lacy shadows. The high walls were covered with books, books spilled onto the low copper tables and carved benches. In the corners of the room pots and vases on the floor or on tile stools were full of beads, shells and old bits of cloth. From the vaulted ceiling brass chains held circular paintings of what seemed to be animals, cities of tiny animals, an ornate and mythical zoo. The room smelled deeply of jasmine.

Yakov Shtern sat on one couch awaiting her, and his wife sat on the other. He stood up as she came through the door and held out both hands.

"Yehudit Rafael," he said. "You know"—he turned to his wife—"I can see Chenya in the eyes."

"Yes." She stood up too. "I'm Alla," she said, "it is so good to meet you."

They sat her down in a huge wooden chair, the chair of honour, Yakov said, and asked her questions, what she read, where she walked, what she did with her friends. Yakov was genial and Alla passionate. He asked about big things and she about details.

"Like her paintings," Yakov said, pointing to the canvases over them, "Alla likes to take something very small and look and look, turn it around and upside down until she knows it."

"Whereas you?" Judith said.

"I"—he tapped his chest—"I'm in the poems. I stand in my small place and look at the universe. Everything is bigger than I am."

"Don't believe his modesty," Alla said. "Don't let it take you in. Yakov likes to challenge God directly, no intermediaries."

"Alla works through one ant, a scorpion, a thread of grass. But her questions are just as grand."

"Anyone can ask big questions." Alla dismissed him, smiling.

"And what are your big questions, maidele?" Yakov said. He sat squat and dark against the brilliant fabric of the couch, a small man with scant grey hair and a belly that strained against his belt. Alla sat opposite, even smaller than he, but her aureole of bright hair and proud bearing were distinct.

"Love," Judith said. "It's always love."

"But you are in love, aren't you?" Yakov persisted. "It is evident."

Judith touched her face. What was evident? She was thinking of Ori, of course, as she always did when she met someone Jewish and interesting.

"It's the light there," Alla said. "Don't you think old birds like us know it still?"

"You despair," Yakov said. "Why should a young girl like you despair?"

"I'm very old," Judith said. "Don't believe my face. I was even older a few years ago," before I met Ori, she was thinking, "I'm working my way down."

They were laughing. "Think how young you'll be when you're my age," Yakov said.

He didn't look so old. He looked the age of her father.

"Such an old man," Alla teased him. "Don't believe it," she said to Judith, "he's only fifty."

"Half a century," Yakov answered, "and besides, a Yiddish poet is always old. It comes from singing to the dead in a dead language. But I'm not going to talk about death to a beautiful young woman."

Judith felt flushed. She had no idea of the time. The dimness of the room seemed to intensify. She thought she heard birds singing the way they do at twilight.

"I have to go," she said, "it must be close to Shabbes. The buses have probably stopped running."

"Stay with us." Alla got up. "Spend Shabbat dinner with us. You'll meet some interesting people."

"That I've already done." Judith smiled. "But I should get back to Chenya."

"I'll call her." Yakov reached beneath the table nearest him and dialled rapidly. "Chenya?" He started speaking Yiddish but Judith recognised her name.

So it was that Judith came to the table of the Shterns, one of the most privileged tables of Jerusalem, Chenya said when Judith apologized. Alla took out an old silver candelabrum and set in seven white candles. She saw Judith's inquiring eyes and explained, "For the days of the week. You're used to two, I know, but this is an ancient custom Yakov and I discovered from Spain." She covered her hair with lace and sang the blessing, Yakov beside her. He uncovered her hair and put his hands over her head, murmuring, she smiling at him. Then they took out an illuminated book and began to chant, prayers and songs Judith had never heard, in winding Oriental melody. They were songs to the Sabbath queen, the bride, from her lover Israel.

Slowly the guests appeared. A nun from a convent outside the city, a Turkish prince who advised the Israeli government. An English Jew who spent all his time getting siddurim and tefillin into the Soviet Union and organizing classes to teach Hebrew secretly there. A couple who had just returned from ten years in Calcutta. A pilot, a potter, a Torah scribe.

"We collect Jews," Yakov said, "and introduce them to other friends." He bowed towards the nun, who smiled back. It was quite an evening. Judith drank wine steeped in oranges and cloves and listened to the talk. Enchanting talk, the first names of famous men, great religious leaders and their feuds, meditative Jewish dance practised in caves, retrieving Prophetic words for day to day. Alla got up and sat down often, bringing trays of twisted challah, dips and fruit, no meat, no chicken, pure food grown in her garden. It was very late when Judith tiptoed into Chenya's house.

"Did you like it?" Chenya's voice came from the bedroom, far away.

"I'm in love with them," Judith said.

"Come here and tell me everything."

Judith sat down on the bed and clasped her knees to her chest. "I've never met anyone like them. It was absolutely perfect, every detail, every word. I can't believe observant Jews can create a life like that. And their relationship. What a wonderful marriage. It's too bad they don't have kids. Imagine being brought up to be Jewish in Jerusalem like that."

"But they do have children," Chenya said. "They have four."

Judith straightened up, astonished. "Are you sure? They never mentioned them, not once."

"Of course I'm sure. I've seen them many times."

"Who are they? What do they do?"

"The boys are very religious. They live in a chasidic community in the Galil, far north, a new settlement they're building from nothing. They're lovely boys, very learned, very fine. They teach in a secular school deliberately, trying to give love of Judaism to our children who know so little."

"What about the fourth?"

"The fourth, the girl, is an actress. A most gifted actress."

That made sense, Judith thought, picturing Alla gesturing vividly, Yakov's voice in the gloom. "And where does she live?"

"In Paris, to her parents' grief, for they love her more than the others, she's the youngest and a daughter."

Judith heard the withdrawing. "But?"

"Choices, there are always choices. For me it isn't troubling, but for Yakov and Alla. She is an actress in Paris, you see, with a huge talent. It is hard to be a Jew with that kind of talent. For me in Polanya when I was young it was hard too, to read poetry on the stage, the daughter of the rebbe. But television and movies and promises of gold. She is living with a French man she'll probably marry and it hurts their hearts."

Chenya saw Judith's face. "You won't marry this English boy," she said, "you know you won't. But you must be careful too. Not all the pleasures of the world can be tasted with impunity. You're young"—she put her arm around Judith—"so taste. Plunge in. I'm not worried about you. But about her I was always worried. I could see her impatience, her terror at constriction. Israel couldn't contain her, she wanted to be all over the world. She's a wonderful girl, everyone loves her, that's why it's so painful. Well," Chenya said, "we must go to sleep. Even for me it is late."

Judith couldn't sleep. She kept thinking of Yakov and Alla and the girl, James, Riva, her ancestry. In a week she was going back to England. The summer was coming. Jessie was waiting. Ori, if only he were here to talk to. He'd love the Shterns exactly as she did. Someday she'd sit in their room with him. She could picture him there, he belonged. It was on evenings like this that she longed for him most, how he'd take to the strange people and shine among them, how remarkable they would be together there, the youngest ones. This was the life she wanted, she had to show Ori and hope he would want to build it with her.

When Sharon realised that Judith was leaving she was dismayed. "You'll miss Independence Day," she said. "It's on May first."

"I promised James I'd be back for May Day, what can I do?"

"Stay," Sharon said. "You can't go back on Independence Day, it's one of the greatest days of the year."

"What will I miss?"

"There's dancing in the streets and concerts and picnics. The whole country takes off to celebrate. It's Israel's birthday, Judith. You know." And she started to sing songs they'd learned in school.

"I wish you hadn't told me. Now I don't know what to do. Of course I want to stay."

"We'll have such a good time. We'll spend the day in the park and hit each other on the head with plastic hammers—"

"That sounds like a lot of fun."

"I don't know why they do that here but they do. You buy these hammers that make a squeaking sound and you walk around smashing people. It doesn't hurt."

"I hope not, it sounds crazy."

"Everyone's in a great mood, it's a real family day. Life here can be so hard, especially with a six-day workweek, that when the holidays come they're important."

Judith knew it was important. She was so looking forward to being with James in Oxford, to seeing an English May Day, the jugglers, the players, the girls with wreaths in their hair. James would have one for her. She would come back brown and rested and be pretty for him. But to turn her back on Israel's independence for the sake of a not-Jewish boy whom she'd never see after this year, to know always that she could have celebrated with Israel, her country, and instead she'd chosen a pagan festival. She cabled Oxford. Israel's sun over English green, she watched the people throng to Kikar Tsion, dancing in rings to blaring loudspeakers, crowding to ice cream and felafel stands, and yes, armed with plastic hammers that popped on the heads of children and short people, Judith being one. In the dry heat that was already summer, she stood with Sharon until night.

England was so quiet. In the airport she stopped beside her suitcase. Nobody came over to talk to her, flirt or bother her. The man beside her on the bus looked resolutely forward. There was no yelling, no pushing, only a discreet murmur and the rustle of newspapers. Her street was sedate, her house was still. Judith walked to the Heath the next day to lie all morning on the slope of a hill. There were a few solitary walkers and none approached her. James was coming soon. His modulated voice on the phone made her weak and she was rallying her forces. He would meet her in the park and she would tell him, she hoped.

She fell asleep in the sun and woke to the coolness of his shadow stealing over her. As soon as she saw him she knew it was impossible. He was as dear as ever. He told her how beautiful she looked, how Mediterranean. She stated her purpose.

"Well," said James finally, "if you're looking to me to acquiesce and make it easier for you, I won't. If you want to end it now, not that I want you to, I have no intention of helping you at all."

"Come on," she said, "be a sport."

He pulled her up, smoothed her dress, and kissed her. "I have a present for you, if you're willing to stay around me long enough to take advantage of it."

She loved the way he said advantage. "I'll be around," she said.

He handed her a square of embossed paper. You and your

escort, it said, are most cordially invited to the Jesus College Solstice Ball, midnight to dawn. Frolic and gambol to the flute and lyre, feast on champagne and strawberries. Dress formal. Come celebrate summer.

She saw herself in a light gown, leaning against his dark suit. Then she frowned at the date. She'd forgotten about such considerations. "Is it a Saturday?"

"Don't worry, it's a Saturday night."

"The Sabbath ends at its latest then."

"The dance starts at twelve. You'll come when you can."

She reached out to him. "I can't wait."

"It seemed a good way to end the year," James said. "It's drawing to a close, you know." She nodded, her body anticipating the delicious sadness of impending farewell.

"We'll stay up all night," she said.

"Thus"—James swept his arm to the sky—"though we cannot make our sun stand still, yet we will make him run. And after the ball I'll take you home."

"But we'll be home." She was confused.

"No, to my parents' house, in the country. You said you wanted to see the real England."

"I don't know." Judith panicked, an alien in his English house. "I'll feel strange."

"They've invited you. My mother will be delighted. She's good with guests."

Judith couldn't imagine it. "I won't know how to act."

"They don't bite." James laughed at her. "Not very courageous, are you? They know you're Jewish." He was guessing—correctly.

"Maybe for an afternoon." Maybe if they're not home, she wanted to say.

"It's too far for one afternoon, it's near Devon. You'll like it very much, there's beautiful country at the Severn. We'll stay overnight and be off, how's that? Then you can go."

Judith calculated. By then her parents would already have left England. Naomi was going with them. Riva wouldn't tell. No visitors were coming. It was a weekday. She was safe.

Hayh

Once upon a time a man and a maid were wandering in an English glade. The man was dark and the maid was fair with nut-brown skin and yellow hair. O where are we going, the maiden said. To my childhood home and my birthing bed.

James was weaving a ballad for her as the train drew them deeper and deeper into the country. Oxford was far behind them now, and slowly the factories and warehouses withdrew. Blocks of flats diminished, highways shrank, and the ancient forest of England surged forward to engulf them. The windows were shrouded in rain that was always falling, falling on fields of horses and sky, on thatched roofs and scarecrows and hay. They drank ale to dissolve the morning, and James sang of lost kingdoms and imperilled love. He was languid against the dark plush of the car, and the pallor of his face, his very white skin, seemed to prefigure a slow refinement of the flesh that would end only in death. A pair of ghost hands ringed Judith's neck and their chill ran lightly along her body, once, twice. She shook herself and moved over to him. It was summer but it was cold.

They arrived before tea and huddled in front of the fire. The house was odd. Hundreds of years before, it had been two separate houses and they'd grown together unevenly, so that small crooked steps appeared at random to mark the union. There was a larder and a cloakroom and a guest room carved into the attic. When Judith raised the lid of the wooden chest to unpack, lavender filled the room. A lace coverlet hid the bed, there were roses floating in glass, and a round window that opened onto a widow's walk, though there was no sea. A weathervane on a nearby gable danced wildly in the rain. Inside, it was very still, except for the measured weight of the clock that pulsed the heart of the house.

James's father wore flannels and his mother wore her knit dress with pearls. During their chat at tea Judith found that his father had served with the British in Palestine in 1948. He was perfectly genial telling her, it was long in the past. His mother served biscuits from an enamelled tin and suggested a tour of the house. James led her through the rooms of his childhood, pointing out the medallions and trinkets that centuries of army life had bequeathed him. His family had always lived in these parts, though they'd fought all over the world, and the cathedral in town held the ancestral crypt where someday he too would lie. It was one of the greatest cathedrals in England and James took her there before dinner to show it to her.

The rain slashed the windshield, and the grey looming bushes through which they drove crowded the narrow road. They walked around the church towards the place where his family was buried. There were many alcoves and corners and all of them were tombs. Soldiers who'd faithfully served, statesmen who in God's name had led their country to triumph, men who had died beneath the cross and were buried under it, thousands of bodies stacked one on top of the other, broken in battle at twenty or thirty, dead for the glory of God. Once these people had breathed and loved, and then their lives had been spent, to add another field to a king's estate, another stone pier to this monument. This was James's life and it was not hers. She had no history in buildings, she didn't know how to revere a building, her people were buried in their own blood, liquid graves, or burned in smoke, tombs of air that the world was still breathing.

At the house the rain finally slowed, and she plodded with him through the vegetable garden, picking tomatoes and greens for the evening meal. Judith left her shoes at the side door and she and James crept up the back stairs to dress. Every night James's father put on a suit to dine. The table was formally set and his mother served them their meat and Judith her omelette from chafing dishes on the sideboard. His parents were very thoughtful hosts and guided the conversation to Canada, to sisters, so that she would feel at ease. James looked nothing like them but the photographs he'd shown her of himself as a child looked nothing like him, so perhaps in twenty years he too would preside over a gracious table.

She helped his mother clear the dishes while James and his father drank brandy, and set the thin china plates down carefully in the kitchen for washing up. The woman who came in would do them with breakfast the next day, James's mother explained. Against the casement windows occasional drops still sounded dully in the twilight. His mother urged her to walk through the grounds while it was still light enough to see, and lent her a slicker that smelled faintly of violets.

They tramped along lanes at the edge of the field, sinking in mud that sucked them down, forced them to walk as if they were underwater. It was work to press on in the dusk, and for some time they walked silently. When they rounded the copse at the far end of the land Judith began to tell him about Chenya. She wanted to explain about the world she came from, what Europe was like before, what was lost, to make sure he knew how, exactly, it had ceased to be. James turned to her as she spoke, he was listening intently. It was a torrent of mourning, so utterly, eternally gone, a life steeped in the presence of God, snuffed out, the image of God in its highest degree, impossible to retrieve. James and she stood face to face and James said: But it was bound to disappear anyway. Between his body and hers she watched the chasm open, the ground in her mind between them split and slowly sundered them, she watched him grow very distant on the other side.

With his parents asleep the hours were long in the silent house, the relentless drone of the clock and the crackling fire were their only company. James wound the ancient phonograph but no music played. She lay at the hearth and drew her shawl over her face. She could see him through the gaps in the weave but to him she was gone. It reminded him of a hiding game he'd played by himself in this house, and he took her into the fruit cellar to rediscover the place. In the light of the candle he carried, the jars of preserves quivered, and the dank air pressed in on her, pressed in. James put his arm on her shoulders, its weight bowed her head. She clung to him.

Still the night did not end. A terrible restlessness seized her, and she felt that if they didn't do something, one final act, she'd be up until dawn in a purposeless vigil, and so they went walking again. Slipping out through the garden, they left the gate ajar and hiked along the river, swollen by days of rain. Mist stung her face and exposed hands as she tried to keep up with him, her breath wrenching the quiet. She would not tell him he was disappearing ahead of her, the dark mass of him shuffling through the undergrowth. He kept going.

The grass was getting taller, it swayed at her knees but soon rose to her waist and then higher. James's body was free and hers almost covered. She couldn't see, spitting wet fronds from her mouth. Beneath her the ground too was rising, and the sky was abandoned to a tangle of shadow. She was about to give up when it broke, the grasses abated, the wind died, she was standing on a mound in the dark and at her feet the unfogged mirror of a silver lake held the remains of the moon. The moon itself was unseen, James was not there, and she was alone on a swelling of earth, bewitched. She was waiting for James to capture her in his arms. She was waiting for the next moment, he behind her, beside her, wrapping her in darkness. She could not enter without him.

But her wild soaring heart. The mist and the hour and the crazy trees, like peacocks, like lions, and then, without James, finally themselves, the treeness of them, the sky that was over, the ground, the lake, naked, not needing, the world as it stood, at night, attained, consummate, unfiltered by love.

SIX

.

Alone in an empty room in New York, bare walls, bare floor, the mattress she was sitting on her only piece of furniture. She had slept in this apartment for one night and this was her second. It was her own apartment until Sharon came, she had found it by herself, walking from building to building, asking questions, trying not to show how scared she was. In a week Sharon was coming from Toronto to live with her, she and Sharon moving to New York, and just days ago she'd said goodbye to her parents, goodbye to her sisters, she'd piled her suitcases into the car and flown to this city. Her parents were sure she couldn't wait to go, she'd certainly complained enough over the years, and she couldn't tell them that when she twisted around in the back seat of the car to look at the house, at her father already going in, at Naomi leaning on the post and Riva waving madly, she could not remember in the blankness, in the terror, that she would ever see them again. I am leaving home meant ending, over, her childhood gone, it meant never running into that house, her room not her room, her clothes, her leftover things pushed aside in the closet, crumpled in drawers until they were given away. Her sisters still lived there and she did not. She'd have another key in her pocket and if she lost it her mother would not have a spare. No more Toronto, no more Shabbes with Bobba and the cousins, no more whispering with Anna, no more long-distance calls to New York.

She was moving to New York to be with Ori. She'd made up her mind, she was ready. She wanted to be an adult and serious, and now she was sitting in her room, watching the streetlights stripe the floor, listening to the traffic. Tonight they were going to make love. Tonight she was going to sleep with Ori, it was going to happen because she'd decided, and she was very still. She had set aside this night, chosen it, and all she had to do was wait.

When Ori came into her room he was late. He rushed in and paced around while he told her what he'd been doing. She looked at him and saw him clearly, the person she had carried inside her for years, the body that had been all her longing. He did not look immortal anymore. He looked like a boy in a hurry. She wanted to slow him down, if he would let her. He might have been nervous. She had stopped thinking. He took off his watch. She stood up. His clothes were strewn on the floor. She undressed herself. They stood side by side, without any clothes, looking, and then he reached over. She made herself fit. His hands were very familiar, she remembered them, and while he moved she watched the procession in her mind. Many old companions were passing by. Her Friday night, and a Hebrew dream of love, and the person she had been the second before she'd met him. She was not with him. Love and the dream of love were more disparate than she'd understood, and her body had to continue without her. One evening could not dissolve the years of anticipation and mourning, they were now what she was, and the hope of Ori, the idea of him, was undiminished by what was spent tonight. Nothing changed, the true hunger of the heart, separate from her body, was not and would not be appeased.

Ori went home and she was left in her room. The night sounds of the city were constant and unflagging, and she opened the window wide to let them in. Although it was autumn the air was still warm, so different from home where September meant the certain death of summer. In New York she could walk in bare legs into October. In the building across from her, lights blazed randomly and music from someone's radio drifted back. All over the city people were wide awake, going places and doing things even now. The old promise of New York filled her to the brim. She would not relinquish it. Somewhere people were turning to each other in the darkness, a woman was smiling to herself, arranging her hair. A man, his suit jacket draped on one arm, was nonchalantly watching. She would be part of it, no matter what. She leaned out into the city until the edge of the windowsill cut into her flesh. It was time to go to bed. She should have been asleep a long time ago.

Daily life with Ori was not transformed. They were always running from one place to another, fixing her apartment, arranging his rabbinical school, her school, buying tickets to the ballet that was months away. There were lines and delays in everything, and it was impossible to meet for more than a few minutes. New York was full of impediments. She could never have imagined how hard it would turn out to be. Judith spent all day cleaning and buying food. She didn't know how she'd have time to do her life. Now on the subways and in the streets she'd stare at the people crowding the platforms and sidewalks, rushing around. All of them were doing it. On Madison Avenue and Fifth, beautiful women held themselves like art, while Judith felt her hair escape, her face drained and grim when she caught it in the mirror.

"Help," she cried on the phone to Jessie at college the day before Sharon was coming. "I can't do it."

"You can do it," Jessie soothed her. "Do what?"

"Life, I can't do life. It takes me a day just to clean and then I have to start over again. How do people manage?"

"They're probably not as particular as you," Jessie said. "Give yourself a break. It's your first time away from home. It'll get easier."

"It won't," Judith insisted. "I know myself. This is the way I am."

"Judith," Jessie cautioned. "Don't do that to yourself. Talk to me a month from now."

"I'll talk to you every day. Thank God we're on the same side of the ocean. There's nothing I'd rather do."

"How are things with Ori?"

"They're all right," Judith said brightly.

"What isn't all right?"

"Everything's fine," Judith told her.

"That's not your fine voice."

"It's nothing. I'm just tired. We've both been very busy, me with the apartment, Ori at school. I'm sure that once it's all settled we'll see each other. Right now it's hard to believe he lives around the corner from me. But that's bound to change, isn't it?"

"You two have to get used to each other," Jessie said. "It's different now that you're in the same city. It's not easy to adjust. After a month you'll be amazed."

That would be November. Judith didn't know if she could wait that long. She couldn't figure it out. She was so angry at him when they couldn't get together and so impatient when they did. He didn't please her, nothing he did was right. And yet if he protested, if he asked her why she was always unhappy, why she snapped at him over trivial things and reproached him for big ones, she could only tell him that it was wrong, she felt wrong with him, she'd expected that being with him would ease the voices that said: This is not enough. This is not love.

"But what do you want from him?" Jessie said. "He feels what he's always felt about you. Maybe he can't express it as well as you'd like but that doesn't mean it's not there."

She couldn't say to Jessie what she was beginning to fear. She was starting to wonder if Ori didn't talk not because he had no words for what was inside him but because he didn't think the way she did. When she pressed him, when she insisted that he talk about her, about them, he didn't know what she meant. He was studying meditation, he was learning vegetarian cooking and shiatsu, he was going to rabbinical school as little as possible. Ori had no time.

Judith hoped that Sharon wasn't noticing. Two weeks after she'd moved in, Sharon had a boyfriend, a New York lawyer who was already nearly living with them. Judith's vision of life with Sharon, shopping together, staying up late, being girlfriends, had to be abandoned. Sharon spent most evenings with him and ate dinner at his parents' house every Friday night. When the month Jessie had promised her was over, Judith was seeing Ori less and less, and Sharon was engaged. She told Judith apologetically.

"It really makes no sense not to get married," Sharon said. "We spend all our time together anyway."

"Well, congratulations," said Judith. She was thinking it was impossible. How could Sharon, the girl she'd known since they were eight years old, before they'd even heard of boyfriends, decide to be with someone for the rest of her life, someone

224

Judith hardly knew and wasn't even sure she liked very much?

"He's a grownup," she told Jessie.

"So are you," Jessie said.

Judith was appalled. "I'll never be, don't be ridiculous. He's settled, he'll buy a house, how can Sharon want that?"

There was no doubt that the ground was shifting under her. Moving away from home was not like visiting. She was always running from the library to school, from school to the supermarket, home and the laundry, exhausted.

"I don't want to interfere," Sharon said, hesitating, after dinner when they were alone, "but don't you two ever spend any time together?"

Judith knew that she would start crying. "It's Ori, he's never around."

"Maybe I'm just out of touch with what's going on," Sharon said carefully, "but it seems to me that sometimes he calls to come over and you're not home."

Judith thought about it. In her mind she did all the calling.

"It's been happening quite a lot lately," Sharon said.

Judith sat down. She was trying to consider it calmly but her fear was in the way. She was trying to figure out if it was possible that she didn't want to see Ori as much as she told herself she did. And if she didn't, what might be her reasons for staying away from the person for whom she'd come to New York in the first place. Ori's face was blurry in her mind. When she closed her eyes and examined it, Ori at seventeen was what she saw. She could not bring him forward to now. The rage was rising, it was choking her, she didn't care if she never spoke to him again.

"I think we should break up," she said to herself out loud in front of the mirror. "Maybe we should split up for a while. Do you think we should break up?" She stepped back. "I think we need a break from each other."

Judith looked at her face as she tried the different versions. How could she be saying the words? She was actually going to end it. In her future was a big blank nothing. Ori had been her only plan.

Her mother cried when she told her, for which Judith felt an immense gratitude. It was too late but it was a measure of love.

Her father said, "Don't rush into anything too soon. It's always a temptation in these circumstances."

What do you know? she wanted to say. But she said, "Don't worry, I don't want to get involved with anyone for a long, long time."

She didn't tell them that she'd been sick from the minute she told Ori. He slept over and in the morning she couldn't stop shivering. Ori kept asking if he should stay, and she wavered between wanting to hang onto him as long as possible and knowing that she should get used to being without him. If only she weren't so weak. She lay beneath the blankets and her body felt as if it were made of many brittle layers that grated against each other when she turned over. Ori was moving about the room helplessly. She couldn't watch him anymore.

"Go," she said. "Just go. I'll be all right."

When she heard the click of the key in the door, the key he would probably never turn in her door again, she pulled the covers over her head and lay perfectly still. What if I were to die now? she thought. What if I suddenly stopped breathing? No one would know. Sharon was gone for the weekend. Her parents wouldn't call for another five days. By then she'd be mouldy and disgusting. Who would identify her body? Ori, and she couldn't let him see her like that. She got out of bed and put on a robe. I'm going to be very rational, she said to herself. I'm going to think very clearly and decide what exactly would be the best thing for me right now. I'll sit in this chair and whatever comes into my mind is what I'll do.

Jessie picked up the phone at the first ring. Judith heard her hello and collapsed. She cried for twenty minutes and Jessie was saying, "It's all right, it's all right."

"I can't talk," Judith kept gasping between sobs.

"Don't," Jessie said. "I'm still here."

"I feel awful. I'm sorry. I'm sorry," she started again.

"Judith, can you hear me?"

Judith nodded at the phone, her tears were wetting the receiver.

"Go into the bathroom and wash your face with lots of warm water. When you can see your eyes, come back to the phone. Just put me down on the table. I'll be waiting for you."

"I love you," Judith managed to say. The next day Jessie came into the city.

"Now, look"—she took Judith's hands in hers—"your life is not over."

"Why do I feel like this?"

"You feel like that," Jessie said patiently, "because you've just ended a relationship that lasted a long time and of course you're shaky. That doesn't mean that you'll never be able to fall in love with someone else. Is that what you're afraid of?"

Judith was shocked. She counted on Jessie to believe in her and Ori, even if they weren't together. "He and I have done this before," Judith reminded her, testing.

"I know." Jessie did not commit herself. "You can't predict the future. But for now you're alone. It can be good. You'll learn a lot."

"I don't want to learn anything," Judith cried. "I just want love. Why is that so bad?"

"You have a lot of love," Jessie said. "It's just one kind that's temporarily missing."

Judith berated herself. She wasn't thinking, moaning about love when Jessie had never even been in love once.

"And stop feeling guilty," Jessie said. "You can say anything to me, you know that."

"I don't know what to do."

"You're living in the most exciting city in the world. There's everything to do. Get out of your apartment and start looking around you, you'll find so much you won't know where to start. What about all the stuff you haven't had time for? Art classes and theatre. Call someone up. Invite someone over. Your life won't stop if you don't let it."

Judith knew she was going to let it. Nothing interested her without someone to share it.

"Where's Sharon?" Jessie asked. "What about her?"

"She's busy with her boyfriend."

"No one's busy twenty-four hours a day. Come on, you can do it. It might even give you a chance to try a kind of life you'd never have experienced otherwise."

"I don't want experience," Judith grumbled.

On the other hand, she walked down the street looking at men.

She dreamed of a city man now, a man who looked good in a suit. She saw him dark and expensive, and not Jewish. Enough of love, she said to herself. She wanted passion. She wanted an affair. But of course it was not possible, first because she could not not think of Ori, whom she hated and craved all the time. And because her dream of the unknown man stopped at the point when she placed her hands on the back of that jacket. She couldn't imagine the removing of clothes. It had taken so many years and she didn't have years now. She felt very old. She couldn't re-member that she'd had any part in ending it. Once it was gone she was deserted. To have poured all she had into a cracked ves-sel, she loathed herself. And she pictured Ori all the time, laugh-ing with women. She hoped for absurdities, that she was thinner than they were, that they would be haunted by her. She hoped he would never get over her long after she had recovered. Except that she never would. Even as she wanted nothing to do with him she thought she'd give anything to have him reach for her. One more try. They'd had their last try.

Judith began imitating his life, to her shame. She slunk into yoga classes, the very room where she and Jessie had laughed so hard at it all. Her heart went crazy each time, for fear he would be there. She swept the room with her eyes and felt her-self plummet when she found he was not. She stopped eating meat and stopped eating with Sharon. She was living her life alone. In school the classes went vaguely by, one following the other without her attention. From the moment of rising until the close of the day she talked to no one. So I'll be alone for the rest of my life, Judith thought, I don't care. But what if I'll be a person who was in love only once? The poignancy of her future brought her to tears. She would be an old lady who gave out cookies to children. She would drown herself in her work, and come home to a television. She would be one of those about whom people said, she was never quite the same after that. And she waited, every day, for the phone call from Jessie telling her Ori had found someone, he had fallen in love, he was marrying. Ori's wedding, never would she be old enough not to feel com-pletely ruined by it. She pictured all her friends whom he should have chosen, went through all the women she'd met since him. None was good enough for him.

She went to the Sabbath services he'd organized, bracing herself to smile and be casual. Ostensibly they were still friends, it was the agreement. She couldn't stay away from what he was involved in, because in her mind what he chose was still best, even as she despised him for being less than she. Being less, but not living less well. He had friends, he had this community that she felt so outside of as she came each Saturday, watching these young New York Jews pray sitting on the floor, singing, dancing together, ardently discussing Torah. She was part of nothing, not of school, not of Jews, and not of Ori, who would always be ahead of her, doing whatever the vanguard was doing while she trailed behind. People were nice to her, they talked, but her pain diminished all kindness.

"In a year you'll look back on this and be amazed how much you've changed," Rachel said. Judith had finally called her after Rachel's letters were piling up unanswered.

"I don't see how that's possible," Judith said, "but that's partly because I don't think I'll live through this year."

"You'll live. People grow and change, and so will you. You're human, you're allowed to mourn. That's what they never tell you about breaking up. It's like any other grief and takes time. A year is what mourners are always given and you should give yourself no less."

"I'll remember that and call you in a year," Judith told her. "I only hope you're right."

"Come visit me," Rachel said suddenly. "Come for Thanksgiving, you can tell me all about it and I'll talk you out of him. I never did—"

"Don't say it," Judith said. "Don't say anything against him."

"Judith, it's over. And it's a good decision. Now I really think you should spend some time on your other relationships. You were away for a year and we couldn't even talk on the phone. I know you've been having a tough time but our friendship has to matter too. I can't have you only between men, and I was around longer. You've been neglecting us."

"Rachel."

"We need time together, just us. A friendship can't be based on few letters and no visits."

Judith could not leave New York. Jessie was coming back for

Thanksgiving and Judith needed her reassurance more than Rachel's challenges.

"I can't, Rachel. I'll try to come really soon after that."

"How about Christmas?"

Judith was going home for Christmas. Rachel would be furious if Judith asked her to visit there.

"Well," Judith said, "Christmas doesn't look so good."

Rachel paused. "You realise, don't you, that we're never going to see each other."

"That's not true. It's just been a very hard year. You don't know what I'm going through."

"Come tell me," Rachel cried. "Give something to me. Don't leave me last on your list, it's too painful. What has become of this friendship? There was a time when you couldn't live a week without talking to me."

That time was over. "I want to know how you're doing," Judith said. "I'm very interested in you and I always will be. But it's not like it was when we were thirteen, and I'm not sure you'd want it to be. I can't give as much as you want now. I have nothing left inside me. Isn't there some kind of middle ground?"

"Not for me," Rachel said firmly. "Forget it. I'm not going to exchange New Year's cards and see you every four years for a couple of days. I'd rather end it than see it become trivial."

"Rachel, all I'm saying is that it can't be as intense as it was."

"A friendship is based on shared life. We don't live in the same place. If you can't share your life with me by visiting, so that we can catch up and spend some real time together, and you can't write letters—I've been going crazy not knowing what's happened to you—then it's worthless."

"I'll try to call more often. I'm sorry about the letters, I just couldn't put it down on paper. There are all these unstarted letters in my head."

"You don't let me in on your life. You don't open up."

"Rachel, you talk about how much you love me, but listen to yourself, you don't sound very ·loving. You sound accusing and judgemental. But I understand that you're upset and you have a right to be. Look, I'll call you next week, all right?"

"Don't call me. I don't want to talk to you."

"You're not serious."

"I am." Rachel was crying. "Unless you change, I don't want to hear from you. It'll just make me more upset."

"If it's not worth it to you anymore, I can't talk you into it"— I don't have to take this, Judith was thinking—"but I am really sorry."

"Sorry!" Rachel said and hung up.

Everything was ending. Judith spent Thanksgiving with Jessie, sitting at the same table as Ori, laughing at his jokes, her insides wrenching. She was afraid of the day when she couldn't keep it up, then she'd lose him forever and ever.

On Sunday Jessie took her out to brunch. She'd made reservations and they were led to their table in a corner full of light. Jessie ordered champagne and they sat on the same side, drinking slowly, smiling at each other and watching the New York people walking past. The room was quiet. They were the first ones there. The people ambling by seemed sleepy, and Judith leaned against the back of the chair and took a deep breath. Finally she was calm. "If I could feel this way always," she said to Jessie, "I'd ask for nothing more in life."

"You're asking a lot," Jessie said.

"It's you," Judith told her. "You bring me peace. Whenever I'm with you, all's right with the world. No harm can befall me, that's how I feel."

"If only you could do it for yourself," Jessie said. "That's the ultimate goal."

"Not in this lifetime."

Jessie said, "Because you do the same for me, that's the amazing thing. When I get off the phone after talking to you I'm a changed person."

"How can I do that for you when I'm such a mess?"

"You're wonderful."

"You're wonderful!"

Judith was laughing. "Let's not argue. I want to hear about you. How's school?"

Jessie made a face. "I can't take it. The people are the same middle-class kids from New York I've known all my life. I really want something different, something I can pour myself into and care about."

"Do you have any choices?"

"As a matter of fact," Jessie said, "something's come up that I want to talk to you about."

Judith felt the fear start slowly. "What?" she said.

"I've been offered the chance to take my second semester in Israel. It's a real honour. Nothing like that has ever happened to me, as you know. I've never been singled out at school."

"It's about time someone acknowledged you," Judith said fiercely.

"Well, you always have and that's been worth a lot. It is a little strange to be getting it from the outside."

"I think you should do it." Judith was sinking.

Jessie shook her head. "I don't know. I've spent a summer in Israel but a year is a long time."

"I thought you said a semester."

"I'd start with that but I can do up to a year if I want. It's a special program for American students. You know, Judith, I'm frightened. I know that's terrible, it's an adventure and all that, but I am."

"You'll do fine, you'll take off. You deserve to be treated as special, and now that you are, let yourself fly."

Jessie winced. "I'm sorry you mentioned that. I'm even nervous about the plane ride."

"I know you, by the time it's landed, you'll have the whole plane thinking they're one family."

"But what about you? How can I live a year without you?"

"You can. Who knows? Maybe I can visit in the summer."

Jessie brightened. "It won't be long."

Judith felt slightly sick. It would be awful not to have Jessie. She didn't see how she'd get through without her.

"Will you come say goodbye to me at the airport?"

"There's loads of time before that."

Jessie looked down. "No, there isn't," she said. "If I go, I have to leave in three weeks."

"Three weeks!" Judith was determined to be good. "We'll have to do as much as we can till then."

"Can you come down next weekend?" Jessie asked.

"I wouldn't miss it for the world."

When Judith told her parents Jessie was going, she detected a note of relief. They would never admit it, but she knew they thought she and Jessie were a little strange. If they dared say anything, she didn't know what she'd do. But they were the same.

"I guess we'll see you pretty soon," her mother said.

"Pretty soon," Judith said dismally. There was nothing to look forward to.

Naomi got on the line. "I got a call from Anna's mother the other day. She wanted your address."

"What for?"

"I don't know. Maybe Anna lost it and she asked her mother to call."

Judith found out very soon. The size of the envelope was unmistakable. An invitation, Judith was invited to a party to meet Anna's fiancé.

"I wanted to tell you," Anna said, "but I couldn't face it."

"Why?"

"I don't know why I'm doing it, Judith. It just seems like the only thing left."

"You're crazy," Judith said. "Your whole life's left. Not to say anything against him"—she didn't want to spoil anything—"but aren't you rushing it?"

"He's really the right person, he's Orthodox but he feels he's on the outside, the way I do. I won't find someone better. And I don't have much choice. I can't move out of the house, it would kill my parents, and they really like him so I may as well get it over with."

Life was falling apart around her. Sharon was getting married, Anna engaged. How could it happen at once? How could they give up so quickly? She wished she could talk to Ori about it, but that wouldn't do any good. She had to ask someone who could explain to her why people she'd known all her life veered away and did these things.

Ori drove them to the airport. He thought it was great that Jessie was going, he was already scheming a plan to see her really soon. He was telling her his favourite places, the places Judith had seen with him, and Judith was waiting for him to look at her, to acknowledge in some way that at least in the past they had shared something remarkable. But he was chattering away, oblivious, and she sat in the back getting madder and madder. The list of his faults drummed into her until she had to dig her fists into the sides of her head to stop it.

"Are you all right?" Jessie whispered.

"I'll just miss you," Judith said.

When Jessie couldn't see her anymore, Judith felt tears start. She didn't care if Ori noticed, maybe he'd finally feel something. But he was halfway down the road to the car and he wasn't looking back. On the way in she counted the days till Christmas, when she could get out of this city.

Before that, though, were the tickets. Ori intended to go to the ballet with her as if nothing had happened, and she was determined to carry it off. She dressed in her favourite clothes, all in black, and put sparkles on her eyes and hair. Ori met her at the subway and they rode down to Lincoln Center in silence. It was night, and the fountain, the courtyard swarmed with shadowy people. Couples were everywhere. None of them knew that Ori and she were separate. They sat next to each other as the theatre dimmed, and then the darkness dissolved to a bare white stage where men in draped voluminous skirts and bare chests began moving to Bach. The music was weighty and sombre as the men moved slowly, the softness of the skirts belying their hard naked chests. There were thick metal belts at their waists, dividing skin from swirling darkness. Judith was rivetted. She couldn't take her eyes off those men, moving in pattern, rigid, controlled, their glinting bodies. The women flew out, they were white, delicate, their small heads perched on thin necks. They were light, fair and trembling, and the men surrounded them, swooped upon them, lifted them, exchanged them, high over their heads, then beneath them. In front of her eyes the men were covering the delicate girls with their skirts. They reached for the men, yearning, and the men with their wet shining muscles held them and bent them and turned them around until the black and the white were over and under, and finally in one swooping breath each man and each woman pressed into each other, ecstatic.

"Oh," Judith heard her mouth say. She could not live through this perfection of women and men before her, her dream since childhood, the indistinguishable embrace. And the bitterness of

234

Ori beside her, once the person for whom it was invented. Ori who saw this ballet as he saw it all, something to do, not something to be.

"I am not giving up," she said to the applause. "It is right to feel so much, it's right." But what on this earth was adequate to such feeling?

She had to go home. She had to think out what was becoming of her. School was not good, she couldn't keep up. For the first time she was not doing her work, even last minute, and she saw no prospect of change. It didn't mean anything, it wasn't important. She was spending far too much time on nothingness. Ori had failed, Jessie was gone, there was no purpose. The year nearly over and winter closing in. When she got home she would do something, Judith resolved. She had to remember what she saw now, the bones of her life, sustaining nothing.

"But you must finish school," her father said. His face was grim. "There's no question of that."

"You're almost done, dear, hang on," her mother said. "You're just up against a rough patch. Once you work it through, it'll all seem much easier."

"I can't do it, and I don't want to do it," Judith told them. She was scared of her father, but she was determined to defend herself. "It's oppressing me and it always has."

"What kind of talk is this?" her father roared. "What do you think university is for? Your personal freedom? You're there to learn. Remember education? University is a privilege. Do you think in my day our daddies took out their wallets and paid? We worked damn hard for university and thanked God we could go."

"I'm glad you could go too," Judith said, "but that was you. You once said you'd never hand us our education on a silver platter, because you didn't want us to take it for granted. Well, I am, and I hate it, so I won't anymore."

"And what does my daughter propose to do?" The quiet, dangerous approach.

"I don't know. Maybe I'll work."

"You can't work," her mother reminded her. "You need a work permit. Judith, I can see you're upset but it's only one more term. Then you'll have your degree and you can do what you want. Hold out till June and I promise we'll have this conversation again."

Her father was about to talk and then stopped himself. Clearly he was hoping. Her mother was crying. She looked at them sitting on the couch. All they wanted was for her life to work out. But it wasn't working out, and their advice before hadn't prevented what happened.

"I'll think about it," she said. They looked relieved. But she knew she wouldn't go back. There was nothing for her in New York. There was nothing for her in Toronto, and no one to help. Naomi was embarrassed by her, Judith could tell. My crazy older sister, Judith imagined her saying to her boyfriend. Riva was going crazy herself. She wanted to drop out of high school and she couldn't tell them until Judith was settled.

"I can hear Daddy now," Riva said. "Two daughters who are quitters, that's all he needs."

"I'm not a quitter. I'm looking for something," Judith insisted.

"Searcher to you is quitter to them. I know you and respect you. I respect me." Riva thumped her chest.

"I wish you'd come back with me to New York," Judith cried. "Maybe there would be a chance."

Riva hugged her. "I believe in you, Judith. I know you'll figure it out. If only you could be less serious. It's fun to be confused."

Judith stared at her. "You don't mean that."

Riva admitted that she didn't. "But it isn't bad all the time. I go out drinking and dancing, and I forget my troubles. Of course I wake up feeling terrible the next day, but it's happy."

"I'll never be like that, I wish I could be. Ori was like that. Oh"—she clapped her hand to her mouth—"and I promised myself I wouldn't talk about him."

"Forget him," Riva advised. "I loved him, I love funny men, but it's over. C'est la vie."

"C'est la guerre," Judith said.

On Christmas Eve the phone rang. "I had a feeling I'd find you there." It was Jessie's voice. "Christmas is pretty quiet in this part of the world, so I called to get a report."

"I'm dying."

"Honey, you ain't dying. You just in transition, that's all."

"I'm dropping out of school and I don't know what to do with my life and I can't face New York and I can't stand being home. I'm alone in the world—"

"You are not. I am here."

"You are there," Judith said.

"So come," Jessie said simply.

There was silence.

"That's the most expensive breathing I ever heard." Jessie laughed.

"Really?"

"Yes, really. Come. The program is great, we live in Jerusalem, we have classes with Americans and Israelis, I'm meeting all kinds of people."

"Do you miss me?"

"Madly."

"But you went to be away, you don't want me to come following you."

"You, my darling, are not what I went to be away from. I said come, I meant it."

"They'll never let me."

"So come here to work, I can find you something. If you could make a little money, would that help?"

"Maybe." More than maybe. It was the best idea in the world. She'd go back to New York to pack up and leave right away. Everything would be fine once she was with Jessie. Judith had never not been happy with her. Her parents wouldn't understand, no one would, but it was time for her to do what was right, whether people understood or not. Her heart was with Jessie, the best of her was there. Jessie was healing, she'd know what to do.

Her father wouldn't talk to her. He loved her, he said, but he could not sanction a daughter who gave up.

"I'm not giving up, I'm beginning," Judith cried to her mother.

"That's how you see it," her mother said, "but you have to start thinking about life."

"You think I don't think about life?"

"Look, we love you and we'll be behind you because you're our daughter. But it's very hard for parents to see their children make choices that will be so much more difficult to rectify later. Here you have the chance—"

"Don't start. I've decided."

She was going. Goodbye, North America, yet again. Another chance at a brand-new life. She had packed her clothes into one suitcase. No more encumbrances. No more parents' voices. No holding back.

On the plane she said the prayer for a journey. She was on the way to her real life.

Vav

The house was full of strangers. Young Israeli men in green uniforms were lounging on the couch, sprawled on the floor, eating and drinking at the dining room table.

"Hey, chevreh." Jessie clapped her hands good-naturedly. "I want you to meet Judith," she said in Hebrew.

Nobody looked up. They were all absorbed in conversation.

"See the one in the corner?" Jessie asked.

"What?" Judith couldn't hear over the noise. She was faint from tiredness and wanted only to find her room, wherever it was, and go to sleep.

"The redhead in the corner, he's mine," Jessie said.

Judith saw a tall soldier gesturing in animation.

"He doesn't know it yet, but I do," Jessie told her. "We only met a week ago in his time off from the base, and we've seen each other every day."

"What's he do?"

"Paratrooper," Jessie said proudly. "It scares me to death. Come, you must be exhausted. I just wanted to make sure you saw him before I start talking about him."

Judith was too sleepy to concentrate. She dreaded having to make her bed, but Jessie hadn't changed that much.

"And here's your room." Jessie flung open the door. There were flowers everywhere and an Israeli poster on the wall, and a tightly made bed waiting for her to crawl into.

"I'm not even going to unpack," Judith said. "Never did a girl need sleep as much as I do."

"You can't sleep yet," Jessie said. "I haven't told you anything."

Judith was already undoing the covers. "Talk to me while I'm lying down. I promise I'll listen."

Jessie sat at the foot of the bed as she'd always done. "I couldn't wait for you to come. There's no one here who'd understand all the details."

Judith didn't want to know. She hoped a night's sleep would help.

"It was a Thursday," Jessie began, "around one in the afternoon." Jessie's story of meeting him drifted at the edge of Judith's mind, mingling with the memory of the long plane ride that her body was still in the middle of and her dread of tomorrow. What would she do when she woke up?

"Something clicked right from the beginning. A friend of mine was sitting in the room and she said that the second he walked in there was an instant connection. I felt it. We kept looking at each other all through the meeting and afterwards—"

Judith felt the welcome wave of sleep. It was starting in her legs and moving up. She was almost gone, in a minute she wouldn't have to think anymore.

"And then on the beach after everyone left we made love."

"You did?"

"We made love," Jessie said shyly. "I can't believe it either."

"How was it?"

"It was wonderful. Of course, it was the first time, probably like all first times, but he cares about me so much, I know that." Jessie was radiant.

"How long did you say you've known him?"

"A week. I'm so scared it'll disappear. You know me, there's a disaster around the corner. But, Judith, this time it's right."

Judith sat up and leaned her head against the wall. "Tell me about him," she said.

"His name is Yishai, like the Bible. He's a sixth-generation Israeli, he knows the country inside out and he's already planning tiyulim for us. You know, hiking and camping. My Hebrew's improved a hundred percent."

"Why didn't you say something on the phone?" Judith said slowly. The room was circling, her head was floating away from her body.

Jessie's voice came to her from very far away. "I was nervous, I don't know why. Not that I didn't think you'd be happy for me. You've been saying for years that I'd finally meet someone who would make it worth all the waiting."

Woe is me, thought Judith.

"I stayed up most of last night before you came. Yishai thought I was crazy. He doesn't understand about us yet, but he will. He needs American training. It'll take time." She sounded totally confident.

"What doesn't he understand?"

"Firstly, Israeli men don't have friendships like Americans do. They have a crowd of people they've grown up with and fought next to, so of course they're close, but they'd never dream of saying anything about it to each other. It would be considered unmanly. Another thing." Jessie paused. "He isn't very religious. In fact, he doesn't know anything, Judith, it's amazing. He's one of those secular Israelis who hate the Orthodox in the government for imposing their standards on the rest of the country even though they're a minority. His friends give me such a hard time. They have one day off a week and they can't get to the beach because there's no public transportation on Saturday."

"But this is Israel."

"I know, but it's not right."

Judith agreed. "Still, how will Israel be special? It's a Jewish country, that's what makes it different. Anyway, unfair as it is, it doesn't affect us directly. One of the things I love most about Jerusalem is how quiet Shabbes is here."

"It makes it tough on me, though. It's the only day we can get away together."

"Jessie, you're not driving on Shabbes!"

"Not yet," Jessie said. "But I don't rule it out as a possibility."

"Listen, I can't talk about this now. It's too important to give only half my mind to. But I don't understand how you can be interested in someone who doesn't have any sense of where you come from or what you stand for. And I can't believe that you'd give up the richest life for this guy. What would you have left?"

"I don't see my being Jewish as only observance. I never was as committed to that part of Judaism as you. Yishai and I have a lot in common—our belief in Israel, and caring about the people of this country no matter what their religious life. His secular friends are the most idealistic Israelis I know. They really want to change the world. Sure, we have arguments, but I hold my own. Sooner or later they'll realise that there's a way to value tradition without being a slave to it. Their lives are on the line for Judaism—driving a car on Shabbat just doesn't seem like a major tragedy in light of that."

"Jessie, I came here to share a Jewish life with you. We've never had a chance to live out together what we believe in, that women have a spirituality that hasn't been tapped, that what women know about relationships and love can transform Judaism, even the way we think about God, remember?"

"It's not the same here." She would not elaborate. "And I'm a very selfish person for keeping you up so late. Go to sleep now. I have classes in the morning but as soon as I'm done I'll pick you up for lunch."

"I love you, Jessie," Judith said.

The room was dark. Judith's body was weighted with stones.

One second later a noise split her head in half. It was brilliantly light even though the shutters were closed, and the noise did not stop, turned into the phone. She staggered out of bed to get it. It was seven-thirty in the morning.

"Welcome to Yerushalayim," a man's voice said. "It's Yakov Shtern."

Judith woke up. "How wonderful of you to call!"

"How could I not feel a change in the very heavens."

She felt herself soar.

"Wonders await you," he continued. "Every minute. Alla and I want to invite you for your first Shabbat here, you'll tell us all you've found."

Ir hakodesh. The holy city. She was living in Jerusalem. "I'd love to come. But I have a friend I want you to meet. Would it be all right if she came too?"

"Of course. Without a doubt. There's always room for an extra soul at our table."

She couldn't wait to tell Jessie. She'd thought of the Shterns so often since she'd decided to come. They were part of it, the new Jewish life she wanted, pure and only possible in Israel.

242

But Jessie couldn't go. She was spending the night at the base because Yishai was on duty.

"Do they have a Shabbes there?" Judith asked.

"Some of them do. Look, Judith, I can't change everything at once. It's a big step for Yishai to be with an American at all, and a feminist is even harder. I can't pile Judaism on top of that and expect him to come out alive. I have to compromise too."

"But this is religion. It's not like who does the dishes. It's not adjustable."

"It is to me." Jessie was stubborn. "I care about it and I believe it as much as ever, even more. This is where it's alive, the place-names, the language. The only difference is in some of my practice."

"I don't see how you can do this. Do you mean to tell me that all the talking we did, all our convictions, were only good as long as you didn't have someone? What about your encouragement and faith when I despaired about Judaism changing? It was you who said you don't have to give up, you can find it without rejecting tradition. You said we didn't have to choose between Judaism and life."

"Judith, I need to do this. I expected that coming to Israel would make me change, and though I have to admit I was surprised by the kind of change"—she laughed—"in a way I'm not. I knew it was coming."

"Why didn't you say anything?"

"I was scared of you. I was afraid you wouldn't approve."

"But I tell you everything. I keep nothing from you, that's why I love you, I don't have to hide."

"We were always very different."

"We were not."

Jessie said, "Wait till you're here for a while. Maybe you'll understand better."

"What don't I understand?" Judith sobbed to Chenya, who took one look at her face after so long and said, "Tell me."

Judith did. She explained her friendship with Jessie, the kind of love they had, irreplaceable. She told it year by year, and when she was done Chenya said, "Yehudit, she has fallen in love. Everything's upside down when you're in love."

"Not these things. Not us. We promised each other. I never let anyone come before her, not even her brother, not even when I was most in love."

Chenya was silent. "She has hurt you," she finally said. "It's not a matter of right or wrong, but she's closed herself to you. And now that it's happened—"

"Maybe it'll change back. Maybe they'll break up."

Chenya shook her head. "It will never be as it was," she said. "But you will see it in a new way."

Jessie was as generous as ever but her soul was absent. She still asked all the right questions, still read Judith's mind, and yet there was a withholding, Judith sensed it.

"I have my own life here," Jessie said when Judith tried to talk to her, "for the first time. When I got to this place I was petrified. I'd never had to be by myself this way. I remember about a week after I came, when I didn't know anyone and the course hadn't started, I stood out on that balcony there and hugged myself saying: I can do it, I can manage. Well, I have, I set up this room and made a home, I found friends, and you will too."

"Jessie, there was never any doubt in my mind you could do it. But you chose to come for those reasons. I came for you. You can't just leave me stranded. It's not that I want your life and your friends, but you have to accept me long enough for me to get my bearings. After that, believe me, I'll leave you alone."

Jessie looked miserable. "You know that's not what I want. I love you, I don't want you to abandon me, I couldn't take it."

"But you are abandoning me."

"No," Jessie said. "It's not that. We can't grow all tangled up in each other."

"What am I going to do?" Judith started to cry. "I don't have what you have."

"Shh." Jessie hugged her. "You're right. It's important for you to be in my life. Then you'll understand. Come to the base with me for Shabbat. You'll meet Yishai and our friends. You'll see what the Army's like from the inside." Jessie was getting enthusiastic, persuading herself.

"I'm going to the Shterns Friday night, where you were invited," Judith said. "I wouldn't miss it for anything."

"That's right," Jessie said, "I forgot. How about tonight? Yishai and I are going out for dinner."

"Are you sure you don't want to be alone?"

"You can join us at the restaurant and then I'll be alone with him after, okay?"

"I'd really like that. I should get to know him."

Jessie nodded. "He'll be around for a while."

Yishai was very attractive. He didn't say much but it was clear he was smart, he had dreams. When he got out of the Army he would go to the university, he couldn't wait to start studying after all these years. He leaned across the table as he explained it to Judith.

"I think I have a different sense of time now," he said. "I don't need years to decide, as you Americans might."

"Canadian," she corrected him. His eyes were startlingly green.

"I have such a thirst, is that how you say it?" He turned to Jessie. She was glowing. "To learn, to get the skills I need, and then—"

"What skills?"

"To help people. To work in communities I've seen in this time, where people have no hope, and to give them some hope. To teach them to use the country well, as I was taught to do. Already I worked in ir pituach—"

"Development town," Jessie said.

"—for a year. Israel needs these people."

He was very opinionated, Judith thought. And he interrupted Jessie. Judith didn't like that. But Jessie didn't even seem to notice.

Judith waited for Friday night with all the longing she'd ever had for Shabbes. Jessie left early for the base on an air force plane that girlfriends and wives could use if there were room, and Judith had the whole day to herself. She spent the morning at the shuk, buying fruit and nuts for her room and staring at the stalls that were piled high with all the delicacies that Jerusalem housewives bought on Fridays. She got tall speckled lilies for Yakov and Alla and a slab of sweet chocolate, Chenya's indulgence. Her arms were stacked with parcels and she kept dropping things. She didn't know that you had to bring your own shopping bags in this country.

In her room she sat and listened to the house. Doors were slamming, people were going in and out on the street below her, their backpacks straining with clothes and presents for the relatives or friends they were going to see. Judith felt the desolation begin. She had two hours before dinner and she had to do something. The city was closing down as the afternoon wore on, and soon the sun would set. She put on her long dress, gathered her presents, and started out towards that old Arab house. She wandered in the direction of the Shterns, passing on the way little girls with white stockings and braided hair, boys with black hats clutching the hands of their fathers. They were going to shul, and Judith followed them. The streets went up and down, and the sound of singing from doors and windows accompanied them. Everywhere there were shuls, stuck over shops, behind houses, in basements, the psalms of welcoming in different accents and formulations. Slowly the people turned in, here or there, until only one son with his father remained. Judith was in a neighbourhood that was not familiar. It was dusk. The man took the child in his arms and they ran towards a square building set back in a courtyard. At a safe distance behind them, Judith entered.

This shul was unlike any other. Wonderful wordless music flowed out and the father disappeared into a sea of black coats and hats that Judith could just see through the open doorway. The men were dancing with linked arms around the altar. She looked up for the women's gallery, but the walls were bare. She walked around to the back of the building, dark with trees. When she had almost completed the circle a low murmuring reached her. Tucked into the corner seemed to be an opening. She approached it with her arms outstretched, afraid of hurting herself against the stone. There was a door, not closed, so she eased her way in.

It was very dim. The only light came from one window set high in the wall over her head. A couple of empty wooden benches were scattered about, and in front of them three or four women were softly praying. Judith stood on tiptoe. In one corner of the window she thought she could see the ark. This room was the women's gallery. The men's prayer was muted through the glass. She had to hear. Judith crept around the room until she was directly beneath the sound. It was faint and beautiful. The latch of the window was undone, and she slowly raised it to bring the music in. A man's face appeared. He shook his fist and, frightened, she let the window fall. Behind her a woman clucked. Judith was interrupting the prayer.

She left in a rage, raced to the Shterns for some consolation. Yakov wasn't yet home from shul but Alla took her into the kitchen, as angry as Judith when she heard the story.

"It's the Bratslav shul, and I wish I could tell you it was unique but it's not. Most of the chasidic shuls are just like that. I stopped going a long time ago," Alla said proudly.

"What about Yakov?" Judith said. It was so good to sit in this kitchen and watch Alla moving gracefully from sink to table. The hot food, wrapped in towels, was piled on a sheet of metal over the gas stove, waiting for the men to return.

"Ask him," Alla said.

He asked Judith first. "And where did you daven, little one?" he said, kissing her hello.

"Bratslav."

His face lit up. "Wonderful! You see, the Shekhinah Herself was looking after you, to lead you to Bratslav on your first Friday night."

"Yakov, I hated it." She explained.

"Ach, I forgot," he said. "I need you amerikayot to come here and remind me. You see, I grew up in a shul like that, and for me it will always be"—he looked for the words—"tasting of heaven."

"I wish it were for me. I want to be part of it too and I can't. Tell me about your childhood," she said. "I want to know what it was like to take it for granted."

"Do you have several hours?" He laughed. "Look, Alla is impatient. She wants us to wait for the guests while she finishes, am I right?"

Alla nodded, preoccupied.

"So come. We'll await the guests and the greatest guest of all, the Shabbes herself, visiting for one brief day. And I will tell you about Bratslav and maybe you will see another side of it.

"You know what tikkun is?" Yakov began.

"Fixing," said Judith

"Well, it's fixing, but it's much more than fixing. It is repairing the world for redemption."

They were sitting in the room she remembered, lit only by one small lamp. Outside the wind had picked up and the trees were brushing against the dark panes.

"Tikkun," Yakov said again. "Before the Creator, blessed be He, made the world, He gathered Himself in to make room for us. In His infiniteness He drew in one breath, He left a small space, for us and what we are to do. Into that space He emanated Himself, into the vessels, forms of light, so that nothing was not filled with Him. But His radiance was so brilliant that the vessels could not contain it. They shattered, and sparks of divine light scattered everywhere. But even the sparks were too pure, and shells of worldliness encased them, hiding their light. Our task here is to crack the shells, to redeem the sparks by our good deeds and prayer so that they can return to the Source of all light, to repair the vessels that hold them for us. When every last spark is redeemed and returned, it will be the days of the Messiah.

"Each Jew," Yakov went on, "repairs in his own fashion. Bratslav prayer is very strong and devoted. You must not underestimate it."

"I don't," Judith whispered.

"Each Jew has his own path, with rising and falling unique to his soul. The daveners at Bratslav have theirs and you have yours. It is wrong to force another's path upon yourself."

"But I don't know what my path is," Judith cried.

"That is why you came to Jerusalem, is it not? This is a city of souls looking for paths. Explore it. You may find roads leading to nowhere, false roads. But open your heart to the sparks, and all your longing for a path will have reward.

"And now"—he rose—"I hear steps on the path outside. Not the highest path, I fear, but still a path."

Judith couldn't move. Yakov's words were before her. What was her task and how would it be fulfilled? At dinner she watched the guests, the way they moved and spoke. Had any of them found it? Everyone seemed more at peace than she. Some spoke of study and some of their work. All had something to do in this world while she sat around worrying.

"I've been wasting my time," she told Chenya afterwards. "On Sunday I go with Jessie and find out what my job is, and in my spare time I want to begin to learn."

Chenya clapped her hands. "Good for you. There is so much here, just start. You'll see how soon you forget your disappointment in Jessie."

"Oh, but she'll do it with me. We always intended to study together, it was our dream."

Chenya looked at her quietly. "Yehudit"—she took Judith's hands in her own small hands—"let me tell you a story. I grew up in a house of great love, as I've told you. But there was always fighting. Now you may ask me, great love and fighting, how can this be? I would say to you then what I saw among the Rafaels, a very unusual house. My father knew many languages. Some he was born with, some he learned from books. But Hebrew he placed above all of them. Yiddish is my mistress, he would say, but Hebrew is the one I have chosen as my wife. My brother laughed at him. He himself chose Yiddish, he taught in Yiddish schools, he dreamed in Yiddish. The fights they used to have! This was in a tiny Polish village whose name is now on no map. And what did they fight over? Which was the true language of the Jews. Which language will be spoken in the Holy Land. Because even then we knew that Eretz Yisrael was our only hope. So, to get back to the story, my father said Hebrew and my brother said Yiddish. And you see that it's not always the son who is ahead of his father, because my father's Zion is what came to be, although he didn't live to hear it spoken on this land. Well, that was only one fight. Then there was religion. My brother didn't believe in the ritual, he thought our future was the language and the land. But my mother was very pious. A tsadeket, she devoted her life to good deeds and fearing God. They too used to argue. My father stayed out of it, he was already under attack for his interpretations of the Law. But my mother and brother—all the time. And still, not an unkind word between them. My brother used to smoke on Shabbat after my mother had left for shul. She went very early to help the old ladies with the stairs. So my brother would smoke when she left the house, but an hour before shul was over he stopped. He opened all the

windows to chase out the smoke. This was in respect for my
mother, whose Shabbat he would have died to preserve although
he had a very different kind himself. And I think my mother
knew, she had a certain softness in her face when she kissed him
on returning. But of course they would never have said anything
to each other," Chenya said, laughing. "And now you should go
to bed, my dear one. There will be plenty of time to talk to
Jessie."

Jessie was in such a rush she barely had time to show Judith
the job. Yishai had arrived in the middle of the night and was
gone at five, leaving Jessie exhausted and happy.

"I'm sorry." She yawned at Judith. "Somehow I'm going to
have to find a way to do my studying and stay awake."

"That's just what I wanted to talk to you about," Judith said.
"Not the staying-awake part but the studying."

Jessie groaned. "Please"—she held up her hands—"even the
word makes me nervous, I'm so far behind. That Yishai will be
the death of me." She leaned towards Judith to confide, "It's getting so good I'm afraid it can't last."

"It'll last," Judith said. "I know it."

Judith's job was research. She had to take the bus every morning to the university library and look up her daily list of books
in the catalogue room. Then she filled out slips with the numbers
from the catalogue, put in her requests, and waited for the books
to appear or not appear one at a time at the desk. It took forever.
Each book had the answer to some question that a student teacher
in Jessie's program needed to know, and Judith had to find the
information, condense it, and deliver it at the end of the day in
time for class. The library was icy. No buildings in Jerusalem
were warm enough and the students gathered in the library as
a refuge from their homes, where the heat came on only from
five in the afternoon to bedtime, or from their dorms, where
there was no heat at all. Judith spent all day alone, sitting by
herself at a table piled high with books. In the middle she went
downstairs to the smoky cafeteria for watery soup and tea, anything hot. The room was full of chattering students but she didn't
know anyone. She left the library in the dark, shivering at the
bus stop, praying for the two lights like eyes to peer around the

corner. If she ran to the stop and saw no one there, her spirits plummetted, it meant half an hour in the cold darkness.

Judith didn't know what was wrong with her. The work was interesting, it was learning without deadlines or marks, but she couldn't like it. Jessie's friends told her it was one of the best jobs to have, that Judith was so lucky, that Jessie had fought for her to get it and everyone was pleased with her. It didn't help. While Judith was stuck in the library, Jessie was meeting people, speaking Hebrew, travelling around. Judith went to bed at ten o'clock but she was always tired. She'd been in Israel a month and she hadn't done anything.

"When does it get warm?" she cried to Chenya. Chenya bustled around the house in layers of sweaters, fortifying herself with tea. She had lived through the siege of Jerusalem, and cold during peace did not touch her.

"Yehudit"—she hugged her—"next week is Tu B'shvat, the birthday of the trees. It's the first day of spring for us."

"I don't believe it."

"You will see. The little children go out to the forests and plant saplings, and the buds appear on the trees. The almond is in flower and we will eat carob and oranges."

Judith huddled under Chenya's blanket. She was still wearing her coat.

"I think you should take a trip," Chenya said.

"Myself?" Judith tasted the blanket. "Myself?" She poked her head out.

"You, my little mouse." Chenya laughed. "Take one day for yourself and leave Yerushalayim."

"But where would I go?"

"Ein Gedi," Chenya said immediately. "It is full of sun there. You'll climb the mountains and get hot. You'll be so hot you'll have to take off your coat. Then you'll lie on the rocks and look at the sky and down at the Salt Sea staring back at you. Then you'll get on a bus and come back, but it'll be a different Yehudit. I will make you lunch."

"I can make lunch," Judith said quickly.

"When do you eat?" Chenya said. "You never eat here, and you don't eat at work, do you?"

Judith admitted she didn't.

"I know all American girls are b'dieta," Chenya said. "But you are too thin."

"I'm not hungry." Judith knew she wasn't too thin. She was just getting thin enough.

"For Tu B'shvat, though, I'll make you picnic yisraeli. You come pick it up on your way to the station. That way I can say goodbye. And don't ask Jessie," she called after her, "she'll want to be with Yishai and you are for you."

"You haven't even met her." Judith came back in. "How do you know?"

"I would like to meet her. She must be remarkable for you to love her so."

"She is remarkable," Judith said in sorrow.

"But so are you," Chenya said. "It could not have happened otherwise."

"My remarkable days are over."

"You haven't even opened the door," Chenya said.

That was what Judith repeated to herself as she got on the bus to Ein Gedi. The Central Bus Station was packed with kids and tourists, yelling and running around, and Judith got the last seat by planting herself in line and refusing to be swayed. It was a dismal day as she left the city, but as the bus descended through the hills, the air began to clear. It thinned, grew translucent, revealing walls of stone that turned from grey to sand to gold. Now the sky was blue, the light was full. There was the Salt Sea, glittering, and on the other side the hills of Ein Gedi. The earth was in flower and across its paths the wild gazelles leapt shyly before they disappeared. There were birds and pools of water, and though it was cold the sun collected in her black coat and she was warm. Children were playing near the water and guides from the field school nearby, but Judith chose a solitary path and started the hike, following the marked rocks without knowing where they'd lead. Her breath sounded in the clarity as she rose higher and higher, sweating, pushing herself. She would get to the top, she would see what was there.

What was there was the source of a river and utter silence. Judith put her coat down near the water, rolled up her jeans, took off her shoes and socks and stuck her feet in. Icy, she laughed out loud, it was so startling. The sun dried her off in a minute. She opened her knapsack and looked inside. The fruit gleamed, there were small surprise packages. She felt Chenya's love leap out, and pulling the sack close to her, she lay down until she felt the heat all over her. Then she leaned on her elbows to look around. Way down there was the sea and somewhere the pillar of salt that was Lot's wife. The desert and the glare encroached upon this place, but where she was, so near the sky, was an empty garden and only she in it. Judith sat up and unbuttoned her shirt. Who would know? Her bare skin in the sun, she lay on the soft lining of her coat and let her mind for once be filled with nothing.

Some time passed. The light was in a different place. A branch snapped close by. There might have been some people talking. She found her watch and packed in a hurry. The bus would be coming from Be'ersheva and would not wait. Scrambling down the path, she thought: How will I describe this day? Telling it to Jessie, for example. Judith's body ached. The climb had been harder than she'd realised. She'd feel it tomorrow.

Jerusalem was clouded in darkness by the time she got in. She had to wait for nearly an hour till her bus came. In her room, alone, her heart was beating in no pattern, she couldn't endure it. Where was Jessie? Why wasn't she home yet? It was too late to call Chenya. Judith had to get out of bed to empty her knapsack. All the food was spoiled from being in the sun. Now she was hungry but only a stick of carob was left at the bottom. She gnawed at it and felt the tears on her cheeks. In a few more hours she'd be getting up to go to work. And Jessie was still not back. She squeezed her eyes shut to stop picturing Jessie and Yishai in the fields, on the grass.

Alla listened eagerly when Judith saw her next. She didn't want to hear about Ein Gedi, she wanted to talk about Judith and Jessie. She wanted to know exactly what Judith was feeling.

"I know how it is to be deserted by one whom you love over everything," Alla said.

Judith didn't want to ask her who.

"People who see you talking with her have no idea, I'm sure, of the difference."

"I hope not," said Judith. It was shameful to feel as she did.

"Why?" Alla said. "She has hurt you bitterly."

"All she's done is fallen in love. We both wanted that for her."

"No," Alla said. "She has turned herself away from you. She has betrayed your covenant."

Judith demurred halfheartedly. She was looking at Alla's painting, not yet finished. Tiny birds were embracing between blank spaces. Alla moved it into the light and Judith could see. The birds were eating each other's throats.

"I like it," Judith said. "It suits me."

"I am drawing the insides of hearts." Alla's hands moved abruptly through her hair. "I am up all the night, I am driving myself wildly. I must finish this soon."

"Does Yakov like it?"

"Yakov's book comes out next month. He is moving from party to party."

"His poems?"

Alla nodded.

"Of what?"

"Soft things," Alla said. "Yakov is still a dreamer. The world has not awoken him. It may never."

Jessie was full of apologies about how little time they had together. She invited Judith to her relatives for the Purim meal and Judith was happy to go.

"Let's go to a café beforehand," she said to Jessie, "and just sit and talk."

"You're going to yell at me, aren't you?" Jessie was meek.

"Of course not. I'm so glad you want to spend time with me."

"I love you, Judith. I really do. You have to be patient, though. Remember what it's like when something sweeps you away?"

"No matter how much I was swept"—Judith was laughing at how that sounded—"you were you, unsurpassed. I still don't understand why you can't do it if I could."

"Maybe it wasn't right to do."

"But I did it." Judith was stubborn.

"We'll talk then, all right?" Jessie hugged her.

Judith felt those strong arms. "All right."

She was nervous Purim morning and frightened by that. "I never thought the day would come," she told Chenya, "that I would be afraid to see Jessie."

"Lomdim mikol davar," Chenya said, you learn from everything.

Judith and Jessie spent two hours talking and laughing in the café, recalling all the funny times they'd had and the words they'd invented to describe them.

"We should write this down," Judith said, "so we never forget it."

Jessie was solemn. "Let's start now," she said. She pulled out some paper and pens from her bag and they each made the same list, starting from when they'd met, and exchanged them at the end so that Judith's was in Jessie's hand and Jessie's in Judith's. Then it was time to go. Judith fingered the list in her pocket right through the meal. They were not going to be at the same seder. Jessie was going to Yishai's parents and Judith would be at the Shterns. This was the last festive meal they'd spend together for a long time.

On Purim the children of Jerusalem dressed up in costumes and walked through the streets. All day people exchanged gifts of sweets and wine and gave money for presents to the poor. When Jessie and Judith got back they found a pile of wrapped cakes and fruit waiting for them.

"From Yishai," Jessie said, her face lighting up. "I explained the custom to him and look what he's done. There's hope for that boy yet in the religion department."

"What do you mean?"

"I think he's a little less angry. Maybe seeing my love of being Jewish has shown him another side."

"But how are you showing it to him?"

"All the time," Jessie said. "Why don't you believe it?"

"It just seems to me that if you're not keeping Shabbes and you spend holidays on the base, he can't see what celebration looks like."

"There's more to it than that. I take my candlesticks. I describe Shabbat at home. I daven every Friday night and teach him the songs. He does read Hebrew, you know"—she smiled—"so it's not like starting from zero."

Judith was sceptical but afraid to say more.

"I wish you liked him better," Jessie said. "It hurts me so much."

"Oh, Jessie, it's not that I don't like him, he seems fine to me. Things are much more complicated than that."

Jessie didn't ask.

"I've lost you," Judith cried.

Jessie shook her head and Judith gave up. She would let her go, she had no choice. Someday Jessie would need her again and she would not be there. That was the most Judith could expect.

Now she was home as little as possible. She worked all day and went to Chenya's or to the Shterns in the evenings. It was twilight that was most dreadful, and if she planned a shelter at that hour when Jerusalem was drained of all colour before it plunged into darkness, she was safe. It was then that the heat slowly entered the houses. Someone was there to give her tea, to make her warm.

Judith stopped talking to Jessie. She would say nothing to her except hello or excuse me if they passed each other in the narrow halls. It tormented Jessie, Judith knew. What was most painful to Jessie was Judith's not letting her in. And Judith could not. When she opened her heart to Jessie these days she felt Jessie steal it. Jessie then knew everything but still gave nothing of herself.

"What does Judaism say about love?" Judith asked Yakov. She had finally begun to study, two evenings a week.

"Love can bring redemption," Yakov said. "Love of God. Seek Him, cling to Him, do not stray from His ways. Each of us is created in His image. If you seek what is highest, most Godly in another, if you try to draw forth the divine sparks in another's soul, if you try to exalt always what is holy and bring to perfection what is imperfect, if you do this for the loved one and the loved one does it for you, then there will always be renewal."

She wanted to ask him if that was what he had with Alla, but he was her teacher, she couldn't.

"Of course this is not possible in our world except in moments. Because we are imperfect, we are in His image but still human and so we fail. But it is a beautiful failure." Yakov smiled. "In a few years you will come to me with a husband at your side and a baby in your arm, and you'll know the rewards of such failure."

Judith wanted sacred love, every moment hallowed. She wanted her love to defy dailiness, so that she and he would be a refuge for each other from the wearing down of passion in the universe. And if that were not possible, if the voices of the world were right, still she would wait for it, it was her belief.

"Why is he so cynical?" Judith asked Alla. "Somehow it must be Jewishly possible or I couldn't have thought it up."

"Don't speak to a man about love," Alla said. "For men it is theory. They talk and talk but they don't know. Women know. A man cannot teach. A relationship can teach. That's the secret of women, a new kind of teacher, not one person but what lies between two, a lived example. Therefore I do not study such matters with him," she said scornfully. "I do my painting and create, not talk. Creation is in the image of God, who created all things and gave us the chance. Seize it, that's all you can do."

"After Pesach," Yakov said, "we will start you with texts. But for now I will give you a taste of the riches, a little of this and of that. To whet your appetite." And he spoke of Jewish history, not the events but the inner life, the story of the Jewish soul. "First the Prophets, and Moshe, the greatest of them, who freed us from Egypt to give us Torah and teach us to love her, no easy thing for such a stubborn people. Then the rabbis and midrash, elaborating the Torah, making stories that grow and change, we must remake them in each generation for Torah to live in us. Then kabbalah, that is the glory, and Luria in Tsfat, here in Yisrael. Your devotion can restore the universe, that is what Luria gave us. And then chasidut, which infused it with joy, because prayer and devotion can be so hard. From the chasidim we learned to sing, to dance, to carry the burden lightly. So, maidele, great things await you. At our seder we shall tell one of the greatest tellings, the haggadah, freedom from slavery, and you will hear it many ways."

Judith cleaned every corner of her room for Pesach, scraping up all the crumbs of bread, purifying her house of leavening to remember the new beginning that Passover was for her ancestors and to bring it about for her. She bought a dress of embroidery and walked to the Shterns hardly shivering. Aviv, spring was coming, the air was mild, the moon full over the land. Once again it was the night of protection, and she was wrapped in chesed and the coming deliverance. She stopped for Chenya and they went on together, slowly to breathe in the flowers.

Chenya squeezed her hand. "Yehudit, I wish you an aviv full of osher, joyfulness, for your soul and your body. Tonight you will eat like a queen. Alla has been working since dawn."

Judith hadn't eaten all day. She was keeping the fast of the oldest sons, traditionally overturned by completing a book of study on this day before Pesach so that eating was required to celebrate.

"But I have just begun my study," Judith explained when Chenya protested. "Next Pesach I too will feast."

The Shterns' house was chaos. Guests were milling around trying to follow Alla's instructions, while in the study the men were starting the evening prayer. The table was not even set. Alla was still adding wine to the charoset and there was no one to clean up the soup that had boiled over.

"Chenya, get off your hands and knees." Alla sank into her chair for a minute. "This is not why I asked you to come."

Chenya brushed that aside and squeezed out the cloth.

"A seder is a lot of work," she said. "No, no, Yehudit, you are wearing a new dress. When you've known Alla as long as I have, you too can scrub her floor."

"You look lovely," Alla told Judith. "Really lovely."

Judith didn't see how they'd ever be ready. But Chenya took over in her modest way so that Alla was calm. By the time the men were done, everything was in its place. Yakov stood at the head of the table surveying his domain. He was wearing a white satin robe only for seder, and Alla at the other end was dressed in the colour of wine. On the chairs were brocade cushions for reclining. There were silver goblets at each place, mats made of woven gold thread. The matsah cover, sewn with stones, was next to the main seder plate near Yakov, encrusted with turquoise and mother-of-pearl. It was the Shterns as she'd always known them. Judith wished she could have walked in only then.

"Tonight we are rich," Yakov said. The seder began.

Judith waited for the harmony of the table to wash over her, for the haggadah and the stories Yakov told around it to carry her out of slavery. But even after the wine and feasting she was not free. There was some trouble there, she didn't know what. Perhaps the children of the sons, who stayed up too late and cried. Even the promise of afikoman presents did not appease them. Or maybe the shadow of the missing daughter was darkening Alla's eyes and making Yakov look at his wife with pain and speak shortly to her, so that when it was over and the last version of the last melody had been sung, Judith declined their offer to stay and left Chenya there to continue home alone.

Only the moon lit her path as she walked Jerusalem. Most of the houses were dark. Here and there the music of the haggadah's end flowed into the street and faded. Judith took her time. She was alone and relieved to be. She let her feet take her this way and that, not caring when she arrived. At the turn of the road she paused and looked. There was a long street staircase, an alley and a lane, and she didn't know which to choose. She stood suspended in that for some time. Each would take her home, it was a matter of the one. She couldn't get past the three openings. To take one would mean leaving the others, and there was no reason to. So she was found by a girl beside her soundlessly.

"Efshar laazor?" The girl offered help.

But how could she help? Judith shook her head.

"Are you waiting for someone?" the girl said.

Her voice was low and pleasant. She was Israeli or American, Judith couldn't yet tell which. The girl was small and slight. She wore a long white dress and her eyes gleamed, kindly lights, opposite Judith.

"I'm Ruth," she said. "You're on your way back from the seder?"

Judith nodded.

"I too. Perhaps we can continue together." Ruth started into the lane and Judith followed. It turned out that they lived on the same street, were both from New York, the first of sisters. Ruth was older, Judith couldn't tell how much. She probably looked as she had years ago, and would be the same in ten, it was the bones.

"It's amazing that we met this way," Judith said. They were sitting on the stairs outside her building.

"It's not amazing, it's His will," Ruth said. "Hashgachah, these things are ordained."

Judith talked to her until the sky began to grow white and Ruth stood up quietly and said, "It's the time of the morning prayer. Go in peace."

"But when will we see each other?" Judith panicked.

Ruth kissed her. "Have faith," she said and pointed to where she lived. "I'm going to a class in Meah Shearim next Thursday. It's on the teachings of Reb Nachman of Bratslav. Would you like to come?"

"But Meah Shearim's ultra-Orthodox. They won't let us in."

"Of course they will. It's a class for women taught by a wonderful man, Rav Gvaryahu. I met him a few years ago and he invited me then. I've only gotten back now. Come to the number four bus stop at eight. I'll wait for you."

When Judith told Chenya about it, she was fascinated. "Of course, I wouldn't go to such a class, I don't believe in separating women from men. But you will learn so much. Rav Gvaryahu is a sage."

"You've heard of him?"

"Naturally. He is from my town in Polanya. I knew him as a young man and even then he was a tsadik. You will see it on his face. I trust you in his hands.

"Tell me about your town," Judith said. "Tell me about Europe." It was suddenly urgent. "Show it to me in words. How is it you know what you do?"

Chenya sighed. "It is all gone. Ah, Yehudit, the riches we've lost, we can never regain them. Every town, not just mine, all over Europe were cities of scholars and devoted ones. Thousands of years it took to refine the spirit to that degree and then, gone, vanished. Is it any wonder we are impoverished? Our souls that should have been wise and aged are just born. They are peeking into the world asking questions that no one alive knows the answers to. We have to start over again. Our souls are crying, Mamme, Tatte, they are orphans. Ach"—she brushed the tears angrily from her face—"I am an old woman."

"Give me your burden," Judith said. "I want to carry it with you."

And Chenya began. "The story lies in the names of the towns. In each town was a rebbe and his followers, in each a different way to the Holy One, Blessed be He. Ger and Kotzk and Apt, where we lived and my father was the rav, Mezeritch and Zhitomir, Berditchev and Rizhin, Medzebozh, Bratslav—it goes on. Some were wealthy and some austere. Some were kingly and some smote the flesh. But all were chasidim. They sung God's praises." Chenya reached over. "Oi, Yehudit, I am tireder than I thought. We will go on with this another day, yes?"

That night Judith dreamt she was floating in a sweetness heavier than air. She was breathing names, recited by her heart to herself in a pattern: Mezeritch, Zhitomir, Ger, Kotzk and Apt. Mezeritch, Zhitomir, Ger, Kotzk and Apt. Berditchev and Rizhin, Berditchev and Rizhin. The names cradled her, they rocked her to sleep. They became her blood without separateness.

It was the next day that she meant to meet Ruth and she almost didn't go. The encounter, looked back on, seemed strange. She thought: I don't know her, and what will I say? She'd have to wear a skirt. It was too cold. All the reasons weighed on her, persuaded her to sit in her room. And yet near eight she found herself hurrying into her clothes. She couldn't be late. Ruth's shining dress under the streetlight drew her forward. Her face was dear. When they got off the bus Ruth led her from the hubbub of the main street into another world.

Rav Gvaryahu taught in his house, a small set of rooms on a courtyard with a well in its centre. It was quiet. There were no electric lights above them, only a sky full of stars. Inside the house the walls were painted in a pale blue pattern. Lace covered the windows and divided the study room from the rest. Somewhere inside were the wife and the daughters, Ruth said. They would come in later. There were books everywhere, all of them sforim, sacred books bound in black or wine with Hebrew titles on the spines. Around the long table a row of women sat, with a row behind them and some standing. Judith and Ruth were the only ones without a wig or kerchief covering their hair. Judith felt naked but Ruth seemed at ease. She smiled at the women and moved to a corner. Judith was close behind her.

When the rav came in everyone stood. He motioned them down with a gentle hand, sat at the head of the table and opened his book. Only then did the women open theirs. Someone passed Ruth a copy and she and Judith shared. The rav did not begin until he saw that everyone had found her place.

"We left off last week at perek vav, starting at the words kol adam. Here rabbenu, may his memory be a blessing, talks to us about the steps to get closer to Him, Hashem Yitbarakh, and how you can be fooled into thinking you are farther than you are."

When Rav Gvaryahu bowed his head to read, Judith stole a look at him. He was dressed in a silk robe, tied around his waist, and beneath it a shirt of white linen. Long greying sidecurls framed an extraordinary face, hollowed and striking, with a fine wide brow. She had not expected beauty.

He began: "Every person in the world, even if he is on the lowliest step, even if he feels himself in the ground itself, when he wants to enter into serving Hashem, he has to go and rise from level to level. Each time he leaves one level, according to his capacity, then all over again the shells of desires, imaginings, confusions and temptations overcome him and spread out against him, greatly, and they do not give him rest to enter the gates of holiness. In this the righteous chasid is mistaken when he sees that suddenly desires and confusions and temptations overcome him, and it seems to him that he has fallen from his level because previously the desires and confusions had never overcome him this way, they had let him be, and he therefore concludes that he has fallen. But in truth it is not falling but only in order to rise from level to level according to his capacity, and at each level the desires, confusions, temptations and twistings of the heart overcome him more strongly, so that each time he must strengthen himself and not fall away from it in his mind, until he overcomes them and shatters the shells again."

He looked up and sighed. "Because, you remember what we learned last week, that the going down comes before rising. From this you understand that you must strengthen yourself in serving Him and not let the fallings of the world and in yourself affect you. If you gather yourself in strength, all your fallings will turn to great risings. Everyone who falls thinks these words are not being said to him, only to righteous ones who are continually rising from level to level. Know, then, and believe that every one of these words is said to the smallest of the smallest and the most wretched in spirit, because Hashem Yitbarakh is good to all His creation, steadily and always.

"The course of the spirit is withdrawal and return to Him, withdrawal and return. When you are in a state of withdrawal you feel yourself to be so far from Him, it is impossible to imagine the way back. But rabbenu, of blessed memory, tells us that He is in every place and awaits you. You understand?"

No one spoke.

"There is nothing more important than this. Prayer and study are the way, and there will be times in prayer when your heart is not in the words and your mind is straying. The straying too is part of serving Him. Do not be frightened.

"If anyone has a question," Rav Gvaryahu said gently, "let her come to me after the lesson."

He went on, reading each Hebrew word so that every letter signified, had weight. It was all about the struggle towards a restful spirit, how hard and ongoing it is. They knew then too, Judith thought. So many years ago they had a language for it. Beside her Ruth closed her book. The lesson was over and most of the women slipped away. Ruth approached him, waiting her turn, to give him greetings from another teacher. His face softened when she told him. Ruth was so calm. A woman, and still she moved with grace through this different world.

Outside Judith asked Ruth her questions. Was it possible that the words were for her too?

"Exactly for you." Ruth smiled. "What rabbenu is saying is this: Do not be despondent, my child. All of us are children, afraid we are unworthy. But that fear is only another distancing. You will find your place."

"I don't know how," Judith said.

"Forgive me for this, but when I was your age I didn't know either. I went to my teacher then, a very old man. What he told me I will give you. When you feel you can't bear not knowing and still you don't see the first step, stand alone in your room and call to Him, out loud. Raise your voice as our ancestors in Egypt did and seek of Him what you need. He will answer, for He hears the cries of Israel."

"You believe."

"You don't believe? Is that why you sat entranced tonight, is that why the tears filled your eyes?"

Judith said, "You are sure. I'm so desperate, my soul flutters about in the emptiness. I've just started to study, I've squandered so much time. And there are mountains ahead of me, I'll never be able to do it."

"Follow rabbenu, what you heard tonight. There is only one step at a time, and each one feels harder at first. Tell me, do you pray?"

Judith shook her head.

"Come with me this Shabbat. I will take you to a place where they know how to daven. Start with me."

"Yes, I'll do that," Judith said.

She couldn't wait to tell Yakov about what had happened, but he wasn't home for their next lesson.

"In Tel Aviv," Alla said. "I couldn't stop him. That man can't resist being wanted. Every reading he's offered, he has to go. He says many apologies."

Judith tried not to feel disappointed. She couldn't expect Yakov to give up an audience for his poems just to keep one meeting with her.

"There will be other lessons," Alla said. "But it will be getting harder to see him. I never see him lately. He is teaching in Tel Aviv this term and he stays there two nights a week. That and the books and the young writers that are always coming to talk and the readings—it's too much, he's not young. But does he listen to me? Not at all. A mule, my Yakov. When I married him he dreamed of family. Mishpachah, mishpachah, all he talked about. Especially after what happened in Europe. I want to make Jews, he used to say. But when it came to who gave up their work to make Jews, that was me. I can never get back the years of painting I lost, not ever."

"But you're not sorry, are you?" Judith said quickly.

"I'm sorry I believed him," Alla said. "He stole my life from me."

"Yakov?"

"Yes, your wise man Yakov. Don't look so dismayed. Do you not know what must be sacrificed for fame? You think a soul can withstand it? What is so fresh to you when you hear it has been said to a million eager listeners. I am hurting you," Alla said, "but you cannot be so naïve."

264

"I had no idea."

"What of?"

"You're so angry at him."

Alla sat down abruptly. "I am very, very angry."

"But what has he done to you?"

"You see, you are fooled too. You think we are equals, right, two artists sharing a life, isn't that what you think?"

Judith nodded.

"Then why in our thirty years has he had a hundred books, a thousand readings, and I, five shows? Five shows for thirty years of work."

"But Alla, it's easier to print a book than to have a show, especially in Israel. That's not Yakov's fault."

"Let me tell you a secret."

Judith felt herself shivering.

"When visitors would come to our house and exclaim at my paintings, you must exhibit, Gveret Shtern, we have never seen such work, what did my Yakov tell them? She is not ready, he said, it would be a crime to expose such a talent before it is ripe. And they would agree, when he is the criminal, he is the crime."

"I can't believe it," Judith said. "He has opened a world to me, you both have. I think I can learn so much from him."

"You can learn," Alla relented, "but don't be deluded by the teacher. He will treat you like a daughter but you're not a daughter. For his own daughter he didn't have the time he finds for you."

"Has he said it's too much trouble? I never realised he was so busy. Maybe I should come just once a week."

"Once or twice, he wouldn't find more time for his own family. It's something in you. You must be careful."

"Alla, I have to go now," Judith said, "but I'll think about everything, I promise."

"You do have some thinking to do," Alla said. "I'm glad I had the chance to tell you now, for your own good."

Judith felt sick.

"Everything I touch betrays me," she cried to Chenya. "No more love. I'm stopping now."

"Yehudit." Chenya was holding her.

"It's not worth it. I've learned my lesson. You won," she called out, "all of you, one after the other, I surrender, I give in. Victory. I am finished with love."

"One lonely woman," Chenya said. "One sad, embittered woman and you're beaten? This is not the Yehudit Rafael I know."

"No more Rafaels either. It's a curse."

"Yehudit."

"Yes it is. What taught me to expect love in the first place? Passion, passion, I should have been a normal person, that was my mistake."

"Who has hurt you so badly? Such pain is not from Alla's tongue alone."

Judith's body was limp from crying. She thought of the list. Rachel. Ori. Jessie. At Jessie her mind stopped. "I can't go on like this. I can't be battered every six months and keep coming back. One day I'll die of sorrow. What do I do that's so wrong? I give my whole heart away, each time, and I'm punished for it. They always said it was too much. Chenya, the world is right. That's the worst of it, all along the world's been right."

"Sit up," Chenya said. "Look at me."

Judith looked.

"What do you see?"

Judith saw love. There was no denying it.

"I must tell you of Rafael laughing," Chenya said. "This is a gift you have that hasn't yet been revealed to you. It is your birthright. Some are given beauty and some intelligence. Of course you have both, without a doubt. But Rafael laughing is your blood gift. And the only way to learn it is to be taught, one from the other. My father taught it to me. I was ten years old, the daughter of the rav of the town, and everybody watched me. Even then I loved to recite and when the theatre came I couldn't not go. So I lied to my mother and told her I was staying with a friend. The next day when I walked into my father's study—no matter how busy he was I could always come in—I saw the elders of the town with black faces. I knew immediately. Someone had seen me at the theatre. My father motioned me to him as the oldest man spoke. The daughter of the rav, he said, at this chilul hashem. You understand how serious this was, the rabbi's daughter blaspheming God. So what does my father do? He throws back his head and laughs. Then he takes me close to him, serious, and says: Gentlemen. Any place my daughter steps in is a holy place.

"Now where did he learn that laugh? From his father. And what does it mean? It means: Gentlemen. You try to persuade me the world is full of terror and the line of safety is so thin. I am not persuaded. Neither must you be, Yehudit."

"I'll try," Judith whispered.

If she could live until tomorrow night Ruth would come and she'd have something to do. Then there would be her class with the rav, that was two things. In between there was work, which took care of the day. But morning and evening, morning and evening. When she woke the next day she was reaching for her siddur.

"Elohai, neshamah shenatata bi tehorah hi." She read the words out loud and slowly. It had been years. The soul you have given me is pure, my God, you created it, formed it and breathed it into me.

Judith took a deep breath. She was alive. The pain was still in her body but it hadn't killed her. As long as she was alive she could offer praise. "Who raises those who are bent over," in sorrow, she thought, but he does raise them. "Who gives strength to the weary." She straightened her shoulders and read on. "May it be your will, that we are able to cleave to your ways. Don't let the voices for damage within us have power, and keep us from bad friends." Keep us from bad friends, that was a real prayer. She stared at the page. Why had she never seen it before?

She said the entire service. She wasn't bored, she wasn't impatient. When she reached aleinu, the great prayer of honouring, she felt the thankfulness stream through her. She didn't have nothing, she had this. While the words were before her she wasn't afraid.

But as soon as she opened her door and stepped out, the panic began. I mustn't think, I mustn't think, she walked to the bus. The faces of Alla and Yakov, the catalogue of loss, invaded her. If she looked up from the desk or took a break at the library the voices set in, mocking her. You can't love, you'll never be happy.

The siddur became just a book, its language died, how had it sung for her only today?

At home she stripped off her clothes and crawled into bed. Blackness engulfed her, she was sunk in it down to the bottom. Jessie knocked on her door, back from some trip or other, and Judith told her to go away.

"But I have to talk to you."

"Too bad," Judith said. "I don't want to talk to you."

Jessie stormed in and turned on the light. She pulled off the covers and started shaking her. "What is the matter with you, are you crazy? Do you think I'm just going to let you go without a word? I'm going to make you talk to me, I'll make you. I'm not leaving this room."

Judith clenched her jaw.

"Please," Jessie said. "I'm begging you, is that what you want? You are killing me, I can't stand it. What have I done to make you desert me so terribly?"

"Me desert you?"

Jessie stared. "You really think I left you."

Judith nodded.

"I came to tell you that Yishai and I have decided to live together. I wanted you to know. Somewhere inside you I know you must be able to be happy for me. I would be for you."

"I'm not you."

"Judith, please, be the self I love so much. You taught me how to show friendship, be that friend for me now."

Judith was trying to figure out what she was really feeling. If she hated Jessie she would say so now and if she was angry she would be. Jessie stood before her dishevelled and anguishing.

"This isn't worth it," Judith finally said. "I'm not mad anymore. I thought I was but I'm not. I'm glad you've found a life and I hope you'll be happy with him. I think you will be."

Jessie was waiting for something else.

"Go in peace," Judith said. She had found Ruth's words on her tongue.

That was the hardest for Jessie, to hear the relinquishing. "It doesn't matter? You don't care?"

"I care that you be able to go."

Jessie sat down beside her. "I can't walk away from you with that calmness in your voice. You are the greatest part of me. I couldn't have loved Yishai before you. He knows that. No matter what, he's in your debt."

"No debts. No owing. Let it rest."

"You don't sound like you. You sound strange."

"You don't know me now."

"I want to." Jessie reached over to her. "Don't you think there's a way we can?"

Judith shook her head.

"You know, Ori may be coming to visit in the summer."

Judith searched herself. A tiny feeling, a taste of bitterness. So she was not quite there. But it was close enough, and Jessie saw that she'd lost.

"Well, I'm not letting go of you," she said quietly. "Everything that leaves comes back, I learned that from you. When your retreat is over I'll be here. I don't care how long it takes. Remember that"—and she was gone.

Again the time of Shabbes coming. Meeting Ruth at twilight, being led through winding streets, to find that where she ended up was Bratslav. This shul with its grey cement room was where Ruth returned each week. Judith thought there must be a mistake. But Ruth entered the dismal room like a sanctuary and her being was light. "Come let us sing to God, let us welcome Him in thankfulness." Judith couldn't, her mind refused to. And Ruth's voice beside her continued, "Do not harden your heart."

Never were the words so beautiful. The murmuring men in the other room accompanied the singing of women. "Come, beloved, to meet the bride, let us welcome Shabbes. Arise, rejoice, to welcome her, bo'i kalah, bo'i kalah.

"God with words brings on the evening and opens the gates. Creating day and night, who rolls away the light in the face of darkness and the darkness before light. Day passes and night comes, and God distinguishes between them. Therefore when we lie down and when we rise we celebrate Torah, the given words."

What can I bring to God but love, Judith thought. I'm brimming with love. This was the start of peace, she knew, to be flooded with the fullness of longing. To know that it was serving, such desire, it was the spirit's crying out: Come to me, and the beloved's reply: Let us hasten.

"Bless me with peace," they sang at the end. The room was dark and transparent with light. The messengers of Shabbes had joined them, malakhei hashalom, the peace angels.

Shabbat was in the streets. Judith thought she could live in it, it was nourishment and shelter, a dwelling place. When Ruth drew her over to meet someone, Judith was reluctant to speak. Let this be always as it is now, she thought, suspended in love.

Yaffa was the woman's name and Ruth talked about her. "She is an Israeli from a kibbutz chiloni, where there was no Jewishness. She was always a dancer, and after the Army she began to perform in Tel Aviv. But it did not satisfy her. Something was barren at the heart, and no movement teacher could help her. So she left and wandered, learning the dance of many countries until finally she was in India with a teacher of yoga who showed her a way. She thought then that she'd found her place but her teacher said no, she must return to Israel and teach what she had learned.

"I'll go back to India," Yaffa said, "I'll have to. But for now I am here."

"Where do you teach?" Judith asked her.

It was on the outskirts of the city.

"If you'd like to come," Yaffa said, "I begin a new cycle next week. I can take you at sunrise."

Judith said yes. She wanted to see what it was like to get up very early these spring mornings, perhaps to say shacharit at dawn if she could. Jerusalem was flowering. Every moment was luminous now, the exquisite warm light of the season, beginning white and deepening to gold by imperceptible degree until late afternoon. The bushes were purple and scarlet, and everywhere cascading vines of brilliant colour lit the houses. The rains were finally over. The sun was a dome of light over the city. Jerusalem was wrapped in the light that had anointed kings, hallowing her citizens each day. Judith was starting to breathe differently with Yaffa, and she felt her body take in the city and release it as she travelled outside the walls to the hills where Yaffa lived.

"Let go," Yaffa said. "Stop clinging to things. Let the world pass through you."

Judith closed her eyes. Slowly her tired body eased as she bent forward and arched back, encompassing within her the directions of the universe.

"Like a lulav at Sukkot," Yaffa said, "pliant, flexible. No inclination can break you."

Time spun out before her infinitely, the minute lengthening as she needed. Judith rose these mornings in the dark and wrapped herself in a tallit. She wound tefillin on her arm in betrothal and prayed for knowledge. Her body grew light. In the silence of the room she was only breath. God, the soul you have breathed into me is pure, she began the day.

"Let go," Yaffa said. "You strive against despair. Give it up. It is attachment that brings sorrow. Relinquish yearning and it will come to you. Leave room for nothingness."

Judith did not always understand. At dawn her words were full of attachment, God of our fathers, Israel chosen, the holiness of land and lineage, this people, this city. This God and no other. She was trying to follow the halakhah, one law commanded by God for a certain hour and place.

Yaffa said, "There is a multiplicity of ways and no one way is God. There are many aspects, called different names by different people, and all are of God. God is formless, so any path can lead you in. What is the point of boundaries?" Yaffa said. "God includes all."

Shavuot was coming, kabbalat hatorah, receiving the Torah at Sinai. Judith was studying kabbalah with Ruth, preparing for the day. She was learning of the sefirot, the ten spheres through which God is manifest in the universe and the names by which God may be known, from the highest Keter to the revelation in the Shekhinah, the community of Israel that we reflect on earth.

"We can know nothing of the top three sefirot, God's aspects that are hidden from us. But through the lower seven, divine life flows, the inwardness transformed until finally, at Shekhinah, God may be shown to creation. Creation, something from nothing, first takes place in God, for above the first sefirah of Keter is the great Ein Sof, the mystical nothing in which God's emerging starts. Through the ten, God unfolds, until at the Shekhinah, closest to the created world, divine life and created life may meet and join.

"Once, the Shekhinah, God's bride and queen, was perfectly united with God. But after Eden the flow of divine life was disturbed. The Shekhinah went into exile, where she is still, where we are. The way to repair the break is by tikkun, our task in the world. When the Shekhinah and God are reunited, there will be redemption."

Judith thought of Yakov, who had begun to teach her this.

"How do you repair the breaks in this world?" she said to Ruth.

"You can only work through Him. Root yourself in Him, cleave to Him, and His light shining through you will enable others to find their way."

"But breaches between two people not even God can repair."

"Then ask forgiveness. Healing in this world is tikkun too."

The life she had led was unredeemed. Then she had been enslaved by longing, now she felt ready to receive. But to go back into the chaos of the past, she was not free enough for that.

Yakov's silence was judgement. She wanted to feel no pain, to be able to say to herself, it was what it was. And yet she trembled that she might meet him in the street. She couldn't talk to Ruth about such matters. Ruth was somewhere past her. She needed no one. Judith kept waiting for Ruth to show herself beneath the graciousness, but Ruth met each person as tselem elohim and saw God's image in every one.

"Living in His love," Ruth said, "is all my desire."

It was impossible not to be drawn to such radiance.

In the houses of Jerusalem on the night of Shavuot the lights would burn till dawn, Jews holding tikkunim, studying Torah all night to celebrate Sinai. But Judith got a letter from Riva, arriving on a kibbutz in the Galil just before the holiday. "It's not a religious kibbutz," Riva wrote, "but they celebrate harvest. We'll have a great reunion, so take the bus up here. I've missed you like crazy this year."

It was a language Judith could hardly remember. Yet the feel of Riva, the warm body of her sister, still held her. She would have her own tikkun up in the north where Tsfat was and return to Jerusalem refreshed. Perhaps there would be revelation.

Judith saw Riva from far off, bounding towards her, sweeping her off the ground in her arms.

272

"What's happened to you?" Riva cried out. Her voice was incredulous.

"I'm me," Judith said, "what do you mean?"

"You're disappearing. You're not here. Where's your body?" Riva stepped back. She looked horrified.

"I don't need a body." Judith was laughing. "I feel wonderful, don't worry. I'll try to explain."

"Mummy and Daddy begged me to tell them anything about you. Naomi made me promise. Bobba's so worried. Anna and Sharon both called before I left. This will take some explanation. I admit that thin isn't my area of expertise, but you look terrible. You're not sick with something you're hiding, are you? You're not dying?" She had tears in her eyes.

"Dying! Riva, listen to me. I have never felt so good, do you hear? Not ever."

"Are you in love?"

"In a way." Judith smiled. "I'll tell you about it."

They sat on the steps outside Riva's room and Judith talked about the year. Jessie and Yakov and Alla. Chenya and then Ruth and Yaffa.

Riva squeezed her hand. "I don't get it," she finally said. "You know me. Choose life, that's the Judaism I believe in. We're not into renouncing, isn't that true?"

"I'm accepting."

"Food and love, the two greatest pleasures. Thank goodness I don't have to choose between them. And you're giving up both."

"An abundance of love awaits me if I'm willing. And it's the kind that lasts."

"Into the grave," Riva said. "What about this world?"

"It should be possible in this world," Judith said. "I'm only starting to learn how."

"Your friend Ruth sounds like a nun. What is this devotion to God without relationships? How can you know what love is except what you've learned with people? We're all we've got. You can only guess at God's love from that. And Yaffa doesn't sound Jewish, she's a Hindu. These are your teachers?"

"Enough," Judith said. "Trust me, that's the most you can do for me now. It hurts me when you cut yourself off."

"Of course I trust you. It's our rule. But you have to realise that I see you doing the cutting, not me. I'm as present as always, I'm right here. But you're floating away."

"That's exactly what I want. And now, my dear, I have to get ready for Shavuot."

"You'll come to the dining room with me. The whole kibbutz will be there and I'll introduce you. I've met some terrific people already. There will be singing and skits."

Judith shook her head. "I'm going to wash and dress for the holiday and go off someplace separate where there won't be outside noise. Somewhere green where I can sing and daven without being disturbed or disturbing you. I've brought my own food, don't worry."

"You know I do."

"Milk and cheese for Shavuot."

"You'll miss the blintzes."

"I'll meet you in the morning." Judith smiled. "I'll find my way back."

"What will I say?"

"Whatever's easiest for you."

Riva looked mischievous. "Would you mind very much if I told them you're crazy?"

Judith laughed. "But I am."

Facing east, the woods were dark. Judith said the evening service while she could still read. Then she spread out her blanket and closed her eyes. She was in Tsfat, where what she thought about had begun. It was midnight and the people were astir, gathered to study the Torah. Dressed in white robes, she sat with them to learn the secrets of the universe. Before the creation of the world was the Torah and before the Torah was breisheet, the first word. Before breisheet was God's name, the word that includes all words. What is Torah but the infinite combinations of God's name? And so the first three words of Torah, breisheet bara elohim, at the beginning created God, contain all words. The Torah begins with bet, the first letter with sound, for alef is infinite, it stands by itself, it points in four directions, taking in everything. But bet is unfinished, empty on one side, and out of its open mouth all Torah flows. It is a necessary emptiness, for only when there is a drawing in can emanation begin. Just this way God drew in to leave a place for creation. The beginning

274

contains all creation, breisheet has the letters of bara within it. It has the alef and bet, the first two letters, and the last three, reish, sheen and tav. And it has the beginning of the great name of God, the yod, ten, for the ten sefirot, all the spheres by which God is known, from the alef of Ein Sof, infinite before everything, out of which the ten come, to the last letter of Malkhut, the last sefirah, the kingdom of God that is the community of Israel, Shekhinah. And so we are born at the end of creation, the tav of breisheet, and are its completion. Nothing will come after us but Shabbat, herself the bet of breisheet between the last letters. This is the pattern of Torah, whose last word is us, yisrael, the name we earn every year struggling to begin again in God.

There was nothing outside the letters. They were mountains shining around her and the night she began in was day. She was trembling in light, her body gone, into the space between the letters, the air of Tsfat, white fire. Now it was time to leave, to choose death, and the letters would not let her go. The spaces were gates but only back into the world, returning to Torah, life wholly in it, the body through which the infinite is known.

A veil of leaves hid her face. She was afraid of what her eyes might see if she uncovered them. But the sun was rising, revealing God's handiwork, and she must rise too, and eat and drink, her spirit returned to the form that held it, her body restored. The earth was filled with glory this Shavuot morning, God's love evident. At the kibbutz they were honouring the harvest, reaping the last sheaves of a field and singing plough songs. Far from the kibbutz buildings, this was what it must have been like under the open sky when the first pioneers came to work the land. Judith saw Riva's flaming hair and ran over to meet her.

"I'm back," she said.

"Don't you love it here?"

The light was still soft, it was so early, and they danced each other round to celebrate.

"I work in the orange groves," Riva said. "Keep me company on my shift, you'll just look."

The sun entered the orchards through the holes in the trees. Riva climbed up on a ladder that reached from the ground to the sky.

"These are the apples of Israel," she said, dropping gold into baskets. Red, orange and yellow spheres, hills of fruit offerings patterned the earth. People were going up with empty arms and returning laden. The light garlanded Riva's hair when she reached the top and hovered overhead till she returned. Judith could have watched her all day. But from the dining room the call for breakfast trumpeted.

"We'll take a break and come back for the second shift," Riva said.

Judith wanted to spend the summer under this hard brilliant sky.

"Maybe you can," Riva said. "You're my sister. I'll ask for you."

In the dining room kibbutz volunteers were waiting on tables and straightening the chairs. Most of them wore their long hair tied back and moved easily across the floor. They stood behind serving carts, faces gleaming from the heat, and joked with the people in from the fields. Judith and Riva lingered after the others had gone, and saw the girls cleaning, partnering their mop sticks in a funny domestic dance. As it grew warmer they stripped off their work shirts to vests and finished the mopping with bare arms and legs. They worked together from one corner to the other, collapsing in a heap when the job was done. Judith listened to their laughing.

"Now they can relax for a little while until they set up for lunch," Riva said.

"Do you think they could use more help?"

"I don't know if you'd like it. It's a really hard job. Not only does it kill your body but you run around all the time trying to please people."

"I still want to do it. Will you find out?"

Riva looked dubious. "I will but I'm sceptical," she said.

Judith started the next morning. After yoga and davening, she ran down to the dining room to learn what to do. It was she who waited on Riva at breakfast, lifting the trays, filling the cart, collecting the dishes when the meal was done.

"I can't believe you like this," Riva said. "Everyone begs to be allowed onto the fields and you stay here."

Judith could not move. Every part of her ached separately. By the end of the day her body did not feel like her. She managed to get through her last shift, amazed that the others were still

276

walking lightly, discussing their evening plans. She was going to bed before dinner, if she could get back to her room.

Riva came to visit and make fun of her. "You don't have to stay, you know. You can try other jobs."

Judith was emphatic. "I'm going back tomorrow." She liked to set up in the empty room, then see people come in so weary, slumped in their chairs, but leave satisfied. It pleased her to be part of it, the dining room empty and full according to the rhythm of the day. She liked to serve and afterwards, in her quiet room, she would sit on a mat on the floor for yoga, breathing the air that had earth in it, letting it through her to straighten her limbs as Yaffa had shown her, and untangle her mind.

That was the summer. Work and prayer. Her body grew accustomed and her mind allied with it, so that morning to nightfall was one pure service. The moon's fullness was eaten away and then in one black night Tammuz was born. This was the peak of summer, fiercely burning, taking the life from the grasses, drying up the water. The end of Tammuz would bring Av, mourning month for the destruction of the Temple, the city laid waste, furrowed with salt. Judith could not do it here, on this secular kibbutz so far from Jerusalem. She called Riva to her and said she'd have to go.

The only ride out was at midnight. Stooped from the weight of her knapsack, she walked to the truck with Riva and kissed her goodbye. Riva hugged her hard.

"Don't forget me," she said.

There was dust in the air, it tasted of ashes. Night made the windshield opaque. Judith could not see the driver. She sat on the floor of the truck and took off her shoes. By the river arose the keening lament of the wind. It was many hours before through her tears she saw Jerusalem.

In the last month of the year, Elul, the time of contemplation towards the great days of awe, Judith started getting ready. She now rose at four to study and pray, and stayed up late examining her deeds. She had much to account for and trembled in the face of coming judgement. Now was the time for repentance, and how could she repair what she had done? To come between a sister and a brother, to close her heart to the pleas of a friend, not to hear the pain of a wife towards her husband, to condemn a

277

teacher, to distance herself from her mother, her father. And still so far from devotion. She did not see how there could be forgiveness.

Chenya insisted she stay with her. "Who will feed you?" she said. "God doesn't ask this of you. Such suffering, to think you're so evil. Tir'i," she said, look. "I have seen evil in my time. You don't know what you're saying. You could only be innocent to imagine such things."

"It's what's inside that condemns me."

"I hereby take upon me," Chenya stood up and declared, "all transgressions, real and imagined, that oppress the spirit of Yehudit Rafael."

"Chenya, don't say that!"

"Listen, dear one, I am safe. Only you see what you see. I pray for you, not to escape the judgement you envision, but for chesed so that you will know the true nature of your soul. You have given me so much, you bring light, how can you not know this?"

But Judith saw only darkness. When she met Yakov on the street finally she could not pass him indifferent.

"Mah nishma, how are you?" He was genial.

"Studying," she told him. "Thinking." She couldn't not try to get him intrigued, to make him talk to her somehow. He must see the hurt in her face.

"You could have called, you know," he said. "We were waiting."

"You didn't call me," she cried out. "I didn't want to intrude. You never even explained."

"There were problems," he said. "Why go into it now? So I thought, now I've learned this about her, it's just a disappointment."

"Yakov, I don't know what you're talking about. Give me a chance to defend myself. What are you saying?"

"That was before." He looked haggard. "There were problems at home, you understand."

"But you were my teacher, what could have been wrong? All I wanted was to learn from you, Alla knew that."

Yakov flinched. "You are very young," he said. "You have to open your eyes. I'll say no more about this. For you I was an old teacher. But I saw you in my dreams."

278

Judith felt a deep shame. She could not look at him, part of her exulting, it wasn't that she hadn't mattered, partly dismayed. It couldn't be of her that he spoke. She was a child.

"I want to ask your forgiveness," Yakov said, "and I want to ask you to do something for me. Pray for me on Yom Kippur."

"How can my prayers avail you?" Judith whispered.

"You are a tsadeket," he said. A righteous woman.

"Oh, no," Judith said, "you're so wrong."

But Yakov said, "Repentance and prayer and righteousness avert the harsh decree."

God, until I was created I was as nothing, and now that I have being, it is as if I were not. Dust I am alive, in my death how much more so. Here I am before you, a vessel full of shame. Let it be your will, God my God and of my fathers, that I will not sin anymore. That what I have already done you will undo in your mercy, but not in great trial, Lord, for I am too small to bear it.

Before the great wall of tears, the western wall, at the deciding hour, when the light of the previous day has already faded and the new day's not yet born, humbled, fallen before you, trembling as all of us have trembled from the beginning of days, awaiting the great judgement, the enormous compassionate unfolding, the opening of the gates. The home of my parents behind me, my sisters, my lovers behind me, I have emptied myself of what was, preparing for you. Lord, I sought refuge and found none. I pleaded with rabbis and teachers and could not find a way. I have broken myself in my floundering, torn loving hearts, a terrible pain. But you are everywhere, and I have come this far.

At the end of my journey, on the holiest day of the year, I wait in Jerusalem for what will be chosen for me. I know nothing, and in the pureness of this day I ask to be created again, only to let my cleansed soul serve you according to your will.

But I'm so weak. My strength is spent, my legs shake standing. Everything dissolves before me in the dusk. The wall that loomed all day, huge flat stones, has begun to fade, the space between the stones wells up and darkens the face, the outside is gone and I am shrouded in that space.

The day turns, the gates of judgement are almost sealed, Lord, open a gate. The day turns, the sun at the rim of the world, let us enter your gates.

So many barriers. Up and down the streets chasidim walked, wrapped in robes designed in other times. They walked in pairs, arms linked, intent, and when their eyes met mine they turned away. They saw a young girl, slight, of modern dress. To me my heart thundered through my skin, my soul lit up my face. They did not pause. It's in my blood, I cried. They would have said I did not know my place.

Their rabbi told me: More and more women are studying every day. But I want more than study. I want a way like breathing, to cleave to God all my days. I want there to be nothing for me but God, alive in my life always. But I am bound by appetite, fettered by desire. I want, I need, I cry like a child. Just this way the ones before me cried for me. And Rachel weeping for her children, through centuries of exile, refusing to be comforted.

We are your children and you are our father. We are your people and you are our God. We are your work and you the creator. We are beloved and you are the love, exalted by you, our exalted one.

The grid of your law and the fire of my passion. A harsh exacting God, particular, certain: The holiest people is Israel and the holiest land, Israel. The holiest city, Jerusalem, bloodsoaked past time. Owned and unowned by us, covetted, wrestled through space. My heart in the east, the Hebrew poet cried, and I at the edge of the west. Longing for Jerusalem, and I drawn farther east. Blood flooding the streets. Never will Jerusalem be divided again, and I so circumscribed. The holy city is a small enclosing place. Walled and turretted with narrow ponderous gates. To get to the wall you wend your way through the marketplace, buzzing carcasses of meat, blind old men on donkeys, going the other way. Christians and Moslems claiming it too. The nuns on the Via Dolorosa, full of desire. Everyone confusing Jerusalem of earth with the greater city, fighting their way in, through Dung, Saint Stephen's, Herod's, Damascus, Jaffa, Zion Gate. Mine, mine, the millions of battles within me and the placid voice of the east saying: Come to peace, my child. Give way. The boundaries are illusion and your apartness is your own creation. The teacher, her heart clear, smiling to me: The great path has no gates. Thousands of roads enter it. Pass through this gateless gate and walk freely between earth and heaven.

There is no tranquillity, the ones who teach taught me. You who want to come into serving God must rise by degrees. With each new step the shells obscuring holiness, the appetites, confusions, imaginings, spread out before you, leaving you no rest, preventing you from entering the gates of sacredness. And so there must be falling in order for rising to take place. Tread carefully, they say, because many are the paths of transgression, but the way of righteousness: Fear the Lord. But I believe, perfectly, in a flooding God of love. Evening comes, my breathing calms, the wall begins to fade. There is a place past walls. Though I have barely touched it, still it awaits me. To bathe in the love of God, outside the wheel of desire. Past longing, past the war, alone in infinite space. A wind of light through what once I called my self, behind, suspending that self in it, rendering what I was transparent until all I am is that through which God's love unfolds, through which God's will be done.

And yet here I am, destitute of deeds, trembling and afraid of the one that Israel praises. To stand, to plead before you of what is to be for us, although I am not worthy of it. Because I am not worthy of it I beg of you, God of Abraham, Isaac, Jacob, awful and terrible God, prosper the journey I have undertaken that has brought me to you, and pour out your tenderness towards us. Do not hold others accountable for my sins, for I am a sinner, and let them not be ashamed of me, nor I of them, but accept my prayer as if I were wise and old, venerable, upright of limb, whose sweet voice can be heard throughout the land. Refuse to let evil enter us. Let our assembling be in love. Let love dissolve our sins. And turn all our fasting, our afflictions, to joy and celebration, for life, for peace. Open us to love and there will be no impediment in our prayer.

Underneath my white dress my body is cold. My stomach is swollen, the skin of my hands withered on the bone like an old woman. It is the hour of deciding who shall live and who shall die, and even as I wait I age, second by second, relentless. My life flung straight to the grave. Last year I stood just this way, scraped of impurities, to begin again, and another year's accretions raced to taint me. Here I am, frail, knowing that even as the gates shut and open I can only become more gross than I am now. And so it will of necessity be.

Nothing but a series of becomings and extinctions, holiness certain to be profaned. Last night, bathed and rested, I feasted before the fast, and left to pray for emptiness. Now, as cleansed a vessel as I will be, when the moon begins to rise, ready to leave the earth I must return to it, to enter a door, to sit among cushions, peopled, at ease. The hammering together of sukkah beams, festival of fruition, ripeness of food and drink one degree from dust. After the holiday, chairs pushed back, sated, near sleep, the table strewn with peels, pits, half-eaten things, who will know that we stood empty and clean so recently. The manifold dyings implanted in our birth.

You created us to lose us continually. Splattered our bloodied bodies over history, the ones who died in their beds, the ones who dug their own graves. The besieged ones who ate their own flesh, or watched their children dashed against walls. A time to be burned, a time to be stoned, a time to be shot, a time to be hanged. To die by water, to die by fire, by sword or wild beast. Lord of mercy, have mercy on us.

When we stood at the foot of the mountain, washed, purified, women and men, we ate only milk food waiting for you. Sinai was dense in cloud, raging fire, shaking enormously, and the shofar sounded over and over again through the darkness. You promised us honey and milk. Listen, Israel, you said, I am yours, I am one. We were hidden from the world by smoke, and did not see the others assembled there. To each of them you spoke as a lover, in their tongue, and each replied: God our God is one. The mountain gone in the haze, no one seeing a neighbour, all the voices in the world declaring their own dissolution, the languages of the world, divorced, various, returning to their source in you. The great breath of the world, only, remained, and what we were drew in and out of you.

Hearing me, you are not apart from me, in the one. Lord, I begin on the other side, not in the awesome thundering but in the small still voice that sounded for me. My fast is over, soon I will rejoin the people, bathe, change garments, accept milk offerings. So your children partake of the world, leave it to be near you, near the death of their bodies to honour your name, and in their readiness to leave, learn their own return. Rise, eat, drink, refresh yourself, one says, return to your house. Sit and eat, says another, abandon your dwelling place. Lord, you are greater than the separate ways to you.

Some reach Jerusalem from the west, and some from the east. Some battle the raging Atlantic, some are carried in the ocean of peace. The womb of the world brought all of us forth, and will take us all at our appointed time. At the end of this day there is no one but you. At the end of all days the mountain of your house will be above all mountains, and everyone will flood to it. Many peoples, crying: Come, let us rise to the mountain of the Lord, house of Jacob's God, who will teach us many journeys. and whose ways we will walk, God's light from Zion, God's word from Jerusalem. Then the mountain, the house, the peoples, the journeys, the light and the word, the land and the city will not be divided again.

God is God, God is God, God is God, God is God, God is God, God is God, God is one.

Next year in Jerusalem.

SEVEN

Judith sat on the porch of her room overlooking the city. Her suitcase was packed. She was ready to go. There would be work, there would be love, Chenya said, and Judith believed her. Soon she would be with her parents. Soon she would see her sister. But first she had to get settled. She was moving to New York to find a place to live. It was time to be on her own.

All day she had walked the streets of Jerusalem. She had seen the first light on the gold and silver domes. She had heard the prayers at the wall near dawn. Piles of St. Peter's fish were drying in the sun. The vendors in the shuk were hauling down their rugs. At Kikar Tsion the cafés unlocked their doors. Bells rang in the schoolyard and the children straggled in.

All day under the sun the people worked. The vendors carrying brass trays on their heads. The women in cafés arranging cakes. The children stooping for their books. The housewives in Machaneh Yehudah, elbowing each other between aisles of olives and cheese. The newspaper boy at the corner, crying Maariv, Maariv.

After Shabbat she was leaving for dailiness. Choose life, Riva said, and Judith was. She too would go to work and be tired at the end of the day. She would ride on buses and subways, scrambling like everyone for a place. There would be friends and she would be uncertain. There would be grief. She would face it when it came, not always well. She would choose fullness, plenitude, and be imperfect for its sake.

In the Valley of the Cross the sun was low. The muezzin was

calling the faithful ones. The synagogues were opening their doors. From the porch of her room she could see the last travellers hurrying home. Whatever was not finished was left undone.

All over the world, she thought, people are getting ready. Between the twilights, labour ceased, everything created in heaven and earth is waiting to rest. God looking back on the work of the week is finding it good. The crown of all days is beginning. We are building a palace of the heart, all of us standing here now at the point between where we have come from and what will unfold from us.